Love of a God of Love

Love of a God of Love

Towards a Transformation of the Philosophy of Religion

Hugo Strandberg

BLOOMSBURY

NEW YORK · LONDON · NEW DELHI · SYDNEY

Bloomsbury Academic
An imprint of Bloomsbury Publishing Plc

175 Fifth Avenue
New York
NY 10010
USA

50 Bedford Square
London
WC1B 3DP
UK

www.bloomsbury.com

First published by Continuum International Publishing Group 2011
Paperback edition first published 2013

Library of Congress Cataloging-in-Publication Data
Strandberg, Hugo, 1975-
Love of a God of Love: Towards a Transformation of the Philosophy of
Religion / Hugo Strandberg.
p. cm.
Includes bibliographical references (p.) and index.
ISBN-13: 978-1-4411-8213-5 (hardcover : alk. paper)
ISBN-10: 1-4411-8213-6 (hardcover : alk. paper)
1. Religion–Philosophy. 2. God–Worship and Love. 3. Love–Religious aspects.
I. Title.
BL51.S67365 2011
212'.7–dc23
2011026072

ISBN: HB: 978-1-4411-8213-5
PB: 978-1-6235-6749-1

Typeset by Amnet International, Dublin, Ireland

Contents

Introduction

In one of her essays, Elizabeth Anscombe attributes this idea to "some of Wittgenstein's followers" (she does not say whom she is thinking of):

> [I]n any sense in which a religion can be "true", which is a pretty odd sense, *any* religion is or can be true. It all depends *who* has it and *how* he has it. He may be shallow ... and then he is missing the boat all the time. He contrasts totally with someone else, who has depth ... and this man has not missed the boat. To alter the analogy a little, he is on some boat of the kind in question. As for the shape and fitment of the boat, they can be of any kind, if we are speaking in generalities.[1]

This is an idea she is critical of, although she does not explain why in any detail. I, too, am critical of this idea, and the rest of the book is an attempt at explaining why. The point is not that one should emphasize the "what" of belief instead of the "how"; the point is that they are intimately connected. This is the theme of this book, which the title already hints at: love is both how and what. Consequently, one should not reject the idea Anscombe criticizes completely; there is an insight in it. Wittgensteinian philosophy of religion, which is not homogeneous, to be sure, and hence is not identical to the idea above, has, to my mind, been the most interesting approach to the philosophy of religion during the last fifty years or so. The task is then not, in conformity with mainstream approaches – in comparison to Wittgensteinian philosophy of religion ridiculous in their shortsightedness – to remain at the hither side of it and criticize it from that perspective, but, so to speak, to move through and beyond it. For that reason, this book will not primarily be a critique – although D. Z. Phillips is discussed rather extensively in Chapter 3 – but a philosophical attempt of its own.

The fundamental idea of this book could be said to be this, in rough outline and in need of modifications. What I believe in and how I believe are two sides of the same coin when it comes to love of a God of love: if I say that I believe in a God of love, but do not do so lovingly, I do not believe, and if I believe in something lovingly but not in a God of love I do not know what that I say I believe in means. How, when and where love of a God of love enters the picture remains to be seen, however. In addition to the criticism of the sharp distinction between the what of belief and the how of belief – a distinction I will sometimes describe by means of the term "formalism" – the fundamental idea of this book involves a focus on a theme which, strangely enough, is relatively absent from the discussions in the philosophy of religion: love.[2] By means of these two points we will see how some traditional questions in the philosophy of religion get a new character and that new, important questions arise: the philosophy of religion becomes transformed. Although the chapters build on each other to some extent – the first part of the book (chapters 1–3) provides a background for that understanding of religious belief which I clarify in the second part of the book (chapters 4–5); in the last part of the book (chapters 6–9) that understanding is brought in, at different places, in discussions of some specific questions; and in the last chapter (10) some methodological issues are discussed – they are independent attempts. As you will see, identical questions will sometimes turn up in different chapters and be illuminated from new points of view; sometimes I start out from religious belief understood as love of a God of love, sometimes this understanding is something which turns up later on, as a way of approaching the theme of the chapter in a new way.

In *one* sense what I try to describe in this book is the religious, faith, as such. Traditionally, the line of thought often goes in the opposite direction: one starts out from different religious standpoints, formations of parties and groups, and the like, and then creates a concept of the religious by means of abstraction. The problem with this procedure is that it presupposes that the religious "phenomena" are homogeneous. But what if some elements in them – elements which may be very common and prevalent – are a result of a problem with faith, of lack of faith? Thus, what I try to reflect upon is instead what the phenomenon of religious faith is as such. Of course, this is a moral/existential question, since it is about *personal* difficulties, difficulties *I* have. In *that* respect, philosophy of religion is not about God, as one may be inclined to believe, but about myself: what am I ready to say religiously. This means, furthermore, that describing the phenomenon of religious faith as such does not presuppose some kind of essentialism; saying that faith is, in an *existential* sense, essentially this or that means *rejecting* essentialism, for essentialism is the idea that self-examination is *not* needed, that the world is simply there to be read off.

I suspect that what I have said thus far sounds very vague and obscure. And, in a way, this is true. This book does not have a definite thesis which could be stated here in the introduction and which the rest of the book is an argument for. It does not attack some obvious ideas which could be specified here in the introduction and which the rest of the book is an argument against. This is no accident. On the contrary, I take it to be an important philosophical point that the most important philosophical tasks cannot be described in such a way. If one is able to state a thesis, easy to understand, which the book then argues for, to specify ideas, easy to recognize in other philosophers, which the book then argues against, to frame a definite question, then the most important part of the philosophical work has already been done, or, which is more often the case, this part of the work is not at all paid attention to. The most important part of the philosophical work is to catch sight of questions we are not already aware of, and describe what these questions involve and why they are important. This is a *result* of the philosophical work, not something that *precedes* it. (The same goes for possible theses one has: what is most important is to describe what they mean – it is pointless to state them in the introduction – not to argue for them.) And for the same reason the most important philosophical work is not to argue against what other philosophers explicitly say, but to uncover ideas implicit in their writings, ideas which we did not already know they had, ideas which may be common to philosophers we previously took to belong to opposite camps. That these ideas are prevalent may to begin with be hard to believe; one may even have a hard time understanding what they mean. Here one has to be patient: when one has worked through the question, when one has reached the point it was so hard to arrive at, one gets that prospect of the philosophical landscape in which everything is both well-known and new, but not before that. Which philosophical ideas one turns against, even the realization that these ideas exist, is a result of the philosophical work, not something that precedes it. Philosophy is not to argue for or against clearly stated theses, theses supposed to be possible to observe in their singularity.

In philosophy the way the questions are put is decisive: this decides the form of the answer. In that sense, it is asking (the right questions) which is central to philosophy, not answering. This is perhaps a bit exaggerated, but nevertheless it shows that it is not possible to start a philosophical investigation with a definite question. To start with a question is an expression of an uncritical, and in that respect unscientific, attitude, since to start with a question is to accept the question as given. To do philosophy critically means starting off in a groping manner, without a definite question to hold onto.

If one realizes this, one realizes some of the problems with much of what is done in the name of philosophy today. Much of it overlooks this most important part of the philosophical work. This is not a simple mistake, a blunder. On the contrary, this is its pride: philosophical clarity and being "scientific" are taken to consist in a formal approach, a certain *style* of writing, but, obviously, this betrays a dogmatic attitude hidden for those who have adopted it. In other words, it is *this* approach which is the unscientific one. What I try to do here, and I stress *try*, is to be true to that philosophical tradition – visible, more or less clearly, in the great philosophers in the history of philosophy – which has wanted to get to the bottom of the questions, think beyond the present debates, make evident those questions which are not asked but are implicitly taken to be answered. Doing this is difficult, to say the least, and not primarily for technical reasons, as if what was needed was some kind of specialist skill. On the contrary, the decisive difficulty is an existential one: to try to liberate oneself from the dominating structures of thought, so comfortable to remain in.

For that reason, what I write cannot be *immediately* intelligible. By remaining close to the present debates, one safeguards one's intelligibility, expressing oneself in their terms and relating oneself to their questions. But what if these terms are misleading? What if these questions are not at all important and interesting? This does not mean that what I write will be unintelligible, but to demand *this* kind of intelligibility would be a mistake. And do not suppose that no work on your part will be needed. Getting an additional element in the familiar structure is easy; trying to think in new ways, and to see elements in the familiar structure which it hides for itself, requires work.

The department of philosophy, Åbo Akademi University, is, as usual, an unusually discussion-friendly place. I am grateful for having the privilege of being here.

Previous versions of parts of several chapters have been read at various conferences. Thanks to everyone who participated in the discussions.

A previous version of Chapter 3 was published in *The Contemplative Spirit: D. Z. Phillips on Religion and the Limits of Philosophy*, ed. Ingolf U. Dalferth and Hartmut von Sass (Tübingen: Mohr Siebeck, 2010). I am grateful for the permission to use this material here.

The work on this book has been financially supported by the Ella and Georg Ehrnrooth foundation.

CHAPTER 1

FORMALISM AND NEGATIVISM

In this chapter I will describe a problem which constitutes the background for that understanding of religious belief I will develop in subsequent chapters (especially in chapters 4–5). This problem is intimately related to a tendency in present-day philosophy. One aspect of this tendency could be called formalism. Shortly put, formalism is the idea that it is possible to draw a sharp distinction between the how and the what of belief, between the way a belief is held and the content of the belief. Formalism emphasizes the first side of this dichotomy; hence "formalism". Another aspect of this tendency is the idea that it is possible to draw a sharp distinction between what one does not believe in and what one believes in: dissociating myself from something is supposed to be fundamentally unrelated to the positive content of what I believe in. The tendency I have in mind emphasizes the first side of this dichotomy; hence "negativism".[1] These two aspects of the tendency go together in a particularly evident way in its way of understanding fanaticism. Fanaticism is here understood as an exclusively formal position, and dissociating oneself from fanaticism – which the formalist/ negativist philosopher does more than anything else – is supposed to be a purely negative movement: the formalist takes philosophy to be neutral in respect of content, but since there are some formal features which are invalid as such, irrespective of content, it is nonetheless possible to show the philosophical untenability of fanaticism.

My discussion in this chapter aims both at explaining what I mean with these terms and this tendency, and at explaining what the problem with it is. In the first section I present typical examples of formalism in moral philosophy; in the second section, typical examples in the philosophy of religion. My point is, generally speaking, that there are some questions to which the formal approach implicitly presupposes an answer, without itself, since it is a *formal* approach, being able to answer them; making the implicit answer explicit would show the non-formal character of formalism.

I. *Formalism in moral philosophy*

In *Freedom and Reason*,[2] R. M. Hare gives an example: one person likes to play the trumpet, but his neighbor cannot stand the sound of it. The example is given in order to pose a problem for Hare's own way of treating moral questions, for treating them as questions possible to solve by means of universalization. Whereas in other cases it is possible to criticize someone's behavior by saying that his inclinations being what they are, he cannot want that what he does should be done to him, this could not be done in this case: if he likes the sound of the trumpet, he is not bothered by the possible trumpet playing of his neighbor. However, there is, according to Hare, a solution to the problem:

> *B* has got, not to imagine him in *A*'s situation with his own (B's) likes and dislikes, but to imagine himself in *A*'s situation with *A*'s likes and dislikes ... The natural way for the argument then to run is for *B* to admit that he is not prepared to prescribe universally that people's likes and dislikes should be disregarded by other people, because this would entail prescribing that other people should disregard his own likes and dislikes.[3]

Hare's understanding of morality then is that it is, as he puts it, a matter of "universalized self-interest".[4] However, this results in another problem for Hare: the problem that there may be persons who do not think in terms of inclinations and interests, but in terms of ideals – persons whom Hare calls "fanatics":

> [H]e must be, not merely wanting to play the trumpet himself, but thinking it good that the trumpet should be played by whomsoever, and that whosoever plays it should not be frustrated, even by *B* himself if he has become so depraved as to lose his taste for the instrument ... For it is when people step from the selfish pursuit of their own interests to the propagation of perverted ideals that they become really dangerous. We shall never understand the phenomenon called Fascism, and other similar political movements, until we realize that this is what is happening. The extreme sort of Fascist is a fanatic who not merely wants something for himself, but thinks that it ought to be brought into existence universally, whether or not anybody else, or even himself if his tastes change, wants it.[5]

(One thing Hare disregards – something I will not deal extensively with in what follows – is that what I like, what I have an inclination toward, what I want, is not at all a transparent question. His understanding of the human being is extremely "flat": Hare could perhaps acknowledge that a human being may not be sure about what it is she wants, but he could not, without giving up his basic way of thinking philosophically, acknowledge the fact that the question about what it is I want may be an inner struggle in which I am in conflict with myself about what it is I want, that the character of that which one part of me wants I try to disguise for myself in this struggle. Such an inner struggle cannot be understood as a matter of preferences in conflict; when preferences conflict – there are two things I would like to buy, but I cannot afford them both – they are on the same level, and that I decide on one of them does not mean that I reject the other one as such).

Thus, selfishness is not the problem for Hare. On the contrary, self-interest is what is basic in his account, and non-fanatical morality is about solving conflict of interests, solving them by trying to find principles to act on which I am ready to accept, also when they are turned against me. And that presupposes, of course, that people hold to what is in their own interest. Self-interest does not become a moral problem until what Hare sees as a logical mistake is made: if one has the disinclination to be done to in the way one does unto others, but one still says that one has the right to do it, the logical mistake of not accepting the prescription which results from a universalization of that which one says one has the right to do, is made. Note that making an unfounded exception for oneself is not a moral failure according to Hare, only a logical one. The real moral problem for Hare is, as the quote above shows, the opposite of selfishness: when one is ready to do something, for the sake of the good, which is not in one's interests. Here, for once, Hare takes a real moral stand, one that is not reducible to logic (and part of the problem in his moral philosophy is the tension that arises here).

All this result in claims which are, to say the least, surprising, for example: "[I]t is one thing for the Nazi to think that Jews are inferior specimens of humanity, and another for him to try systematically to exterminate them. It is upon the morality of the latter operation, not of the mere holding of the former opinion, that the liberal and the Nazi differ."[6] Or rather, they are not so surprising after all, when one takes into account how Hare thinks (which is not to say that the claims are not really strange). It is decisive for Hare not to start the discussion on the levels of ideals, for they are on the same level as wants and interests and not susceptible to argument,[7] which means that the fact that he himself does not share the Nazi ideal is not of moral interest. What he attacks is the Nazi's *fanaticism*, the way the ideal is held and how it is acted out. If Hare would say that the anti-Fascist ideal should not be frustrated, even by himself if he would be so depraved as to lose his taste for it, that it should be brought into existence whether or not he himself, if his ideals change, wants it, he would be what he calls a fanatic, and fanaticism is what he attacks.

This way of thinking, common both inside philosophy and outside, is what I want to discuss here. It may be named "formalism" since what distinguishes it is that questions of moral, or existential, content are shunned and that the important question is taken to be a question independent of the former ones, a question about how beliefs are held. The how of belief is all-important; the what of belief is not important.

In order to begin to show the confusions of such a view and what paying attention to these confusions helps us see – I will come back to this more extensively in what follows – let us try to see from where Hare's tolerance comes. What we then run into is an insoluble tension. On the one hand tolerance is the absence of any ideal. Tolerance is what we get when we let anyone pursue their own interests and ideals as long as they do not interfere with other people's pursuit of theirs, knowing that if I am ready to try to prevent others from pursuing their interests and ideals I must be ready to let them try to prevent me from pursuing mine.[8] However, tolerance is never just an absence of ideals: why would it otherwise be something with a moral weight and importance? To be sure, Hare at times calls tolerance an ideal,[9] but nonetheless he is not ready to express himself in the way the "fanatical" advocate of tolerance would: "If I had this and that 'nontolerant interest,' disregard it."[10] Perhaps Hare thinks that he escapes this problem by understanding tolerance purely negatively, as only a matter of preventing certain violent excesses; but what would the problem with these violent excesses be for someone who had no idea about what good it is he is wronging? What Hare does not see is that his repudiation of Nazism, if it is seriously meant,[11] is itself an expression of that which he calls fanaticism, for the serious repudiation means a repudiation of the interests one would have were one to become a Nazi. And hence tolerance – if this is a good word for what we are talking about here – is not a neutral formalism, pace what I have called negativism, but based on a positive understanding of the good.[12]

Another way of expressing this point is by paying attention to the difference between moral and practical questions. Hare claims that what he says has to do with morality. Thus, he implicitly presupposes a difference between doing something morally wrong (for example, holding someone in slavery) and doing something practically wrong (for example, trying to put together a lamp but doing this in a way which results in the lamp not working). But how should this difference be accounted for? What does it mean to say that a person is something I can wrong (that is, is not a "something"), whereas a lamp is not? This difference is already a moral difference; it is a matter of recognizing something positive.

Hare has been the first example of a prevalent tendency: to think that the way a conviction is held is possible to isolate from its content. My second example is John Rawls. Obviously, his account of justice as fairness is an expression of such a way of thinking from the very start: if one wants to ground a conception of justice from what people would choose, its content cannot limit their choices. Consequently, in Rawls's original position, behind the veil of ignorance, the persons in question do not know their own conceptions of the good.[13]

What is interesting here is rather that what such an account involves is particularly obvious in Rawls. How is it possible for the persons in Rawls's original position, behind the veil of ignorance, to choose the principles of their future society, choose a conception of justice, when they do not know their own conceptions of the good? The obvious answer to this is, as Rawls puts it, that each person is nonetheless concerned to further his own interest: in the original position, each one wants himself to possess more rights and liberties, powers and opportunities, income and wealth, rather than less, and no one takes an interest in anybody else's interests.[14] Not surprisingly, Rawls realizes that this sounds a bit repellent, to which he answers:

> Of course, it may turn out, once the veil of ignorance is removed, that some of them for religious or other reasons may not, in fact, want more of these goods. But from the standpoint of the original position, it is rational for the parties to suppose that they do want a larger share ... They know that in general they must try to protect their liberties, widen their opportunities, and enlarge their means for promoting their aims whatever they are ... The assumption of mutually disinterested rationality, then, comes down to this: the persons in the original position try to acknowledge principles which advance their system of ends as far as possible. They do this by attempting to win for themselves the highest index of primary social goods, since this enables them to promote their conception of the good most effectively whatever it turns out to be.[15]

In other words, what Rawls is hinting at is the fact that a person may take whatever he gets the opportunity to take, no matter whether he needs these things or not, in case they be useful in the future. If it turns out that they are not of any use, nothing is lost: he could always get rid of them. As Rawls himself says, this is a conception of rationality drawn from economic theory.[16] But the question is: is this a good starting point when trying to understand the moral concept of justice?

Rawls is instructive, since what he shows, without this being his aim, is that without a positive understanding of the good, moral philosophy has nothing else than self-interest to appeal to. The attempt to create a kind of moral formalism, in which different moral ideas are supposed to be possible to fit, breaks then down: the framework is in itself an expression of (a lack of) moral understanding and is hence not merely a framework, and the way of thinking which leads up to it is hardly describable as moral which makes it unclear to what extent the framework is a framework for morality. For example, for both Hare and Rawls a central task is to show why I should let others be. In one respect this is morally suspect, if the goal is that people should not bother about each other unless given the permission to. But, of course, in other respects this is something morally important. The question then is: how should this be understood? Answering this question would, I take it, among other things, be a matter of referring to the good of the other as person. In other words, in the wrongness of forcing one's will on someone else, the goodness of the other person as a person shows itself. A lot more could be said about this,[17] but this is not needed here, for the important point is simply that this answer is not the answer of Hare and Rawls. What they do is try to answer questions such as this without referring to the good. The answer is then sought in the field of the practical, but apart from the fact that what is practical is not a question isolated from morality, such an answer fails to address the issue of why wronging someone has a *moral* weight: why is it not just a practical failure?[18]

II. *Formalism in the philosophy of religion: The issue of strong belief*

When it comes to religion, a widespread form of formalism concerns the alleged danger, particularly political danger, of strong belief. The idea that strong belief is dangerous is today often aimed in one direction: "The problem with Islam is that it has not yet gone through Enlightenment doubt, which we in the West have." Philosophically, this idea has been expressed by John Caputo (without aiming at Islam in particular), when he again and again emphasizes the danger of saying anything about what God wants or who, or what, God is.[19] The examples are manifold: Jean-François Lyotard draws a direct, general link between "the fantasy to seize reality" and "the desire for a return of terror",[20] and Richard Rorty writes: "Your devotion to democracy is unlikely to be wholehearted if you believe, as monotheists typically do, that we have knowledge of an 'objective' ranking of human needs that can overrule the result of democratic consensus."[21] The idea is that what is dangerous is not particularly what one believes in, but how strongly, or in what way, one believes. In other words, the way a conviction is held is possible to isolate from its content, it is thought.

Why is strong belief taken to be dangerous? The obvious answer is that a belief which is simply held does not do any damage. What does damage is beliefs acted upon, and the difference between strong and weak belief is simply that the former is acted upon to a larger degree than the latter. As clear as this may seem to be, this line of thought is nonetheless deceptive. A radical change of the present situation needs strong beliefs in its support, and in so far as this change is for the good (or for the bad), this strong belief is good (or bad). It may then seem as if strong belief is both more promising and more dangerous than weak belief, and that the latter is neutral and less extreme. However, retaining the status quo does not *need* strong belief in its support, so weak belief is not neutral.[22] And it is less extreme and less dangerous only to the extent that the present situation is not extreme and dangerous; but, of course, a person with weak belief does not see that it is dangerous, if it is so. Consequently, it is a highly suspect idea that rejecting every strong form of belief means escaping responsibility. Of course, the one who never strays far from what the decent person thinks and believes will only in very rare cases put herself to shame, will only in very rare cases have come to have made something which looks bad in the eyes of the decent person.[23] But it is clear that this has nothing to do with morality: morality means that one could feel remorse, have a bad conscience, irrespective of what anyone else, including the decent person, says. What is important to pay attention to here is the fact that the idea that strong belief is dangerous is *itself* an expression of a strong belief, namely, the belief that that which it is said follows from strong beliefs – suppression of those who believe differently – is really wrong. In other words, the whole issue seems to depend on the choice of examples, or rather on the fact that the examples are not chosen but arrived at through oblivion of other examples. Expressed in another way, if it were really the case that strong belief should be shunned, something would get lost also from the point of view of the one who warns of strong belief; it is only *some* strong beliefs which lead to suppression of those who believe differently.

The idea I have criticized here shares the same strange wavering as we have seen in Hare: what appears to be an attack on fanaticism is almost a defense of the content of the fanatic's fanaticism; the problem is understood to be exclusively about *how* something is believed, and not at all about *what* is believed. Caputo writes that "Fundamentalism attempts to close down the open-ended question 'what do I love when I love my God?' with a fixed Answer, to trap the passion for God within literal formulations, to bind up the feet of faith into a finite form instead of allowing it to open upon an infinite abyss."[24] But does Caputo really mean that their idea of God is quite alright, were it not so *fixed?* Or, focusing on the "infinite abyss", does he really mean that their idea of God is actually part of the answer, not just the whole answer?

However, there may be a specific reason for the rejection of strong belief which may make the rejection appear not as a matter of oblivion. In the discussion of Hare, I mentioned his tendency to think negatively, in the sense of trying to construct a framework which is not dependent on any understanding of the good but merely expresses what should not be done. This is a central formalist idea: the form is neutral in respect of the good, and what it excludes (in Hare's case fanaticism), it excludes in a wholly negative fashion. Expressed more generally: those who reject strong belief do this thinking about the bad things strong beliefs could bring about, but since they think negatively all they want is to get these violent excesses down to a reasonable level, not convert that which is wrong in the exact opposite direction, that is, in the direction of the good. However, as pointed out above, there is a decisive question which the one who tries to think purely negatively is not able to answer: why has wronging someone a *moral* weight? Why is it not just a practical failure? So, once again, the rejection of strong belief is a matter of oblivion, of oblivion of that understanding of the good which is there also in one's negative expressions.

One way of illustrating this is by taking a look at compromises. A compromise may seem to fit the negative account perfectly: in a compromise, what I am interested in is to remove the worst features of the ideas of the one I make the compromise with, not interested in the retention of my positive understanding of the good. Furthermore, compromises may seem to be important for society to function, which means that strong belief – belief which is not up for compromise – is detrimental. However, if one looks more closely at what happens here, one sees that a prerequisite for something being a compromise is that something is compromised, which means that each one of the parties actually believes something to be important. If this were not so, we would not have a compromise. But that something is believed to be important means that for one there is a limit to compromises. If this were not so, one would be ready to do anything, and one's belief that something is important would be empty. (And if one emphasizes the importance of compromises since one sees that talking to each other is better than fighting, this too is an expression of something one believes to be important, something which is not up for compromise). Consequently, a compromise presupposes that there is a limit to compromise. In other words, what might appear to be a purely negative issue is, on the contrary, an issue in which the positive side is absolutely central, even though it might be hidden from view. So in one sense compromises are not as fundamental for society as the remark above suggested: what is fundamental is rather the limit of compromises; that is, that which Hare perhaps would call fanaticism.[25]

The points I have made thus far call forth a question which I hold to be central. To explain what I mean, I will go back a little. Caputo expresses himself in a way which is well known by now – he expresses himself purely negatively: "Faith is faith that we can say that certain things are wrong, are evil."[26] And he emphasizes again and again that one should certainly believe in the good, but this one does primarily by not being too sure that one knows what is good:

> Faith is always inhabited by unfaith … For my faith cannot be insulated from unbelief; it is co-constituted by unbelief, which is why faith is faith and not knowledge. For I do not know what I love when I love my God. Not that I do not love God, for that is not a matter of knowing, but that I am always asking who or what the God that I love is.[27]

This is a typical formalist line of thought. What I have already said is obviously also relevant here: this expressed uncertainty hides a certainty – the belief in the good, as well as the belief in God, must mean something in order not to be merely a phrase, and so forth. But there is something more here, which is important to point out. According to Caputo, as well as to the others we have mentioned here, strong belief is dangerous since it results in one forcing one's will upon others, since one takes oneself to be certain of what the good is.[28] Hence, Caputo presupposes that all understandings of the good are on the same level, that the form "forcing one's will upon others, taking x to be the good" can take any argument. However, is this really true? Is there not an understanding – or rather "understanding"; this word is here not that apposite – of the good which does not fit into this form, that is, one which is not about force and will? (Consequently, is there not a strong belief which is not fanaticism? If so, criticizing various criticisms of strong belief is not a defense of fanaticism, even though it might superficially look like it).

If we take that which I here have hinted at seriously, what we should do is try to clarify what is actually (morally) possible to believe strongly in, and, at the same time, try to clarify the way of belief which is connected to this content. What led us astray was the formalist idea that "believing strongly" means the same no matter what is believed, so what we should do is give up this separation of form and content.

Before we move onto the next chapter, there is a difficulty which has not yet been touched upon and which needs to be addressed: what is strong (and weak) belief? It is clear that one's answer to this question is dependent on one's relation to the belief in question. The person about whom others may say that she believes strongly may deny this, saying that she simply believes, that those who say about themselves that they have a weak belief are hypocrites who merely say that they believe, but actually do not. Someone else may say to himself that his belief is weak; this may be a way for him to express his own feeling of double-mindedness, his doubt, which he at times may see as a temptation, at times as something which pulls him in the direction of the good (and in this latter case, the belief which he doubts is weak, but yet too strong). And in this inner struggle, one may say to oneself that one is a hypocrite. Another person may try to give an account of why someone else acted as she did, explaining this by saying "she believes x, but her belief is weak," without this intimating neither criticism nor praise. And someone may explain his own acting in this way, too. The point is not that we should try to come to some sort of decision here, a conclusive answer to questions such as: Is there a neutral way of measuring strength of belief? Are the above cases examples of some belief or non-belief? What should be said is simply that the question about whether it is a matter of the first or the second is *itself* an expression of one's relation to the belief in question. This is another way in which we should reject formalism, since formalism, is, in a way, the idea that neutral measuring of strength is possible; this is another shape the separation of form and content may take.

CHAPTER 2

THE SOURCES OF THEOLOGY

In this chapter I will describe another problem constituting the background for that understanding of religious belief I will develop in subsequent chapters (especially in chapters 4–5). Whereas the problem in the last chapter belonged to moral philosophy and philosophy of religion, this problem belongs to the philosophy of theology (and thus to theology too, as long as this philosophical question about its own character is not answered). The problem concerns what is often called "the sources of theology". The problem is of importance in its own right, but also relates to a possible answer to the problems I described in the last chapter. A theologian might say that theology has an answer to them, in the special content of theology. My question, however, is how that answer should be understood: what are the grounds for a theological statement?

In introductions to theology, lists of these "sources" are often enumerated in the beginning. The lists are different in different books, but contain similar things. One example: John Macquarrie, in *Principles of Christian Theology*, mentions experience, revelation, scripture, tradition, culture and reason.[1] In what follows, I will use this particular enumeration as a point of departure for my discussion, but I will not restrict myself to anyone's interpretation of them (for example, Macquarrie's); how I understand them will show itself in the course of the discussion.

The heading "sources of theology" is not accepted by everyone; Macquarrie calls them "formative factors in theology" and another name which is now and then used is "building blocks of theology". The mere fact that these lists have different names shows that it is not completely clear what functions they have. Of course, the enumerations can be understood as specifying what theology "is about", in some vague manner. Then it is certainly uncontroversial that something like "scripture" is mentioned in the enumeration, whatever one thinks of its importance. And sometimes some of the sources – if that is the preferred name – are understood as providing a way of expressing theological statements, statements which in themselves are held to be independent of this way of expressing them; the source "culture" is now and then given this role. However, it is clear that these enumerations are not only assigned these roles, but also taken to specify the grounds of theological statements, what reasons can be given for these, and so forth. However that may be, it is the enumerations understood in that way that I will discuss here. My questions are simply the following. What status do these sources have? In what way does their respective status distinguish themselves from each other? Notice that these questions are not epistemological. Hence, the questions are not about how to determine whether a specific theological statement is true or not, how one "knows" something or other, but about something more fundamental: how the claim should be *understood*, what talking about status here *means*. In the next section (I) the possible sources scripture, tradition and culture will be discussed. In section II, I ask: what is the theological question, the question whose answer the sources are sources to? In the next two sections, the possible sources reason (III), and experience and revelation (IV), are examined. Last, some criticism of revelation (section V) and some possible objections to what I have been saying (section VI) are discussed. Before starting the discussion proper, some more introductory remarks have to be made, however.

The mere fact that these enumerations mention several sources shows that the enumerations do not say everything that needs to be said here; an (at least implicit) answer to the questions I have asked is necessary in order for these sources even to be able to have the role as sources. Using them as sources will at least be a matter of giving different weights to the different sources and so calculating the resultant, and since that is an issue about the relation of the respective status of the sources, none of the sources can itself state what weight to give to the different sources and how the resultant should be calculated. This is so also for the source "reason", since it, as the sources are here stated, is only one of the parties litigant. In other words: if reason is a source, how the different sources are related is not a question of reason. Realizing this, one might conclude that the questions are impossible to answer and that one should content oneself by talking about "power of judgment". This is not necessarily wrong, but as long as what this means is not clarified in greater detail, this is only a phrase intended to hide one's confusion.[2]

I. *Scripture, tradition, culture*

Let us leave the possible source "reason" for a while, since it seems to pose the most challenging difficulties. We must discuss several of the possible sources, so we can just as well begin with some other one. In that way we will perhaps get some hints about how the question about reason should be approached.

Starting with the question about scripture, it is easy to see that the status it has is derived, not its own. How should the declared difference in status between, say, the Bible and the Quran be understood? If one says that one of them has status but not the other, is there something more to say about this? One cannot refer to these themselves, to be sure, since it is their status the question is about. It is possible to say that there are no answers to be given here, that the status is simply primitive, but such an answer means that there is not anything to say about what scripture has status *as*, and the answer close at hand for many is here "as the word of God" or such like. Hence, the status of scripture is said to depend on its, in some sense, coming from God. Here, words and phrases like inspiration, an account of a revelation, and the like, are used. In other words, the question about the status of scripture is then dependent on a more elementary one: the question about the status of the originator and/or of the content. And our question is then how *their* status should be understood. The same goes for possible sources like culture and tradition. There are many cultures and traditions, and if one says that one has status but not some other one, this becomes a question of the status of the content and possibly of the status of "the originator" (if one believes that God acts through the culture or the tradition), just as with scripture.

II. *What is the theological question?*

Now we have passed through three of the six sources which were mentioned in the beginning. What we have ended up with are questions about the status of the originator and about the status of the content. To be able to approach these issues, it is wise not to rush headlong into them. It is better to wait a minute and ask a question which has been neglected so far: what is it that theology does? The fact is – and this should not really have to be pointed out – that the question about sources is directly dependent on what one sees as the primary theological question. Becoming clear about the question means becoming clear about what the sources are.

Of course, there are many opinions about what the theological question is, and this may seem to imply that it is not possible to say anything general about the sources of theology. In one sense it is obvious that the question about sources has to become more specific in every single case. But in order to show that it is yet possible to say something here, I want to contrast two ways of comprehending the theological question, and I will illustrate this by means of a concept we have already encountered: "originator".

It may seem obvious – even a triviality – that if God is the originator of something, this something is a source for theology. This would be the case if theology were regarded as a study of God, parallel with geology, meteorology, zoology; that is, if the aim of theology was to provide us with *information.* How one uses the possible results of the study would then not be a theological question. For some, the result would be indifferent. For others it would be something to take into consideration when calculating how to go about to get the things one wants. That the study may – as a result of the investigation – discover a command of God does not change anything essentially. Perhaps the prudent one *has* to take the result of the study into consideration since it is impossible to get out of the reach of God, but this does not make the question about how one should use the results of the study into a theological question. And if the study of God studies certain experiences, on the one hand these would be a source of information too; on the other hand the goal of the study may be to get to know how to cause them, if one wants an experience of that kind. Hobbes is an obvious adherent to this way of understanding theology. As he says, "The Right of Nature, whereby God reigneth over men, and punisheth those that break his Lawes, is to be derived, not from his Creating them, as if he required obedience, as of Gratitude for his benefits; but from his *Irresistible Power.*"[3] This means that there is no "right" here; resisting God's power is simply impossible, and for that reason it is important to get information about it, so that one does not try to do what will necessarily fail. If we discovered that there is a degree to which resisting God's power is possible, there would be no additional question about whether doing so would be right or not. (This is connected to Hobbes's theoretical egoism, but this is not the place to discuss that issue.)

However, theology could, in contrast to the above, be understood as a question of what it is really possible to believe *in.* According to the former way of understanding theology, the question of God – the study of God – is one thing, the question about what is authoritative – about what one should use the results of the study *to* – another. In the latter way of understanding theology, the question of God and the question about what is authoritative are not two separate questions. This does not mean that it becomes true by definition that there is a God, as if God is defined as that which is authoritative, no matter what character that which is supposed to be authoritative has. This is not so, since the question is precisely whether that which shows itself to be authoritative is a matter of God or not; one crucial question is here whether the authoritative is a person, or, as it is often thought, a principle.[1] Moreover, asking the question about what is authoritative is not to place oneself "above" God, to regard God as an object of judgment. On the contrary, the authoritative is what one can *not* place oneself above. It is the former way of understanding theology – in which the question of God and the question about what is authoritative are two separate questions – which makes placing oneself above God possible, since a manipulating attitude is there a possibility.

When we now have two different ways of putting the theological question, is what remains to choose between them gratuitously, to choose between them according to taste? If we in all seriousness really ask the question about how to understand theology, about how to put the theological question, we see that these two ways of putting the question are not on an equal footing. If there is a question about which of the two questions to ask and this question is a theological question, this means that they are not on an equal footing, but that the second one is primary. Asking the question about which of the two questions to ask is to ask the second one, since it is only in asking the second one that the question about authority is asked, and the question about what question to ask is a question about authority. The first question has a place only against the background of an (explicit or implicit) answer to the second one. Therefore the second question is primary. What I say with regard to the question about the sources of theology in what follows is related to *this* question; if one asks another question, other sources may be the ones that are important.

To recapitulate: what the sources are, are dependent on what the question is; to ask the question about what the question is, is to ask the question about authority. Thus, it is the question about authority we must clarify to become clear about the sources. This is not the place for a complete discussion of that question (whatever that would mean); in a way, the rest of the book could be understood as part of such a discussion. What I will do here is to come to terms with some misunderstandings about what it means to answer it – come to terms with some ideas about how the question *must* be, and *cannot* be, answered – and at the same time extract some concepts which are important in this context.

Asking the question "What is it really possible to believe in?" – the question about authority – is to ask this question to all that content I have already mentioned. It is possible, to be sure, to find the answer in some such content; asking this question is of course not to dismiss the content-part of every source automatically, only to say that their status is not their own, that it is derived. Or rather, asking the question about authority often becomes a matter of asking what the content really is, since the meaning of a religious formulation is not limited to what I, or any one else, have taken to be its meaning. But it is true that asking the question about authority is to take a certain distance to every historical form of religion. However, this does not mean taking distance to God: on the contrary, when a religious believer asks herself this question, this is an important aspect of her longing for togetherness with God.[5]

What we must ask – since our investigation is about the sources of theology – is what it here means to "find" an answer, what it means to find a content authoritative, what it means to find that God is the originator of something.[6] When one is confronted with many different contents of that kind, what does it mean to say that they differ in status (in relation to the question "What is it really possible to believe in?")? Having come this far, the sources left are reason, revelation and experience. However, it may seem easy to discard the latter two: to ask the question about authority is to distance oneself from any particular experience anyone has had and to ask whether what was experienced was really something authoritative. If matters are different with the concept of revelation – if one claims that such a distance is not possible here – that is due to the fact that there is always a question to be asked about whether something that seemed to be a revelation really was one, about whether God really was the originator. Thus, provided that this line of thought is correct, is not the only way of answering the questions above about what it means to find something authoritative, to use one's reason; does not what has been said thus far end up in a religion within the boundaries of mere reason; is not what has been said thus far an argument for rational theology?[7]

III. *Reason*

However, can reason alone help us here? Kant – the one to whom the hint in the previous paragraph obviously refers – thought that he in the practical philosophy (in contrast to the theoretical philosophy in which the boundaries for the use of pure reason is drawn) could purely by means of reason, without any content, by starting from the purely formal property of the moral law as law, reach a formulation of this very moral law. However, it is obvious that something essential has been left out in such an attempt. If I wrong someone, is this comparable with doing something irregular, something not possible to state as a law, with being irrational? Wronging someone has a moral weight (is, for example, something I have a bad conscience about), being irrational has not. (How should someone who claims that she has a bad conscience for her irrationality be understood?) In other words, this weight is not something one infers – as if it were something possible to overlook by an intellectual mistake – but is immediately given.[8] This example was one of remorse and conscience; another one could have been of love, in which I immediately turn toward another human being, without any preconceived notions which he/she has to comply with, rejecting all manipulation, having seen something which in respect of authority is incomparable to such manipulation.[9] (Kant's confusion has here a common philosophical form: in order for his account to be about morality (and not about something else), he implicitly relies on something whose importance he at the same time explicitly denies. What he relies on is so central that it is hard to see, and when it becomes articulated it is taken as merely a surface phenomenon.)

IV. *Experience and revelation*

Thus, what we have run into here is something immediately authoritative, something about which some further question about status cannot be asked. Asking a question of that kind would only be my attempt to escape my responsibility; that is, the question is asked precisely since I know that it cannot be asked.[10] Here something authoritative is experienced, and this means that it is *not* possible to distance oneself from. Furthermore, this makes it even clearer why the status of scripture, tradition and culture is derived. In their case, one could imagine that scripture says one thing and tradition another, and the theologian wavers to and fro between them, trying to reconcile them in some way. But experiencing something authoritative *means* that it cannot be weighed against anything else, means that I am experiencing, and not comparing one experience to another one, means that "experience" here does not refer to some medium but to a direct relation to something authoritative – provided that I do not deny the authoritative nature of my experience, of course.

What is most important to notice, with regard to our discussion, is that what is here found to be immediately authoritative is not grounded in something subjective, for example, in what I want or wish. It does not necessarily coincide with what *anyone* wants or wishes. To illustrate this, let us turn to the parable of the Good Samaritan.[11] To strengthen the point, we could imagine that it is not only the case that, as it is written, "Jews do not share things in common with Samaritans,"[12] but that the Jews and the Samaritans were enemies to each other, at war with each other. In such a situation, it is possible to imagine that everyone dislikes that the Samaritan helps the beaten man (although they do perhaps not want to acknowledge that they dislike it). Other Samaritans may think that one should not help the enemy. People outside of the conflict may be afraid of what they see, since what the Samaritan does shows a possibility also for their part – helping an enemy – a possibility they want to hide for themselves. But do not the Jews and the beaten man have to regard what the Samaritan did as good? Irrespective of the fact that they can react in the same way as others – wanting to shut their eyes to a possibility – being helped by someone one sees as of less worth can be seen as degrading, as something one would have rather died to avoid than been subjected to. And also the Samaritan himself may do what he does – helping the beaten man – against his own will, so to speak. He would rather like to pass by, but he *cannot*: a care, or love, for the beaten man is there which he, however much he tries, cannot extinguish.

The authority which is here discovered is not a matter of reason, since it has a definite weight which is not of reason. Nor is it a matter of a liking or an opinion, for the authority – as the example shows – can counter one's likings and opinions. And the Samaritan's possible irresolution is not a matter of uncertainty or tentativeness about what is authoritative but is, on the contrary, conditioned by his certainty: the irresolution is his attempt at defending himself, or his likings and opinions, against this authority. The authority which is here discovered has simply nothing to do with subjectivism, humanism or something immanent – it is, to put it briefly, not a matter of information, which one can do whatever one likes with, which one can use to those ends one happens to see oneself as having. What is the authority then a matter of? A religious believer or a theologian would here, I guess, use the concept of revelation.[13]

("Humanism" is, to be sure, a contested concept. But, in *this* context, I understand humanism as saying that one should leave other persons alone if they want to be left alone: you should not confront their opinions and likings as long as they do not hurt others; you should not save anyone's life, but try to suppress your love for them, if they hate to be given help from an inferior person such as you. "Humanism" is the principle according to which the good person, disturbing the (non)moral order, is collectively condemned.[14] Another example may be that in a society in which some kind of "an eye for an eye" principle prevails, a convicted criminal may herself want this principle to be applied to her case – not doing so would be to disrespect her – which means that this society has *collectively* shut its eyes to what is good. Hence, non-humanism means seeing that such agreements do not have any moral weight, means the rejection of moral inter-subjectivity.)[15]

Since our question is about the character of the theological question, what is the source to its answer, and not about what its answer is, our task is not to find out what our result implies in respect of belief in *God*.[16] That "revelation" is the religious categorization of that which we have found does not mean that the latter task is supposed to be accomplished. Nor does it mean that this source is identified with any historical form of religion; on the contrary, asking the question of authority is to take a certain distance from every such form in its historical form. It is also possible to understand this term – revelation – independently of its religious use, if one notices the following point. Thus far we have been talking about "experience". The term "revelation" could be used to highlight one important aspect of that kind of experience we have been talking about. "Revelation" refers to this more detailed description. The authority which is here discovered cannot be identified with something immanent, as has been pointed out above. This is not a hypothesis about its origin; it is a description of what it means to have an experience of this character. When it is claimed that experiences of this kind could be hypothetically explained biologically, however, the explanation clashes with this character, which means that what is explained is another experience, not this one: a presupposition for this explanation to work as an explanation is that the character of the experience is rejected beforehand. In other words, the experienced authority is transcendent. (Simone Weil[17] talks in a similar context about supernatural love, implicit love of God.)

The concept that "the experienced authority is transcendent" needs some explanation, since many popular religious ways of talking about revelation refer to it as something immanent. For example, this is the case when the authority is said to depend on a command of God or on God as a lawgiver. However, commands and laws are nearly related to what I, in the above discussion, called "information". A command and a law could be rejected: one thinks that what one gains by doing so outweighs the possible risk of punishment. And when a command is followed and a law obeyed this could be done in the same spirit: as the outcome of a calculation. In both these cases, it is not the command and the law which is taken to be authoritative, but something else: one's own good say. The authority the Samaritan in my example experiences is of another character. Here there are only two pos-sibilities: trying to shut one's eyes to it or taking it seriously. If one uses the word "God" here, God, or the existence of God, is no fact in the strict sense. A fact is something it is possible to use in a calculation, but what is here experienced is something of a different character. That this is not possible here is not to be explained in terms of the power of God, as something which in the end overturns all of my plans by means of force; or rather, what it means to talk about the power of God could be elucidated by paying attention to the concept of authority I am here trying to clarify. That the authority has nothing to do with commands or laws is also important to point out since that would disconnect the authority and love: above I said that love is an immediate turning toward someone else, which means that it cannot be mediated by means of a command or a law. The authority is nothing distinct from this immediate turning: the authority is *in* that turning. And this means that, despite its usefulness for bringing about an important change of philosophical awareness – from epistemological questions to existential questions – the term "authority" is in the end misleading: by focusing on the question about authority, we have run into something which is above authority, something more authoritative than authority. (This is obviously an anti-formalist point.) I will return to this theme, especially in chapters 4 and 5.

V. *Objections to revelation*

As I said, revelation is transcendent, not immanent; that is, it is not to be identified with something merely historical. However, does not revelation (or experience) mean precisely something historical, something that occurs at a specific point of time, in contrast to eternal truths of reason?

This was G. E. Lessing's objection to revelation. He gave a role to revelation – an educatory, one could perhaps say psychological, role – but revelation was not something which gave insight into something which a human being could not also gain insight into by himself.[18] This can be summed up with the help of what is now and then described as Lessing's slogan: "Contingent truths of history can never become arguments for necessary truths of reason."[19]

However, something needs to be pointed out here. What Lessing is trying to give expression to is partly a correct point: what ground a statement has is internally related to the character of this statement; that is, necessary truths of reason have their kind of ground, contingent truths of history theirs (provided that we accept this categorization). This means that in so far as a statement does not have a revelation-character, its truth cannot be revealed. As we have seen, however, the source of the answer to the question about authority is not reason. The phrase "which a human being could gain insight into by himself" is certainly not that clear, but the question about authority is not answered by means of inference or derivation:[20] wronging someone is not to make an intellectual mistake, as I have already said.

Lessing distinguishes between the contingent and the necessary, and it is clear that the question about authority is about the latter: it is not as if the Samaritan had bad luck, passing the beaten man precisely when what is authoritative is helping him and not stealing his money. In other words, the necessary and the rational do not coincide. One idea which can make one believe that they coincide is the idea that truth has two and only two sources: reason (the source of necessary truths) and experience (the source of contingent truths). However, moral and existential insights are not a matter of (that kind of) knowledge, not because they are supposed to be less certain, but because the difficulty here is not a matter of one's lack of skill, which is the epistemological difficulty.[21] In other words, and as I have already pointed out, what is revealed is not information, facts, which Lessing presupposes to be the case.[22] Say that the Samaritan passed by the beaten man without helping him. Later on, pangs of conscience strike him. That this is what strikes him means that he is not informed of some hitherto unknown fact: in that case he could, possibly, excuse himself by blaming his lack of knowledge. On the other hand it is now pangs of conscience strike him, now he sees what it is he has done. Consequently, the revelation does not occur at a specific point of time, as if it sometimes gave me access to certain facts, sometimes not; when it comes to the question about authority, what the matter is about is, rather, my own openness for really taking it seriously, and *this* openness is something contingent. In that sense, the distinction eternal/temporal is dissolved here. But precisely *that* I shut my eyes to it – and that I do not admit to myself that this is what I do – shows that the question is not something I am indifferent to even when I shut my eyes to it. If it were really something indifferent I could just pass it by. This means that even with regard to shutting one's eyes to the beaten man, revelation is a precondition *in* – should not, for obvious reasons, be understood as temporally preceding – what one does.[23]

Somebody who hints at all this, without really getting hold of it, is J. G. Fichte. In his *Versuch einer Kritik aller Offenbarung* he is mostly close to Lessing – revelation does not give us any insights, but may have an important psychological role, as an educator – even though his line of thought is very different, completely dependent on Kant. Revelation does not give us any insights, for two reasons. The experience of a revelation cannot, just as little as any other experience, give us any *theoretical* insights about what is not within the bounds of experience, which Kant showed in *Kritik der reinen*

Vernunft. Hence, a revelation is not something essentially different from what we already have access to without it.[24] *Practically* it does not give us any insights, firstly because that would mean moral heteronomy,[25] secondly because the acknowledgement of something as a revelation presupposes the moral law, in the sense that it is only starting from it that the existence of God is postulated.[26] What role may revelation then have? It may strengthen the effect of the moral law, its effect in us, by means of the idea of a holy being; since "holy" is a moral concept this does not result in heteronomy.[27] However, in one section, Fichte discusses a case which does not fit into this schematization. What he had in mind in the above discussion was a case in which someone is already attentive to the moral law, but whose sensibility is too strong and whose will for that reason needs to be strengthened. But how come that we are attentive to the moral law? Could not revelation be what makes this possible?[28] Fichte does not pursue this line of thought any further,[29] but what we are here able to see is a tension between, on the one hand, understanding revelation as a matter of information, which means that is has no essential role, and, on the other hand, as an answer to a question which precedes all this.

VI. *Answers to some objections*

In this, next to last, section, I would like to answer some possible objections to what I have been saying. These objections are expressions of thought-difficulties which I believe are hard for many to come out of. The first one is that what I have written is propagation for subjectivism, or that what I have written, irrespective of what I say, must be so understood. The answer to this is evident, however: read once again my above passage about the Good Samaritan. As I wrote there, the discovered authority has nothing to do with subjectivism, humanism or something immanent. Of course, it is *me* which the revelation addresses, but this is not subjectivism. And, of course, a revelation is something experienced, but an experience is not as such subjective – the distinction between the subjective and the objective is, when that distinction is at all applicable and relevant, a distinction within experience[30] – which means that you have to pay attention to the content of the described experience in order to be able to say whether it is objective or subjective; that is, it is not possible to disregard it by referring to its individual, or even idiosyncratic, form.[31] The difficulty for many is, I take it, that revelation as information seems to be more objective: the line of thought is that since revelation as information is something to which one adopts some or other of several possible attitudes, the revelation as such is in some sense independent of me. But in fact revelation as information is the opposite of being objective: precisely since one here adopts an attitude, a subjectivism is prevalent, a subjectivism which is impossible when it comes to revelation understood in the way which has been clarified in this chapter, as we have seen. Thus, the authority is in the end about considering what it is really possible to believe in, what something means – and what one for that reason cannot choose to understand in another way, whose meaning one can only try to repress – what one in a sense must believe. Here the difficulty is precisely to critically examine oneself and why one tends to believe something (this may have its root in opportunism, in a wish to be original, in fear of a demand, in a wish to take upon oneself a demand in order to elevate oneself, and so forth) and to try to get clear about what cannot possibly be understood as such a tendency (by, say, asking why the points in the preceding parentheses are *critical*, by asking what the good contrast to all of them is).

The second objection is that what I have been doing is metaphysics, that what I have been saying is only speculation: words like "revelation" are metaphysical, speculative. However, precisely this idea – that metaphysics is a matter of what words one uses – is a metaphysical idea.[32] Doing philosophy is not about discarding certain words but about taking any word and trying to understand it as far as one is able to. Thus, disregarding some phenomenon because it looks "queer"[33] is an unphilosophical objection: the philosophical task is to try to understand the phenomenon, however queer it may seem to be, without forcing it into given theoretical frameworks, without declaring it invalid because it does not fit into these frameworks. But if you dislike the word "revelation" use another one: nothing depends on precisely it being used. Here I have used the term only to highlight an aspect of the experience; for the religious believer the term has, I take it, an additional importance. However, whatever word you use, it is important to bear in mind the descriptive, that is, non-speculative and non-hypothetical, points made in our discussion. For example, when I said that the authority the Samaritan experiences is transcendent, that is not a hypothesis about its origin but a description of the character of this very experience.

The third objection is that I, notwithstanding what I have said, in the end hold onto reason as the only source. Is not the line of thought in this chapter a result of using reason, which means that the role revelation has been assigned, it has been assigned by reason, which, consequently, is the ultimate source? Of course, if you want to use the word "reason" in that way, do it; but there is an obvious risk that this expression confuses one.[34] The concept of reason, when it is used in enumerations of the sources of theology, is thought to be some kind of criterion or source of criterions. This means that when we want to say something about their status as sources, we cannot put up some other criterion against them, as yet another criterion. Nor can we choose one of them as a criterion against the others. In short, no external criterion is of any help here. Instead, the question I have asked is a question of understanding; what I have done is not having decided between two, or more, possible positions, but having tried to consider what is a possible position in the first place. So what I have done here I would rather like to describe as a matter of *thinking* (trying to understand what something means), not of *reason* (occupying the seat of a judge). In other words, this is not to advocate rational theology or "religion within the boundaries of mere reason", as has already been pointed out. Nor is it to advocate "religion within the boundaries of mere thinking", since talking about "boundaries" would here be a confusion – thinking is not a criterion, as I said before – but also since thinking could make one aware of something which it is not possible to place oneself above. And thinking itself is not a matter of placing oneself above anything. In that sense, philosophy is not the business of reason, as a contrast to theology which is supposed to be a business of faith. Philosophy has no criterion which it is trying to fight for, against other criterions; it is a matter of thinking, of understanding. If this were not so, philosophy would only be something gratuitous.[35]

The last objection is that what I have said here makes theology as a practice impossible: "If revelation is the only source, is not the only thing one could do to hope for it?" On the one hand, this is not necessarily an objection: perhaps theology is really impossible. On the other hand, starting out from what I said above about "thinking", it is possible to defend theology in the same way. (The difference being that although I would not myself use the term revelation in the philosophical context, in the latter context thinking and revelation would be connected, I guess.) I am the addressed one, to be sure, but this does not mean that revelation is strictly individual, as if what other human beings, or I myself, say in religious and existential matters is completely irrelevant, as if revelation as an address were in opposition to revelation as something to talk about. Asking oneself the question "What is it really possible to believe in?" and, in writing, trying to consider what and why and what not and why not – to do theology – is therefore not at all something purely individual, but is to a great extent to converse with others. That the example we have discussed here – a version of the parable of the Good Samaritan – is clear and seems not to be something to consider (although the philosophical discussion about the parable shows that it contains far more things than might appear initially), is what makes it good as an example. However, when one for one's own part – or as a part of a whole civilization – is really at a loss and tangled in, the thing is different. "But if revelation were the source, what would theology be other than different subjective opinions fighting against each other? How is it possible to show that something really is a revelation and that something other is not? How is this possible if the source itself *is* revelation?" This is not a good question. Try to remember an occasion when someone said something to you which gave you an existential insight! Was this a matter of showing something by means of reference to criteria? I guess not. Nor is it a matter of saying something you are already clear about; often one reacts reluctantly in the beginning, trying to counter-argue what has been said, and only after some time does one realize that what the other person said was completely right. And when one sees this, one also sees that this is not just an opinion fighting against another opinion; on the contrary, what one tried to hold onto was an opinion, but the insight is something completely different. However, and that is perhaps the confusion which gives rise to the problem, the wordings we try to give *of* the revelation is of course not the revelation itself. A wording has no power of its own *as a wording*, which means that the revelation itself is of a different kind.

VII. *Conclusion*

In this chapter, we have got another background for that understanding of religious belief which I will develop in subsequent chapters (especially in chapters 4–5). By focusing on a question about the "sources of theology" we came across the question about authority. The understanding of religious belief I will develop in subsequent chapters is meant to be an understanding which is able to come to terms with that question; that is, it will not be of the kind I have criticized here, not an understanding of religious belief in terms of information and calculation. Before starting to develop that understanding, one more background to the project must be given.

Chapter 3

Phillips and the Idea of a Contemplative Philosophy

That the primary focus of the mainstream of the philosophy of religion is on the "what" of belief – its "propositional content" – is not difficult to see. The "how" of belief – the act of belief, the way of belief, what it means to believe – does not get as much attention, and the same goes for the relation between them. (In that respect, Caputo and like-minded philosophers really do stand out.)

D. Z. Phillips, however, is often seen, and rightly so, in contrast to that which philosophers of religion like Richard Swinburne represent: partly an unawareness of the specific religious character of religious belief, partly apologetics. And on these issues, and more, his contributions are far from being overrated. However, I think yet that what leads him astray, in a way which I will try to describe, is a distorted emphasis on these two points: that there is a religious way of believing which is possible to isolate from what it is the religious believer believes (formalism); that we should not, because of the contemplative and cool nature of philosophy – a description of its nature which I think is partly right – pay attention to the essential differences different (religious) contents bring in. This chapter, which is the chapter most explicitly devoted to the Wittgensteinian tradition in philosophy of religion referred to in the introduction, will provide the last background to that understanding of religious belief that I will try to describe in subsequent chapters.

I will begin the discussion by pointing out an asymmetry in the use of concepts: how one use is parasitic upon another one (section I). This asymmetry is both known and not known by the one who uses the concept in the parasitic way; it is a matter of self-deception. I explain what this means in the next section (II). The discussions about asymmetries and self-deception must be seen against the background of a more extensive question, however, a question about the attitude of calculation, which I discuss in section III.[1]

In the last section (IV), I discuss Phillips's understanding of philosophy and the shortcomings of that understanding.

I. *An asymmetry in the use of concepts*

One way of being attentive to where Phillips goes wrong is by studying what he writes in some chapters in *Religion and Friendly Fire*.[2] In a chapter of that book in which he, in an elucidatory way, discusses the concept of trust, he nevertheless finishes by saying that there are alternatives to that conception of trust which he has been discussing, for example, what he calls "trust in chariots", that is, a warrior ethos.[3] And in a paper published elsewhere – "Ethics and Humanistic Ethics" – Phillips emphasizes that concepts such as "humanity" and "authenticity" may play a positive role also in (what he there calls) a heroic morality.[4] But in both of these cases, Phillips does not bother to make clear *what* role they play. That they could be used to hide something, as a means of self-deception, is not paid attention to by him.[5] That the warrior ethos stands in opposition to that which he has been discussing is clear; however, the question is what role the concept of trust plays in it. Of course, the same *word* may be used for something essentially different. Phillips has then no other choice – if he wants to claim that it is a matter of the same concept in the two cases – than to say that they are *not* essentially different, that the differences are inessential. But saying so is to take a moral stand, and that contradicts Phillips's claim to neutrality. If there is a point in emphasizing the connection, the point lies elsewhere: the warrior ethos makes use of a concept which is not its own, in order to hide its own true nature, a self-deception which, at the same time, expresses a belief in an authority which it is unable to acknowledge.[6] Phillips writes as if we had a concept which is able to contain (partly) different contents and as if the description of the use of the concept in different contexts could be neutral with regard to these different contents. In other words, he does not notice the asymmetry I have sketched.

All this becomes all the more obvious in a later chapter.[7] There Phillips discusses the text by Søren Kierkegaard which in English is known as *Purity of Heart*.[8] Phillips's thesis is, to put it shortly, that Kierkegaard says more than we know in that he claims that the one who does not will the good, or only wills the good to a certain degree, is necessarily double-minded. In other words, Phillips expresses a kind of formalism: to will and what one wills are possible to isolate from each other. This formalism is implicit in much of Phillips's writing on moral philosophy and philosophy of religion;

in a place in which he is explicit about it, he emphasizes the distinction between *general* claims in ethics (concerning *any* kind of moral concern, that is, claims about the form of moral view points) and claims made from the perspective of one *particular* morality (that is, claims about moral content).[9] The similarities to Hare and Caputo are obvious.

Kierkegaard, on the other hand,[10] wants to point out an asymmetry: it is not a matter of the same "will" when it comes to the one who wills the good and the one who wills something other than the good, and it is the latter "will" which is dependent on the first one. Willing the good means willing wholeheartedly, whereas willing something other than the good means willing in relation to an "if."[11] (I will come back to this "if" in a moment).

Phillips seems to have partly misunderstood what it is Kierkegaard is trying to say. Phillips interprets it as a psychological thesis: "Kierkegaard is tempted to say more than we know, namely, that anyone who deceives him or herself ... will, of necessity, *experience* a disharmony in the self."[12] But this is explicitly denied by Kierkegaard:

> Even an atrocious misdeed is committed, even blood is spilt, and many times in such a way that it must in truth be said about the guilty one: he knew not, what he did – perhaps he dies, without ever in repentance really getting to know what it was he did. And does passion ever really know what it does, isn't this deceptive ignorance about itself its ingratiating temptation and its apparent excuse ...[13]

What Kierkegaard is denying here is precisely that the disharmony is necessarily known. However, that there is a disharmony is, I take it, an almost trivial point: if one really believes in the good, does this not mean that one believes that the one who does not will the good in fact misses something, deprives herself of something, namely misses to do the good, which is the most valuable, or rather invaluable, of all? We should here not have a too simplified understanding of the psychological, as if psychological attribution did not express a moral stand (or the lack of one).

The essential difference between Phillips and Kierkegaard is hence not whether the disharmony is necessarily experienced or not, but seems to concern the issue of self-deception: Phillips thinks it possible that someone wills what is not good and yet is perfectly clear about this, whereas Kierkegaard denies this. Now I could begin to scrutinize Phillips's counter-examples, examples supposed to show that a person who does not will the good but does not deceive herself is intelligible; for my part some of his counter-examples do not seem to be about someone not willing the good, and above all Phillips seems to have a far too simplified understanding of self-deception, since the self-deception shows itself precisely in those examples which is supposed to be examples of the opposite.[14] However, such a discussion is rather pointless: the one who thinks that Phillips is right could agree with my criticism of the examples but claim that there are better ones. So the question is better put in another way: what does it mean to say that there is necessarily an element of self-deception in not willing the good?

II. *Self-deception*

I will begin answering that question – what does it mean to say that there is necessarily an element of self-deception in not willing the good – by giving one example of self-deception. The example is not only an exemplification of self-deception; it also serves as an answer to a distorted picture of morality, a picture which gives rise to a difficulty of realizing the centrality of self-deception. The example is the parable of the Good Samaritan (also discussed in Chapter 2).[15] When the Samaritan helps the beaten man, he does not do so because of some sort of choice, conviction, or anything of the like, on his part. If the Samaritan is asked why he did what he did, his answers would be uninformative ones such as "Because he was wounded" or "Because he needed help." What the Samaritan responded to was a person, not a principle. The priest,[16] on the other hand, could be said to be guided by a principle. If he asks himself why he did what he did – this may be occasioned by someone else asking him this – he will answer by referring to some principle, reason, argument, or the like. My first point, therefore, is this: it would be a distortion to describe morality as a kind of conviction or as a system of reasons; that may be a good account of the attitude of the priest, but not of what the Samaritan did. In the Samaritan's case, morality is, rather, a kind of understanding or attentiveness. But that is not all, and this is my second point. Already in the case of the priest, we can see this attentiveness at work, but silenced. That he asks himself why he did what he did shows that he is attentive to that which the Samaritan was attentive to. It does not matter what answer he gives; irrespective of how "convincing" the answer may be, *that* he asks himself this question shows that he sees something which is not based on reasons. If one gives oneself a reason for not having helped him, this shows that the fact that one did not help him is not indifferent to one. A precondition for him giving reasons is this seeing, even though the reasons are given in order to cloud this very seeing. In other words, the point is that the fundamental question in moral philosophy is not about giving reasons for or against some specific course of action or about choosing this or that course of action.[17] The fundamental question is how the fact that something has a moral importance from the very start should be understood. The moral philosopher already relies on the distinction between practical concerns – where doing something wrong has no weight as such, is not connected to concepts like remorse and conscience – and moral ones. In the latter case, a care for or love of that which the question is about – the beaten man in the parable of the Good Samaritan – is internal to there being a moral question at all, and that is so no matter how strongly one tries to shut one's eyes to his needs. Consequently, Phillips has a far too simplified view of use. In the case of the Good Samaritan and the priest respectively, *all* use of moral concepts is hiding something: the Good Samaritan uses no concepts but helps the beaten man; the priest, as I have imagined him here, uses moral concepts, but does so in order to deceive himself.[18]

However, someone might object to what I have said, by claiming that this is a one-sided example, that there are other ones that point in other directions. Is it not possible to imagine a person who never asks herself why she did the evil things, as we would call them, she did, it might be asked. This objection is not a good one, however. For it to be of any relevance to what I have said, it is necessary that phrases like "evil things" are used; that is, it is necessary that what the person in question has done is described in moral terms. But what does such a description mean? Something that just happens, no matter how disastrous the consequences might be, is not a moral evil: think of an earthquake, say. A description of what the person in question has done as evil – in distinction from the description of it as a natural catastrophe – is connected to concepts like blame, responsibility, and the like. But that means that the problem is not a matter of some sort of natural incapacity, of her just happening to overlook something, of lack of competence. In other words, that we describe what she has done as evil means that we see her as not cut off from a moral response of love, in the sense in which I have used it above. On the contrary, such a description is not dependent on one having previously established that she possesses a specific "capacity" (whatever that would mean). Consequently, if what we are trying to understand philosophically is morality, it is not possible to bracket our description of her as deceiving herself as just some reaction on our part, since that would mean bracketing the possibility of that which we are here trying to understand philosophically: morality.[19]

III. *Calculation*

Kierkegaard's more basic point is not about self-deception, however, since if the question were only about that, it would still be possible to say: "*If* it were possible to will what is not good and be clear about it, I would do it." And this "if" is an important subject for Kierkegaard:[20] it is precisely that which his discussion is essentially about. To the sphere of the "if", concepts like calculation, scheming, strategy, technique, skill, bargain, rationality belong. These concepts all stand for something double-minded: it is a matter of doing something in order to gain something else. The good, on the other hand, is that which is not a matter of scheming, not an interest, not goods. The question is then what more can be said about this non-calculation. By discussing this question, we will be able to see those two subjects of Phillips's which I discuss here – trust and religious belief – from another perspective.

It is often said by Phillips that there is something like trust, which is not a matter of reliance and probability,[21] and, of particular interest in this context, religious belief, which is not hypothetical.[22] But how should this be understood? Is it possible to substitute anything for x in "trusting x" or "having religious faith in x" and still have this non-calculating meaning? No. If a Mafia boss says to one of his underlings that he trusts him, after having ordered him to kill someone, say, this is only a move in a psychological game: he tries to get him to do it. Or if the Mafia boss says to himself that he trusts this underling he has ordered to kill someone, this means no more than that he considers it probable that the underling will do it or that he wants to put his own anxiety to sleep by using a concept taken from another sphere. In none of these cases is it a matter of genuine trust, a trust not about reliance and probability. This is not a psychological "not", but concerns how what he does is to be understood: if he understands what it is he is doing, he sees that he does not trust. He orders that someone should be killed, since this is a way of attaining a goal he has, or since this is a way of preventing his plans from being interfered with. It is not necessarily the case that he in fact makes a calculation of what the underling will probably do, in order to utilize this in the best possible way. There are loads of things he will not bother to consider – that his car works, say – but that does not show that they do not play a part in his scheme. What is decisive is whether it is possible for the Mafia boss to see the underling independently of these plans. Of course, one might believe that he will come to do so sometime in the future, but *in* trying to get rid of someone as part of some plan, the fact, if it is a fact, that the underling may not just as well be the victim, is only a coincidence. (However, the Mafia boss will probably feel let down if the underling does not do what he is supposed to do. This shows that the underling is not *only* a part of a plan; if so, he would be no more than a mechanism that went wrong, not someone to be disappointed in.) Consequently the Mafia boss cannot more than *count* on the underling fulfilling his purpose, and not, as a part of a different plan, turning against the Mafia boss. (Of course, they could try to *show* each other that they "trust" each other – by, say, approaching each other without protection – but precisely the fact that this is a matter of "showing" shows that it is a move in a psychological game and hence is not a matter of trust.)

When someone, on the other hand, is not calculating, this may lead to him becoming a part in someone else's plan. For someone who is non-calculating due to pure passivity, this could be said to be a risk. What we are here considering is something active – trust – and here the word "risk" is not that apt, although becoming a part in someone else's plan may happen and is not hoped for, of course. In what hope is it then that the one who is not calculating is active; in what sense is it possible to do something noncalculatingly? The one who does not calculate is not necessarily indifferent to what may come; tying together calculation, activity, wishing, and so on, is based on the idea that anything could be attained by means of calculation. But with non-calculation itself, this is obviously not so: if I try to get a noncalculating relation with someone – and such a relation could be called "love" – I frustrate that relation as long as I try to get it by means of calculation. In these situations, the fact that someone may take advantage of my non-calculation is no "risk"; it is no more than another expression of the fact that everything would be lost if I tried to be in control of the situation.

So, although it is certainly correct that what could be substituted for x in "trusting x" is a name of a person and that trust is not for reasons, which means that what could replace x is not conditioned, one must nonetheless pay attention to the fact that this is not the whole truth, but that in trust, the trusted person is herself in one sense seen as trusting. What does this mean? If we use the concept of authority,[23] we could say that for the person who trusts, what competes with trust is not a comparable alternative to trust. One could say that for the person who trusts, trust is authoritative; her trust shows her belief in trust, shows her vision of it as higher than its opposites. One could say that what she trusts is trust, if that is not understood as indicating some object beside the person who is trusted, not some object that replaces this person, not some object that – in contrast to this person – is the real object.[24] Holding these two directions together – for they are not two *different* directions – we could say that the person who is trusted is herself seen, in a sense, as trusting. The concept of hope is important here, for the possibility of trust is not dependent on the response it gets; rather, it is *in* trust that the trusted person is seen as trusting. I will not discuss the concept of hope extensively here; right now it suffices to say that trust as hoping has nothing to do with making hypotheses, with what is calculatively probable, and is not falsified by what is hoped for not happening.

The same thing goes for "having religious faith in x": if I believe in God in order to attain something or in order to avoid something – punishment, say – this is a hypothetical belief however much I maintain the opposite; God is here no more than a positive or negative object I may have to take into account when calculating. Such a belief is a belief marked by Kierkegaard's "if":[25] if it were possible to attain this, or avoid that, in some other way, this would be an adequate alternative, and the question about the probable success of these other ways then manifests itself.[26] (Of course, one might *say* to oneself that one's relation to God is not a matter of calculation even though it is; this is a typical example of something to deceive oneself about.) Hence, when emphasizing the non-hypothetical character of religious belief, what Phillips has done, without realizing it, is to have pointed out an asymmetry: the calculating and the non-calculating religious belief do not stand on the same level, as comparable alternatives, but the latter one is primary.

If we use the concept of authority, we could say that God is authoritative for the religious believer, that God is what she bows down to, what she ultimately obeys and reveres. When calculating, I do not bow down to anything, or, if we want to say that I bow down to something here, it is to myself or to that which I want to possess. Although the concept of authority is often connected to punishment and reward, this is then a confusion. Authority and non-calculation is intimately connected. But how then should the authority of God be understood? I am not going to enter into a discussion of various attempts at answering this question – but those who want to must scrutinize the various answers to see whether they are not in the end instances of calculation and hence no answers – for it does not matter in this context whether there is one or several answers. What is clear is that one answer to this question has in fact already been given in our discussion, the answer that it is love that is authoritative. Understanding religious belief as love of a God of love avoids those conceptual difficulties I have pointed out here; hence, the theme of this book.

However, how this more exactly should be understood is not completely clear at this stage, and the rest of this book is an attempt at clarifying what this understanding consists of. Right now, I would only like to suggest a couple of questions.[27] What if that which Phillips has described so well – that religious belief is non-hypothetical, is faith, and so forth – not only expresses *how* the religious believer believes, but also *what* she believes, since anything cannot be believed in, in that way? What if this "what" is there, in some sense, also in forms of religious belief which appears to be different? The question is therefore whether "God is love" is a religious expression comparable with other expressions, or whether it stands apart in an essential way from all other such expressions and, if so, whether the philosophical discussion of this belief must take a very different form from the one it has traditionally had in philosophy of religion. As we have seen, Phillips has made an important contribution by drawing attention to the non-hypothetical character of religious belief, but there is, at the same time, something to question there: the idea that the non-hypothetical character does not show that many religious ideas are parasitical upon another one.[28]

IV. *Philosophy and understanding*

Phillips is right, of course, in that it is important with a contemplative attitude in philosophy, and especially in the philosophy of religion: precisely in the philosophy of religion the temptation to adopt a completely unphilosophical attitude to philosophy is particularly strong, an attitude which means that one uses philosophy as a tool in order to convert others to one's own religious or non-religious view of life. And emphasizing philosophy's *own* value, that philosophy is a matter of trying to understand things one oneself does not understand, making insights one oneself has not made, and so forth – that philosophy concerns the philosopher herself and is not only something one uses against others – is then important, and this is part of what Phillips is trying to say, I take it. However, what I have said above goes partly in another direction than Phillips's. This requires some explanation.

A picture Phillips often uses is one of a person who steps out of the battles and tries to get an overview of them from an independent perspective, a person who tries not to become affected by the heatedness of the battles but to remain cool.[29] To be sure, this is a good recommendation to the philosopher in so far as the way she already sees things hinders her from seeing something of philosophical importance. However, Phillips takes it as a *general* recommendation. But is bracketing myself really the highroad to philosophical insight? And what character has this insight; is it really an insight which has nothing to do with me? What Phillips seems not to be ready to accept is that a purely grammatical investigation (a study of the use of concepts), one which is only descriptive, could lead to moral insights; he is not open to the possibility that a description may reveal something it is not possible to choose not to regard as authoritative.[30] I will explain what my criticism is by commenting on some passages of Phillips's, before at the end pointing out a more basic shortcoming in his understanding of philosophy.

One reason Phillips gives for keeping philosophical questions, on the one hand, and moral and existential questions, on the other hand, apart is that struggling with conceptual issues about worship is not the same thing as struggling to worship.[31] There are differences, of course: one of them is that the one who struggles to worship need not be a philosopher. But that they are not the same thing does not mean that they are necessarily unrelated. To be able to say that the struggle with conceptual issues about worship cannot give an existential insight, Phillips must say that one after having answered the first question is as free in respect to the second one as one was before. But this is obviously false. After all, struggle to worship is a *struggle*, and not something one has power over. Furthermore, one's possible lack of clarity about what worship is will have a role in that struggle: if the lack of clarity made it possible for one to keep the struggle at a distance, the clarity will start the real struggle; if the lack of clarity was used as an evasive argument in the struggle, the clarity may bring the struggle to an end. Consequently, the clarity may make it clear to one that one is *not* free to embrace (or reject) that which was made clear, which does not imply that one *will* embrace (or reject) it, of course, for one may try to escape from it (or embrace it to be able to escape from something else).

In his discussion of why philosophical questions, on the one hand, and moral and existential questions, on the other hand, should be kept apart, Phillips writes about "the hermeneutics of suspicion", that is, anti-religious theorizing (and the same goes for its religious equivalent): "It does not see that recognizing possibilities of religious sense need not entail abandoning the anti-religious or non-religious values it espouses."[32] How "entail" should be understood here is not clear. I guess that Phillips refers to something he has just written: "The moral or religious response which comes in the wake of clarity cannot be predicted from that clarity itself."[33] That it cannot be predicted is right, but Phillips seems to forget one reason why this is so: when I see clearly what is the good thing to do, I may try to escape this by deceiving myself, which means that the insight on the one hand vanishes, on the other hand is there the whole time as that which I try to shut my eyes to by means of the deception, since there would be no need of self-deception if one were not sensitive to some kind of threat, against one's complacency, for example. Consequently, there is a point in saying, "It does not see that recognizing possibilities of religious sense need not entail abandoning the anti-religious or non-religious values it espouses."[34] But Phillips is not making this point; it seems as if he is trying to set their worries at rest by saying that there is no risk that recognizing possibilities of religious sense could lead them to feel obliged to change their ways of living. But this cannot be said. Why could not the description of different possibilities – they may be religious or non-religious – result in one coming to see one possibility as incomparable with the other ones?

What Phillips excludes is the possibility that I, when looking at a phenomenon from the cool perspective, come to see a demand not to remain cool toward this phenomenon. (One example of this is the question about authority. If someone really tries to understand what is meant by "authority" I would be surprised, to say the least, if this person did not came to realize that what is often taken to be authoritative is not so. What would investigating such a question be to a person for whom this question had no moral and existential significance?) Here it will not do to talk, as Phillips does, about "personal appropriation".[35] Of course, in many cases this is what actually goes on, but if one wants to do justice to the world in all its variety, one must try to see if that is all that morality and religion come to. Another possibility is highlighted by Simone Weil, when she writes: "[W]hen we project the light of our attention equally on both [good and evil], the good gains the day … There is not a choice to be made in its favour, it is enough not to refuse to recognize that it exists."[36] If this possibility exists – and I take it that Phillips does not deny that possibility – a general use of terms like "personal appropriation" is highly misleading. In such a situation, what comes in the wake of clarity is *not* a matter of personal appropriation, as if the clarity could be applied in different ways. One example of this is remorse, as my clear-sightedness of what it is I have done (and such a clear-sightedness may be a result of philosophical work, or of something else). If I have done something evil and later feel remorse for what I have done, it is internal to this that my later understanding is superior. In my former state of mind, I could be open to different perspectives on what I have done, and precisely this openness shows that I do not understand what it is I have done. When feeling remorse, it is not possible to talk about a clarity which may be appropriated in different ways. No, the clarity is the remorse. It is not the case that the understanding is one thing and its "application" another one; if I do not feel remorse, there is no understanding. (However, it is possible to feel remorse without being able to be explicit about this understanding in, say, writing; in that respect they are different.) When I feel remorse, my relation to my former self is nevertheless to one that did not suffer from an innocent lack of understanding; consequently, my previous lack of philosophical clarity, to the extent it was bound up with my existential difficulties, is not some impersonal failure. Hence, it does not matter whether I would be able to "convince" my former self by means of "arguments" or not. And the same goes for others: that I am not able to convince them does not make my understanding less a matter of understanding. That others do or do not agree is not a criterion in philosophy. On the contrary, their difficulty of understanding is in some situations an indication that I have said something important.[37]

These critical comments on some passages of Phillips's boil down, I think, to a criticism of a more basic shortcoming in his understanding of philosophy. When Phillips says that "[t]he moral or religious response which comes in the wake of clarity cannot be predicted from that clarity itself"[38] and talks about personal appropriation, this is not only a matter of a specific (mis)understanding of morality and religion. What Phillips is also saying is that that which philosophy is actually able to do is not personal; here, impersonal reports about what has been found are possible. To express this another way: against such philosophers who believe that they can produce general arguments for moral and religious theses, Phillips is right in emphasizing the personal nature of morality and religion, but when he for that reason excludes moral and religious questions from philosophy, he accepts these philosophers' understanding of philosophy as something concerned with impersonal truths.

What is it that is wrong with that understanding of philosophy? Let me begin my explanation by quoting Wittgenstein: "The aspects of things that are most important for us are hidden because of their simplicity and familiarity. (One is unable to notice something – because it is always before one's eyes.)"[39] Hence, the problems in philosophy are not, according to Wittgenstein, dealt with by collecting new facts, but by reminding oneself of something already in plain view:

> Not, however, as if to this end we had to hunt out new facts; it is, rather, essential to our investigation that we do not seek to learn anything *new* by it. We want to *understand* something that is already in plain view ... Something that one knows when nobody asks one, but no longer knows when one is asked to explain it, is something that has to be *called to mind*. (And it is obviously something which, for some reason, it is difficult to call to mind.)[40]

Wittgenstein is not talking here about self-deception, but of something with a similar structure: something that is known and yet not known. However that may be, for anyone who tries to do moral philosophy or philosophy of religion in Wittgenstein's spirit, it is important to notice that the reason it is difficult to remind oneself of that which is in plain view here, includes one's own existential difficulties with that which morality and religion are about. (If one is struggling to worship, this will affect one's possible struggles with conceptual issues about worship.) Furthermore, if philosophy is about *understanding* (or about (dis)solving problems one is troubled with) everything depends on whether *I* come to this understanding or not (or whether the problem is no longer problematic for me or not). A philosophical text does not understand; what it can do is, at the most, help me to come to that understanding. What happens with me when I read, or with us when we are together engaged in a philosophical dialogue – *that* is philosophy. The text is philosophical only in a secondary sense. As Wittgenstein writes: "I should not like my writing to spare other people the trouble of thinking. But if possible, to stimulate someone to thoughts of his own."[11]

In that respect, philosophy is very different from science. Of course, understanding is important also in science, but the scientific result is independent of it: one can construct a technological product by applying scientific theories one does not understand, and the same goes for using such a product. One example of this is a mathematical theorem such as the Pythagorean one. We learn to use this in school but few of us are able, at least when we learnt it, to explain why it works; it is like a machine the workings of which one need not know anything about in order to make use of. As I said, this is not to deny the importance of understanding in science, or in mathematics, only to point out that the scientific result is impersonal in the sense that the application of it is independent of this understanding. But this is not at all the case in philosophy. In philosophy, there is nothing besides the understanding; there are no applications of philosophy, only more philosophical thinking. (For that reason, it is not possible to take something on authority in philosophy, as it is in science; it makes no sense to write a newspaper article about the latest "findings" in philosophy.) And understanding is always a matter of somebody understanding something. It is personal.

That it is personal does not mean that it is subjective. If it were subjective, philosophy would not be hard: then one could settle for anything one happens to be satisfied with. Phillips is right in warning against privileging some opinion one has, against not bothering to try to see whether there are other possibilities or not. (That would be subjective: one does not *want* to see something.) But this is a one-sided example. Another form of the subjective is when one wants the question to remain open – one does not want to see anything else but a wide range of alternatives – when seeing that the alternatives are not on a par is, in some sense, frightening.

The above way of describing what philosophy is about has its precursor in Plato, of course.[42] The same spirit is found in the writings of Wittgenstein and Rush Rhees. In their writings, they are themselves struggling with some issues, trying to come to an understanding of them. And their way of addressing the reader is direct (which is most obvious in Rhees's letters): they are not talking as if they are reporting results but are giving something to the reader to think through philosophically. Of course, no particular literary form is needed to do philosophy in this spirit. One could write combatively, as Phillips did, as long as one understands what one is doing and the reader is clear about the fact that everything depends on her own work with the text. But that Phillips excluded the personal from philosophy means that he did not see that. Trying to read him in a personal way would imply that one in one's own philosophical thinking about what he has written would run into a limit, on the other side of which one has to continue one's own thinking but not anymore under the heading of "philosophy", rather under the heading of "personal appropriation". But what the point of such a limit would be, I am not able to see, especially as one's philosophical difficulties are already from the start intimately related to one's existential difficulties, as I have pointed out many times above. Of course, Phillips is right in saying that "[p]hilosophical reflection does not underwrite any specific form of moral appropriation",[43] but this is simply because philosophical reflection does not underwrite anything; philosophical reflection is not a doctrine, but is about understanding. In the end, the possibility of philosophy has nothing to do with the possibility to give reports about what has been found. Instead, what it comes down to is the possibility of reaching an understanding of some issue in a dialogue with another human being: to agree, disagree, see the point, question, and together going on from there. And, one could also say, the question concerns finding that which does not at all *need* to be underwritten.

The questions I have asked thus far in this book – what is the understanding of the good which is the unacknowledged background to the attempt to prevent violent excesses; what positive understanding of the good is tolerance based on; why has wronging someone a moral weight, why it is not just a practical failure; is there an understanding of the good which is not about force and will, a strong belief which is not fanaticism – may seem to be no more than a couple of loose threads. However, they run together in the concept of non-calculation, stressed in this chapter. In that, they are intimately connected. Furthermore, the answer to all of them involves, in different ways, the concept of love, as I have hinted. And in this chapter (at the end of section III), I said that understanding religious belief as love of a God of love avoids those conceptual difficulties we have run into when discussing Phillips and Kierkegaard. There may, or may not, be other ways of connecting these threads, and there may, or may not, be other ways of avoiding these conceptual difficulties. Seeing that the threads can be so connected and that the difficulties can be so avoided, simply means seeing the need of investigating what love of a God of love means. This is what I will try to do in subsequent chapters.

Chapter 4

Love of a God of Love

The questions I have asked in the course of the previous discussions have been given one answer, in terms of love. Against this background, I will continue by trying to give an account of what character such a religious belief – understood as love of a God of love – has.

In the philosophy of religion it is generally presupposed – but not by Phillips, of course – that we are clear on what religious belief is – both in the sense of the act (the how) and in the sense of the content (the what) – and that the task is only to make an intellectual judgment of it. What religious belief is, is taken to be clear, either since one takes oneself to be a religious believer and thinks that one knows what it is one is, or since one assumes that religious believers are clear on what religious belief is and that one is able to understand what they are saying. (A third alleged possibility is that one is clear on this since one takes oneself to have disclosed the true nature of religious belief, which the religious believers themselves are unable to do as long as they remain believers; but such a disclosure is dependent on the second alleged possibility since it is a disclosure of what the religious believers take religious belief to be). But is this at all clear? Is it really possible, for the philosopher of religion, when trying to do justice to the phenomenon of religious belief, to take what religious belief is to be generally clear?[1]

What the clarification of what "love of a God of love" means achieves is not that "God is love" becomes impossible to reject or modify, but simply this: it shows what the one who rejects it rejects. And that is important, since hypocritically saying that one believes in something one does not believe in is not uncommon. And vice versa: thinking one has theoretically rejected all religious belief is a mere sham if one has not paid any regard to such a central religious expression as "God is love" and to what it could mean, however few as it may possibly be who make more than a confession of the lips to it.

My discussion will start (section I) by pointing out the difficulty of saying that one believes, when belief is understood in this way : as love of a God of love.

This difficulty is illustrated by means of the concept of the afterlife in a subsection (I.a). In the next section (II), an objection to this way of understanding belief is discussed: that religion here becomes a religion of works. In the last section (III), another objection is discussed: that the question of the existence of God is disregarded in my discussion. In its first subsection (III.a), this objection takes the form of a question: what difference does belief make? In its second subsection (III.b), this question is partly questioned. Here a connection is established to the beginning of the chapter. In the beginning, the difficulty is one of saying that one believes; in the end, the difficulty is one of saying that one does not believe.

I. *The difficulty of saying that one believes*

A common philosophical picture of belief could be illustrated by the following example. Some people are playing a quiz game. One of them asks the question, "What is the capital of Switzerland?", and the one whose turn it is to answer says, "Zürich", after which his answer is checked and proved to be wrong. Expressed by means of the word "belief", the one who answered showed by answering in the way he did what he believes – that Zürich is the capital of Switzerland – and this belief is false.

However, when it comes to religious belief, especially when it comes to the understanding of religious belief I have began to clarify here, this is not a good picture of belief. The way someone answers questions like "Do you believe in God" and "What do you believe in" does not necessarily express what she believes in, and not because she is trying to deceive us, but because she is deceiving herself. Questions which are usually considered to be central in the philosophy of religion – questions like "Is the belief in God true/correct/rational?" – are not possible to ask until another question has been answered: when is it possible for someone to say, honestly, that she believes in God? If it turns out that this can never be said, the question about whether this belief is true/correct/rational is pointless; if it turns out that it can be said, those situations in which it can be said will be intimately related to what this belief *means*, which is a question that precedes the question about the truth/correctness/rationality of the belief. This point is in line with the criticism of formalism in Chapter 2.

Let me continue by means of another example, in order to illustrate the necessity of asking the question about what someone's religious expressions really express. Say that someone prays to God and asks God to help her become a better person. What could this mean? There are several possibilities here, but let us focus on two. First, the prayer could be a part of a self-deception: the one who prays knows that she is not a good person, but she tries to make it appear to herself that the problem and the difficulty lie outside herself, as if her lack of goodness is a kind of illness she has been stricken with through no fault of her own. Second, the one who is praying could pray honestly and sincerely. In that case, the position from which the prayer is prayed must be expressed differently than in the former case. One possibility is an outside position: she observes herself from the outside and prays for this person, which means that it is not *she* who is praying, as it were. Another possibility is a divided self: a sincere part of her prays for help against the insincere part, in which case it is decisive, if the prayer is to be regarded as a sincere one, that the insincere part is not seen as something outside of her, something which is not her. In both these possibilities we have run into some kind of division. What is important here is that the same goes for saying that one believes in a God of love. If the believer herself is really completely of love, this is obviously not so, but in all other cases, and these are the important and interesting ones, both philosophically and in general, there is a division. Religion should consequently not be seen as an area in which that struggle between love and selfishness characterizing human life suddenly ceases, as if religious corruption did not exist, as if religious belief could not be used in order for one to deceive oneself. Hence, the question is where the belief is located, what it means to say that *I* believe, how the belief and the insincere part are related, and so forth. The example shows what difficulties there are in honestly saying that one believes, since it discloses a division: saying that one believes means, among other things, saying that one does not believe.

Here, someone might protest against what I have said by claiming that I have simply presupposed that there is a connection between the testimony of belief and the life of that person in general. In other words, I should have overlooked the possibility that someone, completely sincerely and without any division, could say that she believes, no matter how her life is in other respects. Therefore, let us try to become clear about what this could mean. (The one who does not think that this is an interesting objection to what I have said may read what follows as an attempt at clarifying how what the believing voice in the one who says that she believes is to be understood).

Hence, is it possible to disconnect one's relation to God from one's relations to everything else? This alleged possibility is what someone relies upon, when she concludes, from the fact that she has expressed the phrase "I believe" or from the fact that she has said "I believe" to herself with a feeling of sincerity, that she really believes. My point in what follows is that such a disconnection cannot be made, since the God which our discussion concerns is a God of love. The point is, more radically, that the question about whether I believe or not cannot be determined formally, since belief is here a *relation*, is *love*, the understanding of religious belief we are here trying to clarify is belief as love of a God of love. (A formal determination of whether I believe or not would mean that the question about whether I believe is a question about whether I have complied with a list of demands, a list which may be seen as short – the expression of a particular phrase – or long).

The line of thought when someone wants to disconnect her relation to God from her relation to everything else could perhaps be this: "That I hate A does not change anything when it comes to my relation to B; I love him all the same. When it comes to God, this is also the case. That I hate A does not change anything when it comes to my relation to God; I love God all the same." This should be questioned also in the case of A and B, but this is not a question I will discuss right now.[2] Here it suffices to point out that this is not so when it comes to love of a God of love.[3] If one says that God is love, this means not only that God loves me – even though this may be a common attitude de facto – but that God loves everything which and everyone whom it is intelligible to say could be loved. (Here it will not do to claim that it is not intelligible to say that A is loved; on the contrary, the example is a comparison in which that possibility is obviously visible in the background. Furthermore, to claim that this is not intelligible would mean that criticism of my unloving attitude would be unintelligible.) Now, someone could perhaps say: "Sure, it is not good that I hate A, far from it, but that I do so does not change my relation with God." One answer to this is that belief is longing to be with God; but dropping love for hate shows that I do not long for this. Expressed in another way: in my hatred I let something overshadow love, I let something take its place, be more important, and then I let something else than God take God's place, since the understanding of belief we are here working with is that it is love of a God of love.

This answer to the idea that one could disconnect one's relation to God from one's relation to everything else is perhaps a bit hard to follow. Therefore, I would like to supplement that answer by another way of saying the same thing, a way which will also shed light on a couple of other questions which are important in this context.

a. *An illustration: the concept of the afterlife*

The idea that one could disconnect one's relation to God from one's relation to everything else rests on the idea that one is clear about what it means to be with God and about what it means to long for this. In this line of thought, one thinks that one is clear about where God is, or, with a different emphasis, that one does not shut one's eyes to some particular possibilities. This could then be *illustrated* by picturing oneself standing in front of the gates of paradise and knowing that one longs to be there.[4] However, the question is: if someone in her life drops love (hates A), why is it not possible that she does that when standing in front of the gates of paradise?[5] Is it because she now – when she does not stand in front of the gates of paradise – does not clearly see what God is? And *why* does she then not see this clearly now? In this subsection I will use this illustration – the concept of the afterlife – to shed light on my discussion in this section.

Someone would perhaps like to answer these questions by saying that there is an essential difference: "Then everyone else will live in love, so of course I would like to do that too, but as it now is, the difficulty is that I do not dare to live in love since I cannot trust that others will receive me in love. Then a change of the *entire* reality will come about; what is now called for is only a change of *me* irrespective of whether something else is changed or not." Apart from the fact that this is an evasion – the problem is here said to have nothing to do with me, only with others (and they can say the same thing, of course) – this is not at all an answer to the problem. If it were the case that I drop love since I am afraid what living in love would bring about, I would still be divided. In that case, I do not see the possibility of love as what is highest, as something worth risking everything for. And I am then still living according to the principle of every man for himself.

What is decisive here is that there is something which is worse than punishment. Some religious traditions have an idea about a place to which one can be banished after one's death (however this idea more exactly should be understood). Such an idea is not possible to combine with the understanding of God as love: love does not banish anyone, but longs for nothing else than togetherness. But togetherness in love could not be brought about by means of calculation,[6] so love cannot prevent anyone from turning away from it. In any event, there could still be something heroic about being banished; it is a destiny one could protest against (which shows that the power to punish does not bring about authority). No, far worse would be if I, *willingly*, dropped the togetherness with God for something else, since I do not see this togetherness as what is highest. It is this possibility – and not the possibility of banishment – which is relevant when we are discussing religious belief as love of a God of love. If the question concerned the possibility of banishment we would still be stuck in calculation. When calculating, ideas of the afterlife would be an additional factor to take into account when trying to determine how I must go about to get what I want. Then I would still be double-minded, as we have seen Kierkegaard say.[7]

 Love of a God of Love

Hence, what I can do is to use the concept of the afterlife – its moral/ existential weight – to shed light upon what role will, love, and so on, have in my life, what they mean to me. In our context, the task is to get clear about those uses of this concept which are intimately related to religious belief understood as love of a God of love. One such use concerns moral responsibility: What I have done and do has an eternal significance. My responsibility does not cease when I die, as if I, if I know that I have only a short time left, could say to myself that it does not matter whether I am mean or not since the remorse will only last for a short while. The responsibility is, so to speak, larger than life. Hence, it is essential that *I* must bear it also when I have died. If others must bear their responsibility or not is in that respect not as central. (This is related to a question about whether to excuse what others have done, a question which it is not necessary to discuss here.)[8]

There is more which deserves to be said about "heaven and hell" here. Perhaps it seems a digression, but hold onto our basic question and you will see in what ways these questions are connected. What is important in this context is not "what happens with me when I have died". Of course, what is important is what such ideas mean existentially, what differences they make. More arbitrary connections are for that reason irrelevant in this context.

What I have said here – that what is worst is not to be banished, but to drop the togetherness with God willingly – may seem to be paradoxical. If I see the fact that I willingly drop this as what is worst of all, then I will not drop it. In other words, it is unclear from what perspective what I have said above has been said. What meaning that which I have said above has is therefore directly connected to the issue of the inner division. In that respect, both these sides – that it is the worst of all, but that I still drop it – can be open at the same time for me.

The idea of the afterlife seems then to point to a situation where the inner division has ceased to exist. And to the extent that someone really identifies herself with that in her which is not corrupt – which is another way of describing the sincere prayer about becoming a better person – she really wants to get rid of that in her which is corrupt. But there are no external obstacles to getting rid of this: it is she herself which is the obstacle. Therefore, getting rid of this is painful, since it means coming to terms with oneself fundamentally. And if I on the contrary cannot imagine a worse place than one in which love is "reigning", the worst punishment there could be would be to be put precisely there. This is another reason why terms such as punishment and reward are so misleading in the perspective of religious belief as love of a God of love.

To understand what is meant by "painful" here, a specific asymmetry could be enlightening. The inner division cannot be regarded as a struggle between similar forces (with reversed polarity, so to speak). The good has no force by means of which it can force me, by means of which it can wrench me toward itself; it wants me wholehearted and stands therefore open, welcoming. Evil, on the contrary, is something which can be described as something which pulls me, tempts me. This is the asymmetry. This description is not partial – not made from the perspective of the good – as if it were possible to change perspective and get a reverse description. That this is not possible is what makes it into an asymmetry. From the perspective of evil, the good is not a temptation, but, rather, an obstacle, a restriction, something which one should try to describe naturalistically: as a social pressure which prevents me from doing what I want, as a whim.[9]

II. *A religion of works?*

What I have tried to do above is to point out the difficulty there is in honestly saying "I believe" when that which the belief concerns is a God of love. This is the fundamental point. Perhaps someone might regard this as a result of me understanding belief as a matter of performing certain actions, which would turn religion into a religion of works. That would be a misunderstanding, however, which I will try to address in this section.

If my discussion would turn religion into a religion of works, that would not as such be a problem. I am not trying to argue for or against love of a God of love. What I am trying to do is clarify its nature, and if that nature is unattractive (if a religion of works is unattractive), so be it. However, understanding belief as love of a God of love is *not* to understand belief as a matter of performing certain actions. On the contrary, it is the one who understands belief as a matter of saying things – uttering phrases, perhaps with a feeling of sincerity – who has not radically enough come to terms with the understanding of belief as actions. The difficulty there is in honestly saying "I believe" is directly connected to the fact that whether I believe or not is not a question which can be determined formally, since belief, understood as love of a God of love, is a relation. How should this more exactly be understood?

The point is fairly simple. That God is love – which is the understanding of belief we are here discussing – means that God's love for me is not dependent on what I do. This is simply a grammatical remark about the concept of love in general. Lovelessness is then here to turn away from God's love, but turning away does not change God's love, of course: this is part of what makes turning away so terrible. When I am no longer turned away – it may be for a moment or for a longer time – the concept of forgiveness has an application, in this sense: it is *precisely* the one who sees her general loveless-ness as a matter of turning her back on God – and not as something with an arbitrary bearing on her belief – who sees her need of forgiveness, sees that "a God of love" means that God's love never ceases. Here it is important to emphasize that love is a relation; that is, love can neither be analyzed as an action of mine nor as something I am not able to destroy by what I do.

Hence, love is not something *I* do. Nor is it something I *do*; rather, what I can do is simply to stop turning my back on it. This is connected to a more general moral asymmetry: the way I am involved differs considerably when having done something evil and when having done something good. To feel remorse for something means that I see it as something I have done, that I do not see it as a result of certain circumstances having their effect, as it were, through me. However, this is not the case when it comes to the good: here my attention is not directed at myself but at the one I meet. If someone would direct my attention to what I do, I would not here describe it as something I have *chosen* to do, as if I could just as well have chosen not to do it.[10] In that sense it is not *I* who acts here; instead, I might say that I am carried by something higher. For that reason, I cannot get out of being turned away by means of exertion, by means of work, by means of a deci-sion, by means of willpower, by means of doing something I see as a burden. In that case, I would still be stuck in what I try to get away from. Therefore, using religious expressions of the kind we are here trying to understand, one could say that a conversion away from being turned away can only origi-nate as a result of the love of God itself attracting me.[11] In other words, being turned away is always a result of the fact that I still, on some level, struggle against that which attracts me. In the next chapter, I will discuss a related question, so whether the understanding of religious belief I try to clarify means understanding religious belief as a matter of works will get a more extensive discussion there.

III. *Is the question of the existence of God disregarded?*

There is an objection that many readers may have already raised against what I say here: "Perhaps you are right in saying that the question about whether I really believe is connected to the question about what I really long for. But such a question – about whether I really long for togetherness with God or not – is only possible against the background of the fact that I already, on another level, really believe: that I really believe that God exists. So haven't you disregarded that question? Or have you presupposed that God exists?" The idea here is that belief in God consists of two "parts", one which does not concern love (but is simply about the existence of God), and one which does concern love (when belief is love of a God of love). What I will do in the remaining section is to show that, and in what way, such an objection and such an idea are fundamental misunderstandings.

In Chapter 3 I pointed out an important distinction: between religious belief as a judgment and as something to which the word "judgment" does not really fit. This distinction concerned the difference between two cases: when belief is a strategy for getting something and when it is not. In the first case questions about existence are central: if belief is a strategy for getting something, a question about the probability of getting this, and the price one must pay to get this, must be asked.[12] In the other case, questions of a strategic kind do not have any application. Since what we are here trying to clarify is religious belief understood as love of a God of love, it is the second case which is of interest to us. And the question is then what it could mean to ask a question of existence in this case.

"But is not the belief that God exists a presupposition for, or at least a part of, also that kind of wholehearted belief?" One could perhaps say this, if one wants to. The important question is what saying this would mean. Pay attention to the fact that a judgment of probability is out of the question here. Such a judgment would make the belief halfhearted – that is, make it into something which it is not. If one would like to say something about the wholehearted belief, one could say that it originates in an experience, but what this means is still very vague, and I will come back to it later. The question about the "justification", or whatever one would like to call it, of the belief is here a matter of the "justification" of this life in its *entirety*. This does not mean that the one who loves a God of love[13] has in some way managed to get hold of some special permit – allowing her to disregard questions of evidence – as if such questions were meaningful to ask here, but that the believer does not have to answer them. The point is more radical: believing wholeheartedly *is*, conceptually, believing without evidence (and I will explain why in a moment). If one demands evidence, one rejects this belief in its entirety. The philosophical question is instead what (moral/existential) meaning such an act of belief has, if any.

The one who loves a God of love does not choose to see God as authoritative.[14] (In fact, one cannot *choose* to see anything as authoritative; this is a conceptual point.) Therefore, the point above can be expressed in the following way. The one who claims that there is a question about whether God exists or not, supposes that there first is a question about existence, a question which is of a hypothetical character, and when this question has been answered in the affirmative an acknowledgment of God as authoritative immediately follows for the believer. But this would mean that the authority is nonetheless hypothetical, since it is dependent on an affirmative answer to the question about existence, an answer which could here never be anything other than hypothetical.[15] To regard the question of existence as an open question means that the question of authority is regarded as an open question too, a character it does not have for the believer.[16] Consequently, there is nothing she could regard as evidence, since what something being evidence means, is that it is related to an open question. However, the believer can see how the authority of God expresses itself, in different ways, and she may try to articulate this, but such expressions are not evidence for her. Nor is it possible for her to use her articulations of such expressions against someone else, since in that case she has to accept the character the question has for the other one, the character of an open question. The task of the believer is not to answer an open question. If she understands herself as having a task at all, this task would rather be to show what it is to believe. However, showing this is done in a language which itself is religious – perhaps she uses concepts such as sin and grace and points to activities like prayer – a language which to the philosopher who sees the question of existence as fundamental presupposes an affirmative answer to this question for its meaning and force. To the one who sees the question of existence as fundamental, what it means to believe that God exists must be possible to express without using religious concepts. And then it becomes completely unclear what this question of existence is really about.

Of course, one could say, if one so chooses, that the difference between the one who believes and the one who does not[17] is that the first one believes that there is a God, whereas the second one does not believe so. (This is not necessarily a neutral way of formulating the difference; the one who loves a God of love may say that this diminishes the difference, since for her losing God would be the worst thing of all, would be to go to hell willingly, not just a matter of ceasing to believe that this and that is the case). However, the problem is the idea that there has to be a shared propositional content – a content which the believer affirms and the non-believer denies – in order for it to be possible to account for the difference between the believer and the non-believer. The consequence of that idea is that one regards the phrasing above – that the difference between the one who believes and the one who does not is that the first one believes that there is a God, whereas the second one does not believe so – as the fundamental difference, and what one then focuses on is a surface phenomenon – the fact that one may get the believer to say something that the non-believer says with a "not" – without noticing the possibility that the believer and the non-believer may mean different things. And that they mean different things is obvious in the case of love of a God of love: to the non-believer that which is believed or not believed has not at all the weight it has for the believer, to whom this weight is love.

a. *What difference does belief make?*

"Perhaps you are right in saying that the question of existence is not asked by the one who believes in the sense of loves a God of love. Perhaps you are right in saying that the difference between the one who believes and the who does not cannot be stated in judgmental terms, as if the believer believed in order to get something. But does not all this mystify belief? Does not belief in God make some kind of difference? If belief in God made no difference, one could just as well take a principle as authoritative, without talking about God. If belief in God made no difference, religion would just be a vehicle for a general message. Must not the difference be the belief that God exists?"[18] Answering this objection is a continuation of our discussion of the question of existence raised above.

Of course, belief does make a difference. But we should not presuppose that this difference is primarily to be found in belief formulations. Do not forget that religious belief is about *life* – and this is especially obvious in the case of love of a God of love – not something purely intellectual in isolation, but something that has to do with the believer in his or her entirety. Hence, religion is much more than a message; it is a whole life in which all kinds of "activities" are involved. What we should try to seize upon, then, is what it concretely *means* to see God as, say, authoritative. Of course, loving a God of love is connected to particular "activities", for example prayer, or in particular prayer if it is here understood, using a religious expression, as being together with God, talking with God, learning to know God better.

"But if you understand religious belief in this way, that is, as a question of life, then it is possible to imagine a person who is not a believer but lives in the same way as the believer, isn't it? Someone who, say, prays?" Perhaps; but what would this mean? What would what this person – who does everything the religious believer does, and does it wholeheartedly, that is, not just as something she could just as well drop tomorrow – says mean? What would "I am not a believer" mean here? Does anything become clearer if we say that what this person does not have is a belief in the *existence* of God? What exactly does saying that this imagined person is not a religious believer mean, apart from the fact that she answers "No" to a particular question? What exactly does this answer – "No" – mean? The belief is not identical with these activities, as if the belief were exhausted by them; what is important for the religious believer is the life together with God of which they are a part. If the alleged non-believer does them in *that* spirit – as something which really has to do with her – it is unclear how we should understand her assurance that she does not believe. The kind of intelligibility this assurance that she does not believe has, seems to be easiest to understand as a way of keeping a certain distance to what she does, to claim, perhaps rightly, that she could stop doing what she is doing, in contrast to those she sees as really religious. In order for such an answer to become intelligible, it must be connected to something: to an explanation of why not, to an explanation of in what way this does not affect what she is doing, and so forth. It is not intelligible simply because it is uttered.

Furthermore, this emphasis on the belief that God exists as the difference between belief and non-belief could be connected to a particular idea about prayer: that the point of praying is connected to the existence of God. If this is supposed to mean that without God prayer does not pay, it is confused, to be sure: the religious believer does not understand prayer as something one resorts to since it pays. What one does is here not a matter of calculation, of course: it is not a matter of doing something to get something. Rather, the point is that praying is an aspect of one's belief in God. If a non-believer asks a believer "Why do you pray?" the answer "Because I believe in God" is not an explanation but a rejection of the question. The answer means, I suppose, that no reason is needed; believing is praying. The answer "Because I get this and that" is, as I have said, an expression of calculation, and the more probable answer – "Because I want to come closer to God, because I try to make it up with (myself before) God" – is already a religious way of understanding prayer and cannot be used to explain its point in the way the non-believer had required. The more general question – "What does talking about *God* as authoritative add, why does it not suffice to say that what is authoritative is that which one sees God as (love, say)?" – is hence potentially misleading. It is as if the believer has to see the belief as paying in some way, and, as I have said again and again, it is part of what "authority" means that one does not think in that way.

The central question is then what demands my imagined objector makes upon the difference that belief has to make in order for her to be satisfied. What exactly must the difference be for it to count? The non-believer could argue in this way: "If the difference is possible to describe in naturalistic terms, this shows that religious terms are not needed. The only difference which really shows that belief makes a difference is a difference which is not possible to express non-religiously." The problem with this line of thought is obvious, however. The result of it is that there are only two possibilities for the non-believer: either the difference is expressed by means of non-religious terms which shows that the difference is rejected as being too small, or the difference is only possible to express in ways which she does not (yet) accept which means that the difference is rejected as being illusionary. This line of thought makes religious belief impossible a priori. Even the divine as a reality to encounter would then be insufficient, since it is possible to describe that without using the word "God"; instead words like "strange" would be used. In other words, it seems, on the one hand, as if the word "God", in order to be possible to use in a justified way, must be possible to define by means of non-religious terms; on the other hand, this means that the word "God" does not have a function: it is only an economical way of expressing something which could just as well be expressed non-religiously.

The problem here is a way of understanding language, an understanding according to which a particular experience does not have a meaning as such, but can be spoken of in whatever way as long as the concepts used cover what has been experienced according to their definitions. Religious and non-religious ways of expression are then different ways of covering the same subject matter; in other words, there are no religious experiences, only religious ways of describing experiences which as such are not religious. However, the confusion in this way of understanding language is precisely that experiences, despite everything, *have* meaning. An example could illustrate this, and I will quote Cora Diamond, although the point she makes is a bit different from mine:

> [O]ne might, for example, meet George Eliot, and find oneself, during the encounter, recognizing her to be beautiful, but not beautiful as one had understood what beauty was. She, that magnificently ugly woman, gives a totally transformed meaning to "beauty". Beauty itself becomes something entirely new for one, as one comes to see (to one's own amazement, perhaps) a powerful beauty residing in this woman. She has done something, something that one could not at all have predicted, to the concept of beauty ... I have not so far used the word "literal" because it is frequently a source of confusion, but I should be happy to say that the application of "beautiful" to George Eliot is non-literal, in the sense that the application is not justified by the previously established practice, nor intended to be justified by that practice; yet the word is a necessary word.[19]

> The fact that one is no longer using the word "beauty" as one had done, and as
> the other person [who does not think she is beautiful] still does, does not mean
> that "really" one is not contradicting the other person.[20]

The central point here is that the particular word may be essential; that is,
that it is not just a "word". An experience does not have to fit into one's pre-
established categories. To quote Wittgenstein in *Culture and Value*:

> Life can educate one to a belief in God. And *experiences* too are what bring this
> about; but I don't mean visions and other forms of sense experience which
> show us the "existence of this being", but, e.g., sufferings of various sorts. These
> neither show us God in the way a sense impression shows us an object, nor do
> they give rise to *conjectures* about him. Experiences, thoughts, – life can force
> this concept on us.[21]

(The "e.g." here is important, of course). In other words, if the demand
upon what should be counted as "God" could be expressed in a definition,
it would be uninteresting. Then I could just as well use the lengthier expression. Rather, one possibility is that one comes to see the point in using the
word "God" in a particular context, and not necessarily because that which
one wants to use the word for corresponds to a definition one already possesses; on the contrary, one comes to see that it is precisely the demands
one had made upon what "God" must be which has to be rejected. This is
particularly the case when God is understood as infinite. Before this person
became a believer, there was perhaps nothing which she would count as an
experience of something infinite, simply since she had the idea that any
experience, by means of definition, is finite. But when she became a believer
the infinite becomes a dimension *in* human experience. What difference
belief makes is then not independent of the belief itself.[22] The believer may
describe the difference as infinite – the God she sees herself as encountering she sees as infinite – but that is not the way the non-believer would
describe the difference. Even if the non-believer would describe the difference as a matter of experience, this difference would nonetheless not be
described in the same way.

The philosophical task is not then to try to reach a place where one has to
use the word "God", a place where anything else would be impossible.
Instead, the task is to describe some of the ways in which it is used. In other
words, the task is *not* to make demands upon how great the difference must
be to be acceptable. To someone who is calculating, a particular idea about
difference is clearly central: the belief is here a means of getting something
one wants, and the belief makes, to the extent the belief is a good means, a

difference. In other cases this would be a mistaken way of approaching the issue. The subject matter of the description is instead the religious life in its entirety, which means that if one wants to say something *general* about the difference, this would simply be that the meaningfulness of the belief is connected to the meaningfulness of this life in its entirety, *not* the other way around. *In* this life, one could see what talking about God comes to, if it comes to anything at all. (Fairly typical in the discussion of these philosophical questions is that one takes something to be philosophically informative – the isolated utterance "There is a God", say – which disconnected from its context is puzzling. The content the utterance has, it has in its religious context – and this is implicitly made use of, without one paying attention to the fact that it is made use of, when one regards the utterance as informative – a context which the answer was supposed to be a foundation for).

b. *The difficulty of saying that one does not believe*

However, this answer to the imagined objection is perhaps too simplified. The objector probably realizes the problem with seeing belief as a means by which one gets something. What my imagined objector fears is, I suppose, that "God" is here no more than the name of an abstract principle which as such is not of a religious character. In other words, it is not the word "God" which is religiously important, but the actual reality it is used on, a reality which the religious believer claims is, precisely, a reality. The question is then: is the reality which I encounter in love of such a character, such that it (he/she) could be called God?

When we have asked the question in this way, we see that it is just as much about the one who asks it. The question is about what I am ready to use the word "God" on. Of course, nothing – no philosophical treatise, say – will result in the word "God" being a word one is forced to use, in the sense that not using it would prove one's incompetence. As I have already pointed out, there is no general question about how great the difference must be to be sufficient;[23] what I can do here is merely to point out *some* aspects. That someone uses the word "God" or does not use it, is not what is philosophically topical. In other words, it is not at all clear that religious expressions make any difference, not even religiously speaking. The idea that religious expressions do make a difference presupposes that what one encounters in love is *not* something religious. But what one encounters in love may in fact be religious irrespective of whether the word "God" is used or not. That what one is related to in love is independent of the religious way of *expression* does not imply that it, by necessity, is not religious: here a religious element may show itself, also in those who do not call themselves believers. One cannot presuppose that the non-believer does not de facto relate to something in a religious way, just because the non-believer says she does not. It may be the case that already the belief in love as authoritative contains a religious element which only is made more explicit in the (possibly merely apparently) more religious case; this is a question we have not at all discussed yet, a question the answer to which we cannot presuppose. This is the question of this last subsection.

Here I will only point to *some* things which may be involved when God, rather than a principle of love, is seen as authoritative. In general, the point is that love is of an existential nature and cannot be described in empirical terms.[24] In a sense, my discussion in its entirety – both what has already been said and what will come – is a way of trying to clarify this. This clarification could be said to be the second part of an attempt to blur the distinction between belief and non-belief: whereas the first part of this chapter was about showing the difficulties there are in saying that one believes, this part is about showing the difficulties there are in saying that one does not believe. Therefore it would be a misunderstanding of the character of my discussion to say that it is an argument for some kind of "side". On the contrary, the point could be said to be that religious belief – understood as love of a God of love – is not something one decides for or against after having studied different arguments.

Here I will only mention some things which may be involved when God, rather than a principle of love, is seen as authoritative. There is no question of completeness, of course, neither here nor in my discussion in its entirety. Some of these things have already been mentioned above. Generally speaking, it concerns two complexes: a negative one and a positive one.

When I have wronged someone, *who* is it I have wronged? Or, expressed more precisely, what does it mean for what a person is that it is someone who can be wronged? What distinguishes a moral wrong from a practical failure, a failure in which what I did was not an efficient means for getting what I wanted? A vague answer to these questions is that the person has a weight, an importance. But saying this is still not clear; what weight and importance are we talking about? Three things need to be pointed out here. First, the weight we are talking about is not something I add. In that case I could just as well remove it, if that would serve my practical purposes. Second, this weight is of a positive character, otherwise there would be no moral meaning in saying that it should not be removed. This weight is her as loving and trusting, what I direct myself toward when I direct myself to her in love and trust.[25] Third, in a sense it is misleading to talk about a weight a person *has*. In that case, if the weight were something external to her, it would be it I wronged and not *her*. In other words, it is not her as falling under a particular description that I wrong or some part or aspect of her – for example, her body, her reason, or other philosophically-loaded terms – I wrong. (From this follows that her goodness is not external, but is what she really is; evil is in that respect, and in other respects, different.) One way of expressing this is to say that it is her soul I wrong, and from what I have said follows how the term "soul" here is not to be understood (as a part or an aspect, as something external, and so forth)[26] and is to be understood (as something good and connected to love). This means that the question about whether someone or something "has" a soul or not is not a theoretical question, is not a question which makes moral descriptions possible and legitimate only when it has been answered in the affirmative.[27] On the contrary: if a moral description *is* intelligible – and one cannot choose to see something as intelligible or not, which means that there is no question about legitimization here – this means that what the description is about has a soul. In other words, if it is intelligible to describe what I have done as exploiting, that means that what, or the one, I have exploited has a soul. Consequently, it is not at all strange to say that even the inorganic nature has a soul, since the intelligibility of saying that someone has exploited a mountain, say, has carried out ruthless mining operations for profit and left behind a devastated landscape, is not dependent on an affirmative answer to the hypothetical question about whether or not there are human beings who will actually be affected by this.[28]

Moreover, and most important in the context of this chapter, it must be pointed out that the soul is here not something countable and isolated. If I have wronged a person this is not isolated to her, as if it were impossible to understand that someone else may feel affected by what I have done even though it was not directed at her. (The opposite would be to claim that what the wronged one has been subjected to is simply loss or harm; that would obviously only concern her. However, then one has failed to see the difference between the practical and the moral, as if there were no difference between hateful violence and an accident which results in the "same" injuries.[29]) Hence, there is no theoretical borderline here, a borderline enclosing the wrong I have done to only one person. On the contrary, one could say that doing wrong always directs itself toward the good in its complete generality, that is, for the one who sees God as love, toward God. God is then not a principle: a principle cannot, as I have pointed out, be morally wronged, only what "has" a soul. This expresses the infinite importance doing wrong has: that it is, for the believer, always a matter of turning one's back on God understood as love.

A positive meaning in speaking about God as authoritative, rather than a principle about love as authoritative, is the following. Love does not come from me. It is not a decision, not a matter of willpower, not of my own making. It is, in a sense, not I that love. At the same time, it is something I can shut out. Love is something that, in a sense, is independent of me: it is something I am possessed by or something I shut out. It is not my merit, but it is I who does not give it any place; an asymmetry in my relation to good and evil. All this is obviously connected to many of the things I have said previously in this chapter.

What I have just said may be misunderstood, however, as if the point was that the "I" is evil by means of definition. On the contrary: love means that it longs for response. It is the other one as loving I direct myself toward in love,[30] and, as I have pointed out a couple of paragraphs ago, love is that which is not external, that which someone, morally speaking, really is. In love I am turned outwards – the question about myself is not raised here, is uninteresting, has no application – and in love I am carried by something that is larger than me, that addresses me and makes me turn outwards.

Perhaps someone might say that what I turn toward, the one I love, is only a single individual person, and not something larger than that. As we have seen, however, my love for a single person is not something that exists in isolation from everything else: the problems I may have outside this relation – when I hate someone, say – are not really outside, for it is possible that the person I love takes the hated person's side. And this is connected to what I said some paragraphs ago: wronging someone is not to do something to one person in isolation. More positively speaking, love of a single person is still directed to something more all-encompassing. This would not be so if love was conditioned by something specific in the person I love, as if *this*, some property possibly only existing in her or in her and a few others, was what I wanted. In that case, requited love would be a mutual exchange of goods, two parallel processes in which each of us would give the other something she wants. But then love would not have the personal character it has. So one could say that in love we meet each other in something that is larger than us two, in something that is not exhausted by a description of us. It is precisely the unity in love, in contrast to mutuality, which shows what it means to say that love cannot be understood without a direction to something more all-encompassing.

For the one who is a religious believer – for the one who loves a God of love – this means that what I direct myself to in love is God. What I direct myself to is not something abstract, nor something particular, as we have seen. In that sense God is both personal (that is, not abstract) and all-encompassing (that is, not something particular). Consequently, for this believer love is not a principle but a person.

For the one who understands religious belief hypothetically and evidentially, God is, at the most, only personal in principle, however. A personal relation with God, on the other hand, and it is here emphasizing the personal character of God has an importance, means that the relation is *not* hypothetical and evidential. This is precisely the point of love of a God of love.[31]

And that means that the objection raised at the beginning of this subsection is answered.

CHAPTER 5

FREEDOM AND CHOICE

In the previous chapter, I discussed whether religious belief understood as love of a God of love is a religion of works. In this chapter, I will discuss a kindred question. It concerns a difficulty pertaining to that which, in a sense, is the theme of this book: to understand belief, faith. On the one hand, faith cannot be understood as an object of choice. If I say that I have chosen faith, either this is a bad description of my relation to faith, or it indicates that I am at a distance from faith and thus do not believe. Saying that I have chosen faith is strange in the same way as it is strange to say that one has chosen to be committed or in love. On the other hand, it seems to be necessary to describe it as a choice: otherwise it is something which has simply come to happen to me and does not have anything to do with me. This difficulty is a general difficulty of understanding the concept of freedom. This is what I will discuss here. To my way of thinking, this question is more interesting and fruitful than the more common philosophical question about the freedom of the will – related to determinism, prediction, and so forth – but it is not altogether unrelated to it. My point, generally speaking, is that understanding religious belief as love of a God of love dissolves the problem of freedom concerning religious belief.

In my discussion I will use Luther's *On the Bondage of the Will* (*De Servo Arbitrio*) as an interlocutor. That this text serves as an interlocutor means that I am not interested in doing some general exegetical work. I will not discuss one aspect, obviously central to Luther: to what extent some outlook has a biblical foundation. That question is not philosophically interesting. Furthermore, I will disregard much that is not important for my purpose. In other words, it is not the text *On the Bondage of the Will,* Luther's writings in their entirety or him as a person that interest me, but some lines of thought in this text. Exegetically speaking, this means a distortion of it. Consequently, the objection that I have misinterpreted Luther is a good objection only if that which I in that case have failed to notice would be an important observation in any case, that is, even if it was not to be found in Luther's text; in any other case, the objection is irrelevant.

In the first section, I start the discussion by asking a couple of questions and by drawing some distinctions. In the second section, I discuss one of these questions – does God save me if I meet certain criteria – and concepts such as merit, worthiness and criterion will be contrasted with love. In the next one (III), I discuss another question asked initially: how the basis of me being good or evil should be understood – how come I act, think, feel, in the way I do? Again, the question is contrasted with the perspective of love. In section IV, I discuss the concepts "will" and "choice" and their alleged centrality in this context. Against the background of that discussion, I discuss (in section V) Luther's understanding of the power of God and his distinction between the revealed God and the hidden God. In the last section (VI), I leave Luther behind and try to show the connections between love and freedom by means of a discussion of Kant's moral philosophy.

I. *Questions and distinctions*

The difficulty with understanding Luther's discussion in *On the Bondage of the Will* is to a great extent dependent on the fact that he wants to answer two questions, the connection between which is not at all clear. On the one hand, the theme is salvation: does God save me if I meet certain criteria? In that case, salvation would be a kind of reward, for, say, having acted in a good way. On the other hand, the theme is how the basis of me being good or evil should be understood: how come I act, think, feel, in the way I do? These two questions have no immediate connection, unless one believes, either, that God's salvation is based on criteria and these criteria are about my goodness and badness (the question is then whether it is beyond my power to see to it that I meet these criteria), or, that God's salvation is not based on criteria but that it is nevertheless so that the saved one is the one who acts in a good way and the non-saved one is the one who acts in a bad way (one idea would be that salvation is given without criteria, but that the evil one does not want it, since salvation is something good, and that being evil is something that God causes, without criteria). The point of distinguishing these two questions is that doing so makes it obvious that answering one of them does not automatically answer the other; in fact, it is possible to answer one of them and reject the other as a misleading question, a question that should not be answered.

"Without criteria" can mean many things, however. On the one hand, we have the haphazard, the arbitrary, the capricious. Understanding the rejection of criteria in this way is not to reject the possibility of criteria, however; in that respect, this is the less radical form of the rejection. On the other hand, we have the complete rejection of criteria, as we find it in generosity or love. Luther writes: "[L]ove … always thinks well of everyone … we ought all to be regarded as saints by one another according to the law of love."[1] This thinking is not based on criteria – it is not the case that someone is thought well of since she behaves in this way but would not be thought well of if she behaved in that way – but is obviously not capricious either. In this context, the God of love (the one who loves and in that respect saves without criteria) could be contrasted to the capricious God (understood as the one who is the fundamental cause of the good acting of the good person and the bad acting of the bad person). This contrast has a connection to Luther's distinction between the revealed God and the hidden God. I will return to this.

II. *Does God save me if I meet certain criteria?*

If we start with the first question – does God save me if I meet certain criteria – we have already come to see that understanding religious belief as love of a God of love means dismissing that question. God, if God is love, always turns toward me in love. I have already discussed this in Chapter 4. What may be in the way of salvation is then only my own rejection of it, when I turn away from it. (How this rejection should be understood – as a result of free choice or not – is a question I will come to later on). But how is such a rejection possible and intelligible? Is not salvation something obviously good? The difficulty with understanding this is dependent on the idea that my relation to love, to God's love, is independent of my relation to salvation. Salvation would then be something I would always see as a good, no matter what my existential standing; it would be like a gift I accept since I want it even though I despise the person giving it to me, find her generosity stupid, and thus turn away from *her.* However, what one does not notice if one sees things in this way, is that what I receive is not the same thing, in an important respect, if I accept the gift despising the giver – then it makes no difference to me that it is her who is the giver – that is, I do not see it as a *gift*; if possible, I could have procured this thing for myself in some other way – as if I receive it in joy at her and her giving. If salvation *is* God's love, then there is *nothing* external to God's love in salvation, nothing the yearning for which is independent of one's relation to God and God's love. And, obviously, to the one who loves a God of love this will be what salvation is, since to her there is nothing higher: what I *see* as salvation is not independent of my existential standing. Vice versa, there will be nothing worse to her than having turned her back to God's love: this would be punishment, which, just like salvation, is here not an external consequence of some *acts* – God's reaction to them, something one deserves, reward and punishment respectively – but something internal to my way of *being*.

Possibly, someone may find the criterionlessness of love – later on, I will describe this as its freedom – repellent, especially concerning God: it makes it possible to count on God's love. However, the question is who would do such a thing. The one who loves a God of love lives in the belief in the eternity of God's love, but this is not to count on it, since "counting on" something involves taking advantage of something, exploiting something. The one who does not love a God of love may take advantage of God's love, but by doing so she loses it. And to the one who loves a God of love, what this person wins by doing so is nothing compared to this loss; that is, she does not "win" anything at all. If God seems to be immensely weak here – I may desert God again and again without God preventing this by forcing me to submission or without God refusing me to return – this is on the contrary, from the perspective of love, in contrast to the perspective of force, an expression of strength: treachery is unable to defeat it. As Luther writes: "[I]t is in the nature of love to be deceived, seeing it is exposed to all the uses and abuses of all men."[2] What is shown in an objection such as this is a way of relating to love, to keep it at a distance. For whether something is strength or weakness is not a theoretical issue. What might appear to be a question about God is then as much a question about myself.

Luther connects, in an ambiguous way, to what I have said here. He says that "the Spirit and grace are offered ... freely, and by the sole mercy of God" but then continues "unworthy as we are".[3] Thus there is something like being worthy, though nobody is in fact worthy; thinking in terms of criteria is not completely rejected. In the same way, he writes, "If you consider worthiness, there is no merit and no reward. ... the good will, the merit and the reward all come from grace alone".[4] In other words, nobody gets merit through worthiness, for everyone is unworthy, and by one's own efforts one cannot become anything other than unworthy; so it is still meaningful to talk about being worthy and unworthy. In that sense, the one who loves a God of love rejects the relevance of free choice in this context in a much more radical way than Luther does. Furthermore, Luther is somewhat unclear about whether salvation should be understood as something internal or external to the reception of the Spirit of God, if it is this that salvation *is* or if salvation is something given over and above this reception (but not a reward given on the basis of worthiness, of course). The logic of his line of thought[5] points in the former direction – as when he writes: "[T]hose who do good things do them in no servile and mercenary spirit for the sake of gaining eternal life, yet they are seeking eternal life in the sense that they are on the road by which they will arrive at and find eternal life."[6] But the concepts he uses – consequence, result – are taken from a way of thinking in line with the latter direction. Phrases like "follows necessarily"[7] and "necessary consequence"[8] seem to mix the two ways of understanding the question. Understanding religious belief as love of a God of love is a radicalization and more consistent form of Luther's line of thought in this context.

What confuses the question about merit and worthiness is the fact that it is fundamentally unclear from what perspective the issue is seen. Besides, it seems to me that the difference of love, in comparison to the case in which one really talks about merit, is not sufficiently paid attention to. One example could be where someone who has won a race may afterwards, when being interviewed, express her gratitude to her trainer. By doing so, she expresses her awareness of the fact that she would not have been able to do what she has done, were it not for the trainer; what she has done is not only her own merit. And she may express this by giving away the medal to the trainer. From the perspective of some member of the audience, another runner may be a more worthy winner: that she has come as far as she has done, despite poor conditions, is a greater achievement. But what the runner who has won the race has done, and it is precisely she who has done this, is to have won the race: the fastest runner was not the trainer, nor some other participant in the race. Besides, it is possible to win the race irrespective of the trainer, even despite the trainer. To that extent, the help of somebody else is not at all necessary. Finally, there is a question about the correctness of the judgment: irrespective of perspective – the runner herself, the other competitors, the trainer, the audience – one can, if one has knowledge of the relevant facts, make a judgment about how important the contribution of the trainer was. In this example, merit, reward and worthiness have obvious places. As to love, and love of God and God's love, however, this is not at all the case. It is easy to go through the example and point out differences, one after the other. I leave that to the reader, and will only point out some things I find particularly important.

That merit, reward and worthiness have obvious places here depends on the fact that it is a competition; there is a difference between the violinist who, when he has won a competition, gives credit where credit is due by mentioning his teacher, and the violinist who thanks his teacher for her having made the joy of playing music possible for him. In the latter case, no question about merit, reward and worthiness arises, and consequently not about giving credit where credit is due either. Such a comparison – with playing the violin – may make us blind to the differences also to this case, however. The main difference is that love is not a doing, an action, in the sense that running fast or playing the violin well – however different these are among themselves – are actions: the latter two are a matter of succeeding in doing something, that is, there is a difficulty which requires effort, skill, and so forth, to be overcome, and for that reason there is a question about how it came about that I succeeded in doing this, but that is not so in the case of love. When I love, I answer directly to the presence and existence of someone, and it is that presence which everything is about here; without it, this love would not exist at all; that is, it is not the case that without it an inferior form of love would exist. The "contribution" of the other is not superfluous or contributing to something I would, in principle, be able to manage alone; for the same reason, it would be wrong to say that it is the other who does everything and that I am completely incapable, since one would then still remain stuck in a perspective where it is meaningful to talk about being capable and being incapable. But if the point is that the other is not independent of what the issue is about – as the trainer is independent, irrespective of the dimensions of her contribution, of what it means to win the race – the case of a therapist, who is capable of helping me with my relations to other human beings, seems to be different. Of course, there is *something* to this, but the comparison risks being misleading. If the one who helps me is a friend of mine, our relation will change in this; what happens is not external to our friendship, even though the question may concern a third person. The therapist is, at least in principle, different, since her relation to me is supposed to be wholly professional, a relation the goal of which is that it should come to an end when I am no longer in need of therapy. *If*, and this is really a big if, there is a place for talking about merit and worthiness here, that depends on the fact that the therapist is supposed to stand outside all of my relations, to be completely external to them. But it is precisely that which is not possible as to the relation with God: for the believer there is no human being who is able to take up such a position – a human being the relation with whom would be independent of my relation with God – and God does not take up that position either, since God is not understood as someone I shall leave behind when I am no longer in need of such a relation. Since God is here understood as a God of love, this is all the more obvious: "of love" means that my possible loving relation with God is part of our togetherness.[9]

III. *How should the basis of me being good or evil be understood?*

However, more central in Luther's line of thought is that the will is incapable of changing itself, of choosing its motivation. What Luther sets out to do here is answer the second of my two questions (in section I). He writes:

> [W]hen a man is without the Spirit of God he does not do evil against his will, as if he were taken by the scruff of the neck and forced to it, like a thief or robber carried off against his will to punishment, but he does it of his own accord and with a ready will. And this readiness or will to act he cannot by his own powers omit, restrain, or change, but he keeps on willing and being ready; and even if he is compelled by external force to do something different, yet the will within him remains averse and he is resentful at whatever compels or resists it ... This is what we call the necessity of immutability: It means that the will cannot change itself and turn in a different direction ... This would not happen if it were free or had free choice ... By contrast, if God works in us, the will is changed, and being gently breathed upon by the Spirit of God, it again wills and acts from pure willingness and inclination and of its own accord, not from compulsion, so that it cannot be turned another way by any opposition, not be overcome or compelled even by the gates of hell, but it goes on willing and delighting in and loving the good, just as before it willed and delighted in and loved evil ... Thus the human will is placed between the two like a beast of burden. If God rides it, it wills and goes where God wills ... If Satan rides it, it wills and goes where Satan wills; nor can it choose to run to either of the two riders or to seek him out, but the riders themselves contend for the possession and control of it.[10]

My will is not something external to me, something I make use of and change by means of working on it. Or if it were, there would still be a more fundamental will in me, the one which comes to expression in my attempt at deciding the character of my less fundamental will.[11] Good and evil – being ridden by God and being ridden by Satan – are not characteristics which pertain solely to one level, a level I could come beyond and outside by placing myself on a more fundamental level where I could decide on them from an external viewpoint. In that sense, it is not possible to choose my motivation or change my most fundamental will: if a change happens, the change has not its origin in the will. Or to put it another way, behind all doing good and doing evil, there is a being good and being evil (in me), which it is not possible to change by means of some doing.[12] (What Luther is saying here is also an expression of a specific way of understanding God (and Satan): God is in no way external to the good, cannot be understood in any other way, and the same thing goes for Satan and evil).

However, if the change has not its origin in my will, why must it have its origin in God? Why should we think in that way? Why is the question about the origin of the change at all important? Luther answers, that otherwise there would be no hope:

> Christian faith is entirely extinguished, the promises of God and the whole gospel are completely destroyed, if we teach and believe that it is not for us to know ... the necessity of the things that are to come to pass. For this is the one supreme consolation of Christians ... that his [God's] will can neither be resisted nor changed nor hindered.[13]

Thus what appears to be God appealing, in the Bible say, is God acting: "It has thus pleased God to impart the Spirit, not without the Word, but through the Word ... things that he could of course do without the Word, but does not will so to do."[14]

But from what perspective does Luther say this? The one who is "ridden by Satan" does not see any need of this hope and this consolation, for to her it makes no difference – or rather, it would be a good thing – if Christian faith were entirely extinguished, the promises of God and the whole gospel were completely destroyed. Or if she sees such a need, if such a hope and consolation would be important to her, then this would be marked by the fact that she is ridden by Satan and would not express its good meaning. The one who sees this good meaning is the one who is "ridden by God" and thus she does not need this *hope*: the change has already come to pass. Consequently, there is no one who hopes that God will change her will, who would despair if she were given up to herself. Either my hope is not external to my will, but is determined by the more fundamental will which is already good or evil, or it is external to my will – but then there is something in me which determines this will, something in me which is more fundamental than it, and the problem Luther is discussing would then not have the character he initially described it as having.

To clarify this, let us discuss an example of a man who realizes that he does not love his wife anymore. What can he do about this? To be sure, he cannot decide to love her, as if what was missing was an exertion of will.[15] But what does it mean to ask the question "What can he do about this"? If he does not see the fact that he does not love his wife anymore as a problem, he will not ask this question, and if he sees it as a kind of problem other than the one we had in mind, the question means something else, if he asks it. He may find it difficult, practically speaking, to leave his wife, or he may find the conflict that could arise frightening, and therefore he asks himself the question. But if this is what the question means, then he is in fact able to solve the problem by means of a decision, by means of an exertion of will: he could, say, stay with her and *act* lovingly. But if this is not the case, if he really sees the fact that he does not love his wife anymore as a problem and this problem does not have this practical character, what does that mean? I would say that this shows that he still loves her. The solution to the problem is not to say that it does not exist, of course, but there is something to this: if he does not notice the nearly non-existent character of the problem, he will not be able to approach it at all.

As to the religious case, this example shows that to the one for whom despair for one's own evil will is intelligible, the problem does not have the radical form Luther sees it as having. I am not completely corrupted; there is something good in me. But if this is so, it is misleading to say that the change must have its origin outside of me, in God acting on me externally. If I love a God of love, or if this is what I long for – if I am comparable to the man above who grieves at not loving his wife anymore and thus still loves her – then I understand the good, possibly flickering, that is in me, as an expression of God: it is not external to God. But it is not external to me either. In other words, it is not God who acts on me externally or I who choose this in an external way (and hence no "cooperation" since this would only be to add together these two outlooks): this distinction is not applicable here.

Let us discuss another example, this time from the opposite perspective. If someone is about to hit me, what am I able to do? Of course, I may flee, ward off, or hit him before he has hit me. These are all possibilities, which, one could say, are causal: I put in some cause or other which should – I act in this or that way in order to – prevent what he is about to do to have the effect he wants it to have. Are these the only possibilities? Must all possibilities be variants of these? How about appealing to him? If appealing to him is comparable to the other possibilities, its effectiveness depends on my skill. In that case, it would be a matter of pulling at the right strings, psychologically, just like some people know what they should say in order to get some person upset. This is a possibility, of course, but it is not that possibility I have in mind when I talk about appealing to him. What I have in mind is awakening the other's love, mercy, and so on. If you understand what I mean, you see that this is in *contrast* to pulling strings psychologically; what it means to say that he changes his mind in love and does not hit me, is that he is in what he does, is not manipulated by someone pulling at the right strings.

(If you find it obscure to say that there is something which contrasts to
the causal, do not get stuck on this word! (But if your attitude is that "the
causal" is a concept which covers everything, you must ask yourself if this
does not mean that this concept has a highly metaphysical role for you.)
Instead, pay attention to the distinction I have tried to make between hitting back and appealing, between manipulating psychologically and appealing! If you understand this distinction, and take your time to describe the
difference, you see what I mean by "non-causal".)

Another way of shedding light on this difference, continuing the discussion of this example, is as follows. Against his will, I may prevent him hitting
me, by, say, holding fast his arms. I may prevent him hitting me without
recourse to force, by holding forth something I know (or believe) that he
will be attracted by and choose instead of me, by, say, paying him not to hit
me. However, in the latter case I still do what I do with focus on the calculation: I try to change the result of the calculation by bringing in an additional element. Within the framework of the totality of what he wants, my
attempt at changing the direction of his will is done. Appealing, on the
other hand, is something for which this totality is not relevant. Love of
neighbor is not an additional element for him to take into account when
carrying out the calculation, but something which counters this calculation
as such; it is this which I try to awaken in him (and in this very context it is
not important whether this means awakening something which already is
there or means kindling something new in him).[16]

Appealing is about something *different* from the examples I have discussed
here, and should not be understood as variants of them. Preventing someone physically, pulling strings psychologically, and holding forth something
someone will be attracted by, are all a matter of skill. Appealing, on the
other hand, is not more or less skillful, but pure or impure. It is pure and
impure in two respects, nearly related: first, to what degree it is a matter of
appealing and to what degree there are other elements present there (of
pulling strings psychologically, say); second, to what degree I appeal in the
spirit of love or not. Salvation, in the sense in which I have used it previously
in this chapter, is about a goal: this goal may be called, say, "eternal life".
However, salvation can refer to the way to this goal, the necessary transformation. In some ways of understanding religious belief, these are two different things: salvation in the latter sense is God's transformation of me so that
I become worthy of, or at all capable of, receiving the reward which is salvation in the former sense. However, when religious belief is understood as
love of a God of love, this is not so: the transformation and the goal is in
both cases God's love. More precisely put, the transformation is God

appealing in love. God's way of acting is then not different, as compared to human beings' way of acting, by being more skillful, by being a more effective form of manipulation. The difference, if one understands religious belief in this way, is that God's appealing is purer, or is pure.

This means that there are no guarantees when appealing, as there can be when acting causally, in which case you may be more or less skillful. But is it then not possible to say that God's love is so strong than nothing can withstand it? Yes, it is possible; I can imagine one who loves a God of love saying such a thing. But notice that this is something which is said *in* that faith; it is not something said as an expression of sorrow, since in that case one has shown that it is in fact possible to withstand it. As long as one believes in what one says, one cannot apply this saying to oneself and check whether it is true, by comparing my "strength" to God's: the very attempt at checking this shows that one does not believe in what one says. Furthermore, love of a God of love means absence of distrust of other human beings, the kind of distrust which shows itself in the attitude that there is no love at all in some specific human being, that she is evil through and through. In that sense, the one who loves a God of love will not take as evidence that which for someone else is evidence that it is really possible to withstand God's love. Thus saying "God's love is so strong that nothing can withstand it" is not a theoretical report, the result of an investigation.

Luther's mistake, to sum up this section, is not that it is in fact possible for the will to change itself, for me to choose my fundamental motivation. The mistake consists, besides the fact that he seems to underestimate the extent to which the motivation is mixed and unclear – the extent to which I am divided in myself – in him not entering deeper into the *differences* between different ways in which a motivation may change. On the contrary, he makes all such changes into a matter of acting: "impart the Spirit", "God works in us". God and Satan are not – to the one who loves a God of love – simply two different riders, but ride in two completely different senses and try to become masters of "the beast of burden" in two completely different senses (which means that it is just one of them – Satan – which is really "the master of"). Once again we see how we risk being misled by a kind of formalism, the idea that it is possible to distinguish sharply between the content (who the rider is) and the act (what character the riding has, how the attempt at becoming "the master of" is made). This does not mean that the power and control are in the end entirely in my own hands. On the contrary, think of someone who expresses her joy at being saved to love by someone![17] And the same thing applies even more to the one who loves a God of love, for the relation to God, of course: how God has saved her to love. But once again we must distinguish between genuine joy and something which superficially appears to be joy but in fact is a result of manipulation. The first side of this distinction – genuine joy – is not chosen joy (whatever that would mean), but joy as an aspect of love. This distinction is then only possible to make for someone who is open to the possibility of love; the distinction, and the rejection of it, are in that sense not neutral.

For the one who loves a God of love it is an important point that faith is not of her own making, something she is able to produce on her own. But this does not mean that it is of someone else's making (or that is of their joint making, in cooperation). It is not at all a product, a matter of *making.* The problem is that the idea of faith as a matter of the will[18] is still preserved, but is placed differently: it is now a matter of the will of *God.* Instead, faith is for her a matter of "the heart", which means something radically different. This problem is evident also in the one I have taken this expression from: Pascal.[19] For him, the faith of the heart is a result of God acting,[20] and it is merely due to sin that this is necessary; if sin had not damaged reason, reason would manage everything on its own.[21]

IV. *"Will" and "choice"*

Luther writes further:

> God has assuredly promised his grace to the humble … But no man can be thoroughly humbled until he knows that his salvation is utterly beyond his own powers, devices, endeavors, will and works, and depends entirely on the choice, will and work of another, namely, of God alone.[22]
>
> [H]oly men … whenever they come to pray or plead with God, approach him in utter forgetfulness of their own free choice, despairing of themselves and imploring nothing but pure grace alone.[23]

Some of this could be said by someone who loves a God of love, as we have seen: love is a direct answer to the presence and existence of someone, and it is this presence which everything is about here. Love is not something I do. In love I am, one could say, attracted by the good, and the direction is away from me, toward that which I am attracted to. Enough has been said about this, however, and I want to point out another thing, which Luther hints at.

The concept "will" could be used in two different ways. The first one is the will as a specific phenomenon, as when it is contrasted with, say, being humble. Then it is not at all strange not to will anything: this is simply to reject one way of being, in contrast with other ways of being. The philosophical problem arises when this use of the term is mixed up with another one, where the will is said to precede everything *I* do, in contrast to what I am, say, forced to do. To reject the will, if it is at all possible, would then be to reject myself as a living, existing being. The "will" is here taken to be the name for that, whatever it is, which makes an action *my* action, or rather, makes it an *action*. The concept is taken to distinguish between what I am responsible for and what I am not responsible for, that is, what I am forced to do, what I cannot help, and the like. In that respect, to reject the will is a matter of willing.

However, one should notice that the latter way of speaking about the will – as something that precedes everything *I* do, in contrast to what I am forced to do – is somewhat strained. That something has to do with me – that it is my fault, that I have a bad conscience for it – need not mean that it was something I *did*: it may be something I did *not* do. And that something has to do with me – that it is my fault, that I have a bad conscience for it – need not mean that it was preceded by anything in order for one to be able to say that I was not forced. Furthermore, these two points can be important at the same time. If I am reading, and a friend of mine asks me to keep an eye on his kid when he is away for some hours, and the kid runs away without me noticing this, me being absentminded, the problem is not what I did but what I did not do, and what I did not do is not necessarily preceded by anything, as when I *decide* to disregard the kid. The problem may be precisely my inactivity and thoughtlessness. And notice that they are *mine*!

This observation means that the concept "will" is not at all as central as it is often taken to be in philosophy. My point is not that we can do without it (or that we cannot do without it), but simply that it is not needed in order for us to be able to make the distinction I talked about in the preceding paragraph, that using the concept "will" is not that good a way of making this distinction. Instead, we can focus on, say, the spirit in which something is done or not done, where this includes, among other things, such things as inactivity and thoughtlessness, but also, say, love. What makes something mine is the possibility to describe it in some of these ways, in contrast to what happens independent of these "spirits", such as when I am forced to do something. Obviously, this means that the question about *what* makes something mine is rejected. However, this is also in fact so when the answer "the will" is given. Either this answer gets its content from how we are already able to distinguish what is mine from what is not mine, and is then only apparently an answer to the question, or else it has an independent content: but which one?

A problem in Luther is that he does not distinguish between these two uses of the concept "will" clearly enough.[24] As we have seen he sometimes talks about the first one, when he talks about being humble and rejecting one's will. What it is to trust in God's grace is connected to this. But we have also seen how God's grace, God's work in us, and the like, become concepts used to give a general description of everything I do, to the extent it can be described as good, and a corresponding account could be given for the evil things I do. However, pointing out this confusion is not to say that this second project is misguided – that is a question which must be discussed in another way – only to say that there is no immediate connection between them.

Luther makes an important point when he says that goodness and evil cannot be understood as choices I make. (Here, one could, instead, talk about the spirit in which I do something.) He writes, "It is ... a mere dialectical fiction that there is in man a neutral and unqualified willing ... if God is in us, Satan is absent, and only a good will is present; if God is absent, Satan is present, and only an evil will is in us."[25] (Here Luther again underestimates the degree to which I am divided in myself, but that is not important at the moment.) There is no neutral position from which the choice can be made; it is not possible to stand, without any moral standing at all, and choose one's way. How and when I choose, which alternatives I see and on what grounds I take my stand to them, is not independent of my moral standing. (One could, somewhat paradoxically, say that if I choose between good and evil, I have already dismissed the good.) This is something stressed also by Kant and Schelling, when they refer to an evil decision preceding all evil acting, a decision made outside time and space, that is, something in which sense it is at all a "decision" is highly unclear.[26]

Another way of expressing this is by saying that love is not chosen. For the one who loves a God of love and thus sees God and love, a God of love, as the good, the relation to the good is not seen as a result of choice. At the same time – and once again this shows that the concepts "will" and "choice" are not as fundamental as one might be tempted to think – love is not something that simply happens to me, which has nothing to do with me. On the contrary, the one who loves a God of love could say that in this love, she is really herself and free. For her, her "will" is not what she is at bottom.

However, Luther does not accept this. I have said that goodness (and evil) cannot be understood in terms of choice; Luther, on the other hand, says that it should be understood in such terms, in terms of *God's* choice. He may seem to be radical, philosophically speaking, but this is merely apparently. The concepts "will" and "choice" are as central to him as to the rationalistic tradition; he merely gives them a new place. In one sense, they are even more central to him: his above point, his criticism of the idea that we choose our way, should have made him question the centrality of the concept "choice" in general, but that he then feels himself forced to give it a new place shows that there is something almost compulsory to his focus on will and choice. He writes, for example, "It follows now that free choice is plainly a divine term, and can be properly applied to none but the Divine Majesty alone; for he alone can do and does ... whatever he pleases in heaven and on earth."[27] And it is this which is the cause of me being good (or not): "that hidden and awful will of God whereby he ordains by his own counsel which and what sort of persons he wills to be recipients and partakers of his preached and offered mercy."[28] Has Luther suddenly forgotten what he has said about "choice" and "will"? Expressed in the way I started section III, is the will of God something external to God, something God can give some or other character to by means of choice? In what sense is it then a "will"? Is God able to choose between good and evil without already being good or evil? However, Luther has an answer to these problems. It is God who decides what is good and evil, and thus it is God who decides the character of God's own will: "For it is not because he [God] is or was obliged so to will that what he wills is right, but on the contrary, because he himself so wills, therefore what happens must be right."[29] This is not an answer to the problems, however, even though it might seem to be one. What Luther says is in fact that it is senseless to *characterize* God's will as good or evil – it is good by definition – which means that God does not *choose* between good and evil. To say that "free choice can be properly applied to none but God" is consequently misleading. In the same way it is misleading to say that this is an account of my possible goodness, since what Luther here is referring to, in the ultimate instance, is a "decision" beyond good and evil: this is simply to say that there is no explanation. (I will return to the question about the hidden will of God and its arbitrariness in a moment.)

There is another answer to the problems, however. Luther connects God and the good by means of something he says is a choice, a decision, even though it is unclear what this means, as we have seen. The reason for this, as we have seen and will return to, is that he wants to see to it that there is nothing higher than God, an obligation God has to comply with, say. For that reason, he places God higher than every obligation, suggesting that it is God who decides what is good and evil. The other answer to the problems is now evident: it is to place them on the same level. What this would mean as long as one talks in terms of obligation is unclear, but it is evident if one understands religious belief as love of a God of love: there is *no* gap between love and God, nothing needing to be bridged by, say, a choice or a decision. To the one who loves a God of love, it is talking about God's choices and decisions which is "blasphemous", since love is "higher" than all choices and decisions: according to her, talking about God's choices and decisions is as "degrading" to God as talking about God as obliged is according to Luther.

One reason Luther sees for his account is that without it evil is inexplicable. Saying that human beings have no free will is a way of understanding how evil persons go on being evil despite the fact that they have been proved wrong, how it is possible that everyone, even the wisest person, does evil.[30] Partly this is right: it shows that morality and faith cannot be understood as a matter of rational considerations, as if evil was a mistake, an expression of incompetence.[31] However, the problem is that Luther does not satisfy himself with this observation but tries to give an explanation. This explanation is in terms of God's actions. But as we have seen, this is only an apparent explanation. If the explanation was that God imparts the Spirit in some and not in others, this could be seen either as a purely causal explanation – evil as a tragic fate, a comparison actually made by Luther,[32] or as a disease – and the explanation should then be questioned, since it eliminates the moral character it was supposed to explain, or it could be understood as having a moral character in referring to something else having that character. In the latter way one should understand what Luther is trying to say, I take it, since he does not operate with some concept of a causal mechanism, but with the concept "God's decision". However, the problem with such an explanation is that it has not explained the moral character – good and evil – but only placed it on another level which in its turn waits for an explanation. Here Luther cuts off the regress by bringing in a new element in the explanation, saying that God's decision is right by definition. But in that case, would it not be just as good to say that evil is inexplicable? What additional insight has been reached by bringing in the concept of God? My point in this paragraph is not that Luther is necessarily wrong, only that if one wants to give support to his outlook by saying that without it evil is inexplicable, one cheats oneself. Instead, what one should say is that evil is still not explained, and that this is not a drawback but quite in accordance with the subject.

In the end I would say that the problem is trying to adopt a general perspective on evil. Here one tries to say something about evil from a position outside of oneself, so to speak, and it does not make an important difference whether this perspective is taken to be "scientific" (studying the world, understood as a causal nexus, in its entirety), "theological" (from God's perspective), or "philosophical" (a perspective from which one looks down on both God and man). Instead, the point is that I, morally speaking – and this must be central to the question of good and evil – never leave the first person perspective; whatever I say, whatever perspective I claim to have adopted, what I do, is always possible to characterize morally. Evil in its entirety, hence including my own, is inexplicable not because it is an object of explanation which we have not found an explanation for yet, but because it is not (morally) possible to see it as such an object. It does not help using an abstract concept of truth and insist on the explanation given being "true": if something is not possible to say, that is, if the explanation is not possible to *give*, it is not an *intelligible candidate* for truth, whatever support the explanation, partially considered, may seem to have. (The case I am thinking of is not of this kind: "He *is* fat, but don't say so; that would be impolite." In such a case what one should not say is still intelligible: it is precisely for this reason this person says that it should not be said.[33])

Instead, all I can say is that both goodness and evil are primitive. I cannot stand outside of them and choose, nor is it the case that they have nothing to do with me, something that, so to speak, strikes me (fate, a disease). However, one could say that evil is mine in terms of responsibility – here it is important to see what I have done as something *I* have done, but that is not the case as to goodness, where that question is irrelevant – but not mine in terms of moral nature – the opposite would be an attempt at escaping my responsibility by claiming that I cannot help being evil, and, furthermore, goodness could be said to be mine in terms of moral nature, since I cannot evade responsibility by saying that I lack goodness.[34]

V. *The power of God*

That an idea of the perfection, above all, power, of God has an important role for Luther we have already seen, when he objects to the idea of an obligation God has to comply with. For that reason, God is the one who in the end works all in all:

> [H]e [God] foresees and purposes and does all things by his immutable, eternal, and infallible will.[35]
> For God to will and foreknow are the same thing.[36]
> [E]verything we do, everything that happens, even if it seems to us to happen mutably and contingently, happens in fact nonetheless necessarily and immutably, if you have regard to the will of God. For the will of God is effectual and cannot be hindered, since it is the power of the divine nature itself; moreover it is wise, so that it cannot be deceived. Now, if this will is not hindered, there is

nothing to prevent the work itself from being done, in the place, time, manner, and measure that he himself both foresees and wills.[37]

This means that some questions do not arise here: whether the future is an object (possible to have knowledge of), whether the future already exists in some sense. No, God's foreknowledge is the kind of knowledge about the future I may have since I intend to do something. (A: "In a minute, X will lie down on the floor." B: "Why do you believe that? What basis do you have for your prediction?" A knocks X down.) Furthermore, one should notice that what is here said about God means that it is misleading to say, as we have seen Luther say, that "the riders themselves contend for the possession and control of it".[38] The power Satan has is in the end given by God; it is no real contention. This is something Luther himself stresses, by means of this example:

> [I]f God foreknew that Judas would be a traitor, Judas necessarily became a traitor, and it was not in the power of Judas or any other creature to do differently or to change his will, though he did what he did willingly and not under compulsion, but that act of will was a work of God, which he set in motion by his omnipotence, like everything else. For it is an irrefutable and self-evident proposition that God does not lie and is not deceived.[39]

In order to clarify this, Luther makes a distinction between the revealed God and the hidden God:

> [I]t is this that God as he is preached is concerned with, namely, that sin and death should be taken away and we should be saved ... But God hidden in his majesty neither deplores nor takes away death, but works life, death, and all in all. For there he has not bound himself by his word, but has kept himself free over all things ... Thus he does not will the death of a sinner, according to his word; but he wills it according to that inscrutable will of his.[40]

This "second" God – the hidden God – is, since the issue concerns what works all in all, closely connected to fate. In this context, Luther approvingly quotes "heathen poets" and writes, as a comparison to the hidden God, "Fate counts for more than all the endeavors of men, and therefore it imposes a necessity on both things and men".[41] What Luther gives us are two very different understandings of God: on the one hand the good God, close to the God of love; on the other hand the God who works all in all, the capricious God, the almost pantheist God, the fate we ought to submit to.

The problem is not that this is "not consistent". Rather, why should this be *believed?* Why is it important to say that God is what works all in all? There is one point in emphasizing the "hiddenness": loving someone means not seeing this person as a set of properties, means not seeing her as defined by what I experience. As S. L. Frank writes:

> The genuine essence of a person slips away from us insofar as we try to know him as an "object," to expose his inner essence in a set of determinations.[12]
> The fact that I encounter a "thou," that the gaze of "another being" is directed at me, that I stand before the presence of some "other soul," some "other consciousness," is given to me in a much more primary and immediate way than the knowledge of what precisely occurs or is contained in another soul. True, this general presence of "thou" is given to me together with a certain perception of its psychic state at a given moment or, more precisely, together with the qualitative character of its directedness at me ... we can to some extent know the "content" of this reality, penetrate "into" another soul. But this knowledge is somewhat uncertain, inaccurate, shaky, more or less obscure ... Even our closest friend, whom we think we know quite well, can sometimes astonish us with something we could never have expected from him ... the inner content of "thou" is unattainable and unknowable for us in its essence and concrete fullness.[13]

What Frank writes is somewhat misleading, giving preponderance to epistemological considerations. The main point is not that the knowledge I have about the "thou" is necessarily inaccurate and shaky, but that my relation to her is not an epistemological relation. In some situation, I may know what she will say, but this does not mean that, as far as I am concerned, she could just as well keep silent since I do not need to be informed about her state of mind. On the contrary, talking to each other is a way of being together. But that the person I encounter is not defined by what I experience, by what is revealed to me, that I relate to her as someone in some sense new every moment, does not mean that there is necessarily something she keeps hidden. Luther claims something more than this good point. Furthermore, even though Luther says that one should not pry into this hidden will of God,[14] the existence of this hidden will is evidently important to him, something the Christian in that sense must relate to. But why?

At bottom, the reason for this is fairly simple. Luther writes that "God is omnipotent ... otherwise he would be a ridiculous God".[15] What is meant by "omnipotent" is not self-evident, of course – as could be seen from my discussion, the problem is about what *character* the power of God has, not how *much* power God has; the problem does not disappear by one claiming that God does not have all power, if the kind of power one is talking about still has a problematic character – but in this context it is clear what Luther is thinking of. If God is not also the hidden God, if God is not the one who in the end works all in all independent of every obligation, then God is ridiculous. What we see here is one of my basic points: what might appear to be a question about how God should be understood philosophically is rather a question about myself; love being ridiculous since it does not force me to submission and lets itself be deserted again and again is how the issue appears from *one* perspective, a perspective which is not the perspective of the one who loves a God of love.

VI. *Love and freedom*

One reason often appealed to when wanting to emphasize the philosophical importance of choice and will, is that without them there is no such thing as moral responsibility. Erasmus writes, "If the power to distinguish good and evil and the will of God had been hidden from men, it could not be imputed to them if they made the wrong choice. If the will had not been free, sin could not have been imputed, for sin would cease to be sin if it were not voluntary."[46] This need not mean that the existence of choice and will must be possible to establish empirically or metaphysically in order for it to be possible to talk about moral responsibility; it could just as well mean that seeing someone as having done what she has done freely and willingly is internal to ascribing moral responsibility to her (when blaming someone, say). In the latter case, choice and will are not seen as psychological/metaphysical phenomena, but as *moral* ones.

However that may be, it is clear that when I am divided in myself, when I think about what I should do, when I am tempted to do something I do not, in one sense of the word, want to do, then it is hard to understand, to say the least, what it would mean to say that I am not free, if that is supposed to mean that reflecting on the issue is pointless. Saying that it is pointless is not neutral as to the reflection, but is to recommend one way, of many, of relating to the issue; this way of relating to the issue is tempting to adopt when I want to silence a doubt concerning what I usually do as a matter of course. However, talking about being "free" in this sense is not necessarily to talk about choice and will.

What has appeared here is two ways in which choice, will and freedom may be taken to be morally central: first, as connected to ascribing responsibility to someone; second, as connected to taking one's responsibility (in contrast to trying to escape it). Both these ways are important in Kant's moral philosophy, and I will end this chapter with a discussion of it, leaving the discussion of Luther behind, especially since a critical discussion of Kant's moral philosophy may make it clear how love and freedom could be said to be intimately connected. In that way we will see that even though the one who loves a God of love agrees with Luther's criticism of free choice in many respects, there is for her still something important in freedom.

Kant's Copernican revolution in philosophy consists, as he himself says, in turning from the objects of our intuitions to the constitution of this very faculty of intuition as such.[47] One example of this, an example with importance for his moral philosophy, is his way of approaching the question about the freedom of the will. The opposite of freedom here is that everything is causally determined. But from where comes the idea that everything is causally determined? Is it a statement of experience? No, the idea expresses the way in which we approach the world when we investigate it empirically, one could say. That what happens has a cause is not a result confirmed by empirical research; on the contrary, that idea is a presupposition for empirical research. That everything has a cause is not an empirical description of the world, but is an idea internal to the empirical outlook as such. But since this outlook is precisely an outlook, it does not automatically take precedence over other ways of seeing things, where everything is not seen as causally determined, where I understand myself as a moral being acting in freedom.[48] If these two outlooks are clearly distinguished, philosophical problems are avoided. Distinguishing these two outlooks means among other things that one should not try to prove human freedom theoretically; that there is no such thing as a theoretical proof here is evident from what was said above.[49] Kant's philosophy could be described as an attempt at clarifying the character of the different perspectives. The theoretical perspective, on the one hand, searches for laws of nature and employs concepts such as cause and effect within the boundaries of the sensible; in the practical perspective, on the other hand, a law for freedom, a supersensible, intellectual law, is active. The latter law says how things should be done, in contrast to the laws of nature, which include, among other things, psychological laws about what simply happens.

Formulations of such a law for freedom – summarized in the categorical imperative – Kant arrives at in different ways. One way is as follows.[50] A rational being acting practically does not do what she does by chance, but for reasons. Giving a reason may be to refer to a desire: the reason why I ate a banana was that I was hungry. But this is not necessarily the endpoint of a chain of reasons. In some situations additional questions could be asked. If the banana I ate belonged to someone else, if I stole it from someone, saying that I ate it because I was hungry is not enough; in such a situation one could ask why I did not find something to eat in some other way. Hence, being hungry is not something which forces me to act in this or that way, but something I take as a, good or bad, reason for what I do. Kant then draws the conclusion that the fundamental reason for the practical action of a rational being is not some particular end – questions about such an end can still be asked, as we have seen – but the formal property of every reason, that is, its generality as law. This means that Kant takes himself to have connected the concepts "freedom", "reason" and "good will"[51] in the categorical imperative.

Someone who does not act from a maxim in conformity with the categorical imperative is neither free nor rational. She is not free – or, rather, she relates to herself as if she were not free – since the only reason she is able to give for what she did is, in the end, that she felt herself forced to do what she did, forced by some desire say. She is not rational, since the maxim she gives for her action is not one she is able to will as a universal law; that is, she has made an unfounded exception for herself.[52] (Here the difference between autonomy and heteronomy becomes obvious: the categorical imperative is, according to Kant, the only thing you can make into a law for yourself, the only thing you can obey for its own sake, and not for, say, fear of punishment. The good will, freedom and reason are connected in autonomy.[53]) But if reason then is impartial, between whom is it impartial? According to Kant, it is impartial between the rational beings, since only they have a non-relative worth. Something has a worth for me if I desire it; if I did not desire it, it would not have a worth for me. This means that what I here take to be of non-relative worth is myself, and the same goes for all other rational beings.[54] What we get is this formulation of the categorical imperative: "So act that you use humanity, whether in your own person or in the person of any other, always at the same time as an end, never merely as a means."[55] Hence, every person becomes an object of respect.[56]

What is important in Kant is, for my purposes, the idea that morality and freedom are intimately connected. A common idea is that morality is some kind of limitation, that complete freedom would be immoral, that morality is some kind of external constraint I submit to for some good purpose. The question is, however, what such a freedom would be: if I am about to do (say, think) precisely what I want, what is it that I really want? Is this a question which is easily answered? Is it always obvious to me what I want, in contrast to what I have imagined myself to be wanting? And is really what I want the fundamental entity, as if I never regretted that this was something I wanted? This does not mean that I should submit to some external constraint instead: what I would do in such a case would simply be something I did not believe in. On the contrary, the point is that morality – in one sense of the word – is not at all a limitation to freedom. Kant emphasizes this point: only when doing good is one acting freely.

How shall this goodness and this freedom be understood? To Kant it is obvious that this cannot be a matter of love. He criticizes the idea of love of neighbor: feelings cannot be commanded.[57] This may be true, but the question is whether *the commandment* is the elementary form of morality. For it is clear that I may be sorry for, find fault with, criticize myself for, what I feel and do not feel, or what I felt and did not feel. (However, it is clear that an external legislation in that direction would be absurd, but that is not what our issue is about.) What is important here is that it is *myself* I criticize. The "pathological" is not something which happens to me – as if, say, hatred was something that simply struck me – but my feelings are *mine*. Kant is right in that becoming more loving is not something I can *decide* myself upon, as if what was needed was simply pure power of will; on the contrary, love is antithetical to power of will and one could in many cases suspect that it is precisely the will, when one hardens one's heart, which is the problem.[58] But this only goes to show that the center of the self is not the will, with everything else as arbitrary attributes.

Even though Kant criticizes the idea of love of neighbor, it is not altogether clear that this idea is of no importance to him. To explain what I am hinting at I will make what might look like a digression and consider Hegel's criticism of Kant's moral philosophy. In that way we will come back to the idea of love of neighbor and its relation to freedom.

In a central paragraph in *Grundlinien der Philosophie des Rechts*[59] Hegel claims, after having expressed his appreciation of Kant's moral philosophy, that adherence to an exclusively moral position, without bringing in the concept of "ethos" (*Sittlichkeit*), means an empty formalism. Only when some content is brought in from outside, that is, is not solely derived from the idea of "duty for duty's sake", will one arrive at specific duties. If one goes along with Kant and simply understands duty as absence of contradiction, one will not arrive at specific duties. When Kant tries to arrive at specific duties, the result is strange, Hegel goes on. For a theft is only a contradiction in relation to the institution of property, but the absence of this institution is no contradiction. Only when some content is fixed are contradictions possible.

However, it is clear that Hegel has misunderstood Kant's point. The point is not that stealing is wrong since it dissolves the concept of property, which would happen if stealing were to become a universal law. If that were Kant's point then Hegel would be right: that no property exists is no contradiction as such. But Kant's use of the categorical imperative should not be understood in this way. His point is that the one who steals wants a world in which the maxim is universalized – that is, a world in which no property exists; this follows from the first formulation of the categorical imperative – and at the same time wants the maxim itself, and that presupposes that there is property. If I steal something, money, say, I want to be in possession of it. In that sense there is a contradiction here. The same thing could be said about lying: when I deceive someone in order to achieve some goal, the efficiency of my strategy presupposes that this is not the general way of achieving this goal.

Although Hegel's criticism is based on a misunderstanding there is something right in it, however. Kant's ethic is essentially a negative, prohibiting ethic.[60] It does not say anything about what is good, and that is its point: to introduce a positive content would always raise a question about the authority of this content, about heteronomy. Or rather, Kant's ethic says next to nothing about what is good, as we will see in a moment. Precisely its formalist character, that every content is disregarded by means of abstraction, and the role of contradiction within it, shows that what is decisive here is not an idea of the good, but of some minimal prohibitions. For that reason, what may seem to be of positive nature is expressed negatively. Helping others is to Kant to not withhold one's help from someone when one is needed.[61] The happiness of others, as an end which is my duty, may seem to be something positive, but is expressed negatively: it is everybody's own business to decide what his or her happiness consists in.[62] The question I have asked in previous chapters[63] – why is it that bad to treat someone badly? – becomes difficult for Kant. A contradiction is a contradiction, to be sure, but may be trivial. How is the moral weight which I experience in remorse to be described? To feel a pang of conscience for having contradicted oneself, for simply having related to oneself as if one were not free, for being irrational, would be absurd! What is it that is awful here? The question is whether this is really possible to understand if one does not acknowledge how treating someone badly means sinning against something good, something positive.

By paying attention to something strange in Kant's line of thought we could get a hint of the solution to this problem. As we have seen, one of the formulations of the categorical imperative is this one: "So act that you use humanity, whether in your own person or in the person of any other, always at the same time as an end, never merely as a means." The background for this formulation is the understanding of human beings as rational beings, as free. But as we have also seen, freedom is not possible to experience theoretically; in other words, "humanity" is here not an empirical, biological category. To say that someone is a rational being, that her freedom is an object of respect, is something which emerges from the practical use of reason. But Kant is silent as to how this comes about. What we have found here is something which *precedes* the categorical imperative: the recognition of someone as someone to care about. In other words, Kant presupposes something positive which he never makes explicit.[64] And this is what makes treating someone badly awful: it is to sin against *someone*.

If one has said this, one has also said that the Kantian phrase "duty for duty's sake" is misleading.[65] To be sure, if I refrain from swindling someone since I believe that the swindle will not be successful, that being a swindler is not profitable, this shows something suspect in my attitude. But this does not mean that what is good is to act for duty's sake. Why is duty that important? Instead, the point is simply that I do what I do because I care for *someone*; this is what is good. Perhaps Kant would object to this by saying that this makes morality into a matter of skill: what I do is good to the extent I succeed in achieving what is good for someone.[66] And this would, as I have said, have absurd results, since that would mean that my lack of moral skill would make me morally innocent. For this reason, it is important to see that solicitude and care have nothing to do with skill or with achieving some end. Care is what it is; it is not an attempt to achieve something else. And another word for this care is, of course, love of neighbor.[67] (The basic problem may be that the only thing Kant does not understand as sensible is reason, which means that everything else is simply objects for empirical psychology. But if I am right, there is a point in saying that love is supersensible in the Kantian meaning of the term.)[68]

What then is the relation between love and freedom? The task is not to find some necessary connection; how one understands freedom is not independent of one's moral standing. Certainly, the completely self-centered person will not see a connection. (But as I said (Chapter 3), it is not at all clear from what perspective one takes such a person to be possible.) To her, freedom is nothing but the possibility to satisfy her own preferences, and that these may change from one moment to the next is of no importance to her. The point is simply that such a way of being is, from the perspective of love, a *limitation*, means *refusing* oneself the pleasure of love. Love will not, as long as she is stuck in her completely self-centered perspective, be a possibility for her; she may take part in something with superficial similarities to love, but caring for another human being is here an impossibility. (Even to obey a constraint, a juridical law, say, is to her to do what she wants, within the limits of this limited freedom. To do what I would do if this constraint did not exist has by the constraint been connected to something I do not want (punishment), which means that obeying the constraint is what I want; what the calculation shows is that this is the best thing to do given the circumstances).

This self-centered perspective is not Kant's. Officially, his perspective is not the perspective of love, but a purely formal one; as we have seen, however, it is very unclear how the weight of morality should then be understood. But is not the perspective of love necessarily heteronomous, that is, unfree? No, saying so would be to miss a few things.

As we have seen, love cannot be understood as sensible, in the Kantian meaning of the term. In that case remorse for my lack of love would be unintelligible; in remorse, love and its absence is not seen as a result of a natural mechanism but as something which has to do with me. Love is not self-centered, not a preference I try to satisfy instrumentally. Nor is it, and this is especially important in this context, a result of a decision, in which case one could, with Kant, ask for the reasons for this decision – they may be of a heteronomous or formal character. Love is not the result of the application of criteria. What we have here is something which does not fit into these categories. This means that love has those non-heteronomous features crucial to Kant. Love is something I am wholehearted in, where I mean what I say and do, without this implying that it is self-centered. This is the freedom of love.

Chapter 6

Togetherness and Community

In philosophy of religion, it is often taken for granted that religious belief must be analyzed as something individual. Believing is taking something to be true, and taking something to be true is something I do. I may take the same, or a similar, proposition to be true as someone else does, and not until then some form of religious community, togetherness, and so on, arises. What then arises is consequently secondary, and the individual belief is primary; other human beings enter the picture secondarily. (One possibility, when thinking along these lines, is that the content of something I take to be true is that I should worship together with others, as the content of a commandment from God.) This picture of religious belief is seldom expressed so explicitly, but it is still a picture presupposed in many standard discussions.

What one fails to notice, when holding onto this picture, is this: to the calculating one – the one who relates to everything as something to take into account when considering how to get as large a gain as possible – solipsism becomes a real problem. It does not help to refer to physical experiences of resistance,[1] these still being part of the same perspective: the physical experience of resistance is only another element to take into account. Those entities here postulated – words fitting in this context – are postulated with the starting point in the solipsist perspective. To "believe" in God is here to believe that the existence of God must be taken into account, and the relation is characterized by such things as fear, punishment and reward.[2] The opposite of the calculating one is the loving one. The lines of direction have here not me – my wishes, desires and interests – as their starting point, as is the case when calculating; rather, when I love someone, the lines of direction start in her. The grammatical terms may here mislead, since they may seem to intimate that "love" is something some subject does, with something else as an object. It would be better to say that love is something "between" them, and this also goes for a case of unhappy love. In any case, what is important here is that the following picture would be highly misleading: the existence of the loved one as given as an intentional object, as always already there in the act of love.[3] The belief in God – when understood as love – can consequently not be understood as mediated by an ideology – then it is the ideology one relates to primarily and not God – nor as an action one of them – the believer or God – perform in isolation from the other one, which means that belief is not the reciprocity of such actions either. Religious belief, when understood in terms of love, is an *encounter*, and an encounter cannot be analyzed in such terms. But does this mean that the belief is individual in another sense? The relation to God is not individual, since it involves *both* God and the believer, but is it not individual in the sense that it does not involve anyone else, that it is independent of the believer's relation to other human beings? This would be an erroneous conclusion; having a non-calculating relation to God means, in a crucial sense, relating non-calculatively generally. Loving God is not independent of my relations to everything else.

In the first section, I try to show that belief had in togetherness cannot be analyzed as consisting of many individual beliefs which are "added together". In the next section (II), I contrast that togetherness to what I call "community". In its first subsection (II.a), I discuss one aspect of community: ritual. In the next one (II.b), I discuss communities, as such and in relation to togetherness. In the third section, I show what consequences what I have said in this chapter have as to one discussion about reductionism, before coming to a conclusion (section IV).

I. *Togetherness*

The point is not that it is impossible to be a believer on one's own. It is not hard to imagine a lonely person who is a believer, or a person who is religiously isolated. (But it is important to notice that the loneliness and the isolation – if the believer is a believer in the sense in which I understand religious belief in this book – do not come from her but are a result of other people's reaction to her, which means that the loneliness and the isolation are, in a sense, apparent: she is still directed toward togetherness.) Instead, what I will try to show in what follows is that belief, when it is belief together with others, cannot be analyzed as consisting of many individual beliefs which are "added together". As to belief together with others, it is not the case that the individual belief is primary; isolating the individuals from each other would result in something qualitatively different. This does not mean that I am an adherent of some kind of collectivism; this should already be, and will become, clear. On the contrary, making belief together with others clear makes it possible to distinguish sharply between this and collective forms of religion, what I will call (religious) communities: what I will try to do here will, hopefully, make the *distinction* between togetherness and community obvious. I will describe two possibilities – which does not necessarily mean that these are the only possibilities, that mixed forms does not exist, or that it is always easy to characterize an empirically given case – in order to make their *differences* evident.

The very question about whether there is belief which cannot be analyzed as an addition of several individual beliefs hangs on the possibility of finding examples. My examples are the following. If a factory is about to close down, it is an important difference between the case where the workers – those of them that pray – pray about their problems – possible unemployment, say – each on their own, and the case where they pray together; that they pray each on their own means that there is a set of individual problems that happen to coincide, whereas that they pray together means that the problem they pray about is a problem they have together. If two parents thank God for their newborn child, there is a similar difference between the case where they do this each on their own and the case where they do this together. In brief, there is an important difference between the case where the persons in question do a "religious action" – prayer, say – in relation to problems and subjects for rejoicing each on their own, and the case where they do it together.

The nature of the difference may easily be misunderstood, however. The difference is not that the prayer – this being our example – brings about their togetherness, as if it were a means to this end. On the contrary, if I tell someone about some subject for rejoicing *for some reason* – sharing it with her in order to bring about something else – that would not be an example of what I try to direct your attention to here. In such a case, I may tell you about this subject for rejoicing in order for you to admire me: I tell everyone about something I have succeeded in, not because I am glad that I have, but because I want to get others to look up to me, this being the aim of what I say. The doubleness in such a situation is evident, but complex. On the one hand, I distance myself from my own joy at what has happened, by making use of it for other purposes; on the other hand, the admiration I possibly succeed in arousing is not one we can be together in, due to the asymmetrical character of the situation. But when I am simply glad and say this, or express this generally, to everyone I meet, there is no *reason* for doing so: the expression is simply an aspect of me being glad. If others rejoice with me, this is then not a case of individual subjects for rejoicing which happen to coincide, but a joy we have together. This means that prayer, when it is really a prayer in togetherness, is not directed toward the group – then it would simply be a means to an end – but is the way in which they are directed together toward God. Prayer in togetherness is not a means to group formation – if some persons pray in order to unite themselves, that would be something different from what I am talking about here – nor does it consist of individual prayers which happen to coincide. Rather, one could say that in praying together, the problem is no longer the same, but this does not mean that the prayer is a means employed to change the character of the problem. In other words, that some group prays does not mean that they pray together, in the sense in which I have used the word here; there are other possibilities, as we have seen. The point is that there is an important difference between the case where two persons have, each on their own, problems and subjects for rejoicing that happen to coincide, and the case where they are together in the problems and the subjects for rejoicing, and praying together is not the means of bringing about the latter – on the contrary, seeing it as a means pulls them apart, expresses how far they are from being together – but is simply what they are here together in.

What may make it difficult to see this, is the common idea that the religious belief is, in a sense, empty: the religious belief is at bottom a "pure" belief in God – this is the starting point – which, once established, may have consequences, that one submits one's problems and subjects for rejoicing to God, say. But is this the case? Is it not in doing such things that it shows itself what belief means? What would belief be without such things? (The vagueness of "such things" is important – the belief is not exhausted by an enumeration – since what it means for a relation to be alive is that neither it nor its future are formally determined.) What would it mean to encounter religious belief if it did not relate to anything outside of itself? The idea of the empty belief is merely another expression of the idea of belief as calculation: when the belief in God's existence is there, this belief could later on have any role whatsoever, depending on what my interests and desires are.

"Sure, you may be right in saying that religious belief is not 'empty', but is it not possible to analyze its content in terms of the individual? Even though your two examples above work to some extent, they presuppose that the workers, praying about their problems, and the parents, expressing their joy at their newborn child, first believe each one on their own – that is what is primary – and this fact makes it then possible for them to pray together; is that not so? What then arises is something none of them could have created on an individual basis – you are right in that – but that this is so does not change the fact that individual belief is primary." The risk is that such an objection makes one forget what here "arises". But what is more important to notice is this: this objection seems to have forgotten what I said in the beginning of this chapter. The understanding of religious belief I am trying to get clear about is belief as essentially non-calculating. Saying that a calculating belief is individual is unproblematic. Furthermore, the belief I am discussing here is not mediated by an ideology. An ideology may be shared – many could agree in their ideological ideas – but is not a matter of what I have called togetherness. Even though belief in the sense in which I discuss it here – as non-calculative – may be held in loneliness and isolation, it involves the believer's relation to every person she meets, as I have said. Furthermore, the question I am working on right now is rather that *if* the belief is had in togetherness, the idea of a distance – of something as primary and of something as secondary – is misleading. I will try to explain this in more detail.

The question is not, why should I relate to others, what do I gain by doing so? Such a question is asked from the perspective of "each one on her own" which means that we do not reach the belief had in togetherness by finding an answer to it. Nor is it the case that we have, on the one hand, problems and subjects for rejoicing together and, on the other hand, individual belief, a belief that not until this togetherness comes to exist acquires this new character: that would mean that the belief and the problems (the subjects for rejoicing) were originally unrelated, that is, not as intimately related as they are in this situation. Rather, this belief, had in togetherness, and these problems and subjects for rejoicing, had in togetherness, determine each other mutually as being had together. (The following example could illustrate this. Someone goes on a journey together with someone else not because each one of them does a calculation – "I guess I will have more fun if I take X with me" – but because they are already together and it is going on a journey *they* want to do. And if the issue concerned each one of them individually, or one of them together with a third person, what she wanted to do could be something completely different, but "when it comes to *us*, this is what I want".)

All this means that one cannot decide on having a belief in togetherness. One cannot decide on having some problems and subjects for rejoicing – and these are not exhaustive, there are other examples, to be sure – in togetherness.[1] The transition from "each one on her own" to "together" is not continuous: if I were really completely stuck in the first perspective, the transition would be unintelligible since it could not be adequately expressed in terms of such a perspective. The difficulty may then be, for some, that this makes the transition obscure. The idea is that there are only two kinds of human relations: either the relation is one I have brought about (chosen, decided on, and so forth), or it has been forced upon me against my will (and has then been brought about by someone or something else). But it is distinctive of togetherness that it is not "brought about". This does not exclude the possibility that it has its background in a group compounded by someone, but in so far as togetherness exists here, *this* is not brought about by this person. (Compare this to love, which has all these features too. But "too" is misleading since the starting point for my discussion is religious belief understood as non-calculative.) The togetherness has simply arisen. In any other case – if there are no problems or subjects for rejoicing (or something else) we encounter each other in, if the problems and subjects for rejoicing emphasized are not real and genuine – belief is something different: it becomes, for example, something had in common. A religious community is born; in what follows, I will contrast togetherness to this. And it becomes even worse if one tries to bring about some emotions by means of rituals, if one tries to bring about them being had in common; these can then only be closed, directed at the emotions themselves (sentimentality) or aimed at the group itself (sociality), in contrast to emotions directed outwards (to God, say).

II. *Community*

One reason for discussing belief had together is that this makes it possible to distinguish togetherness from collective forms of religion. These are not the same. The differences are important to see, and when emphasizing individual belief, the rest easily becomes lumped together and seen as one phenomenon. In this section I will, consequently, contrast togetherness with what I call "community". First, I will discuss one aspect of community – ritual – before entering into the issue of community proper.

a. *Ritual*

As is evident from what I have said thus far, problems – or subjects for rejoicing, or something else – had in togetherness are central. Praying in togetherness is something those who believe together can be together in. This prayer – and there are other things to be together in too – can take many forms, artistic and bodily, say. (Or rather, it is always bodily when it is genuine, since it is then meant, that is, felt; problems and subjects for rejoicing as something purely "intellectual" are not *problems* and subjects for *rejoicing*.) In any case, no part of oneself is shut out; one comes to God, and to the others, with one's happiness, sorrow, and so forth.[5] Rituals – as I use the term here – are different, however: they are a matter of aesthetics, are a way of trying to bring about – in contrast to "express" – some emotions.[6] The ritual is, generally speaking, like a *Gesamtkunstwerk* affecting all senses by means of strong *Stimmungen*. (It should be noted that banning figural art is also a matter of aesthetics; even though doing so does not necessarily aim at bringing about some emotions, the point is nevertheless to counteract or obstruct some emotions. Thus it is part of the same perspective.) The question here is not how common togetherness and aesthetics are in religion – the answer to such a question one could speculate about and have diverse opinions about – but what these different possibilities mean, irrespective of whether some of them are, de facto, existent or non-existent.

The ritual – as I use the term here – is, as I said, a way of bringing about emotions, bringing about them being had in common. In order for the community to be more than an agreement in ideological ideas, something additional is needed, and the emotions become the means of keeping up the unity, and the means for bring about them is the ritual.

If it is the case that the ritual is such a means – one of many – has this some connection to the regularity of the ritual? (This regularity could be said to be part of the definition of "ritual", but there need not be some definite lower limit to this regularity. There may be a large space within the limits of this regularity – and how large this space is depends on for what purposes the regularity is described – but as long as there is some kind of "style" one has to hold on to, we have a ritual; the regularity is unproblematic only when it is accidental, when the problems and subjects for rejoicing have been expressed in a way which simply happens to be (more or less) regular.)[7] One answer to the question above could be that the regularity of the ritual depends on something unrelated to this and that the community makes use of the regularity since the regularity already has some kind of strength. Another answer could be that what we have here is simply a psychological coincidence: what is regular happens to be efficient. But what does this strength mean and why is it fitting in this context? And how should the effects of this psychological coincidence be described?

That the ritual has to be carried out in a *particular* way, shows that it is not a direct expression of the problems and the subjects for rejoicing: something, not related to the problems and the subjects for rejoicing, enters and determines the form of the ritual. Consequently, the difference between the ritual and the expression is that the problems and the subjects for rejoicing have their own importance in the latter case and do not have to take it from some other sphere. One possible reason for the need of regularity is then that doing something in a precise and regulated manner gives one the impression that what one is doing is important. Furthermore, focusing oneself on the rule means that other ideas and emotions are held at a distance; possible differences within the community are then out of focus.

Above all, within the community a strong *feeling* of community is created. Despite, or rather due to, the fact that we are still within an individual perspective – the community being the agreement of individual ideological ideas[8] – there is a much stronger feeling for the group here. The community, since it is an agreement in ideas, has a limit: those outside of this limit, those who do not share these ideas, are not part of the community. (The togetherness is different: here the term "limit" is not applicable, since the togetherness means being open for an immediate relation to anyone (and to God). I will come to this issue later on.) In that sense, the community need not be oppressive at all – what I have said has perhaps given that impression – but may, in a sense, be much more pleasant than the togetherness.[9]

A common idea is that religious belief is always a matter of rules. What I have said is meant to show that this is not so. In the divine services, and the like, of the togetherness, there are no rules. (Perhaps it is true de facto that religious belief is always a matter of rules, but it is *essentially* false: if the rituals did not address the problems and the subjects for rejoicing *at all*, they would not be efficient, which means that the ritual is dependent on the togetherness.) The point of describing the community is then not only to obtain a clearer understanding of this possibility, but also to have our eyes opened to the possibility of its contrast, togetherness.

b. *Communities, and their relation to togetherness*

In the former section I described one aspect of the community: the ritual. However, the community does not necessarily make use of rituals. The ritual is a means for the community, but it need not make use of this means. Here I will enter into a discussion of other, and more central, aspects of the community.

The fundamental difference between the community and the togetherness is that whereas the latter is not held together by anything – the persons are simply together – the unity of the former is kept up by something: that is, the relations between the persons in the community are mediated by this something. The limits of the community are a (possibly implicit) *judgment.* This is most obvious when this something is an explicit ideology: being a member of the community means having adopted this ideology. In what follows, I will work with this example – the ideology – but it is only an example. In many cases, the something which keeps up the unity of the community is not an ideology in the usual sense of the word. A racist organization may deny someone membership on "racial" grounds, even though this person has adopted its ideology. The point is simply that the community, insofar as it is a community, establishes a difference between those who are part of the community and those who are not. (It is possible that a community de facto includes everyone, but this is then a coincidence, since its being a community means that some conceivable person is excluded.) Of course, there may be a grey area – is this particular person a member of the community or not? – as long as those areas which this grey area is in between are distinct. The something which keeps up the unity of the community need not be explicit either: nobody is able to explain in detail why some person is a member of the community and some other person is not, even though it is obvious to everyone where the line should be drawn. Furthermore, a group could have an unclear and changing status: sometimes, and in certain respects, it is a togetherness – and then not really a group – but otherwise a community.

But, as I said, ideology will be my main example of this something keeping up the unity of the community. This ideological feature is dialectically related to another feature of the community: its focus on number. The community wants to grow, but without losing (what it calls) its soul. To the extent it says that it does not want to grow, it has determined who its members are in a new way. The dialectics consists in a shifting emphasis, now on the ideology, now on number: it might seem to be a contradiction between them, but they presuppose each other.

That number presupposes ideology is evident: it is only possible to count how many members a group has if it is meaningful to fix a boundary for it. On the other hand, the ideology presupposes number in a more intricate sense. There are many opinions I have, but this does not necessarily mean that I feel that I am a member of some community consisting of those agreeing with me on this or that issue. Such a feeling of community arises when the opinion is taken to be important, as in some way threatened and contested, as characterizing those who have it, and so forth. A lot more could be said about this, but we see that the opinion – which is here not anymore an opinion, strictly speaking, but an ideology or part of an ideology – is now important, in the sense of being something to work for and in terms of identity. In that respect, we could say that without a focus on number, no ideology. A community which does not think in terms of number at all has no longer an ideology and is then no community. To be sure, it is not impossible to imagine a community which does not believe growth to be possible, but this belief only underlines the importance of quantity for the community. (The *feeling* of community I talked about above may be stronger in a small group; in that sense the isolation of the group could be wanted and seen as a problem at the same time.)

However, that there is a tension between ideology and number is clear. This comes to expression, for instance, in a common lack of clarity concerning what believing in the ideology really means. The focus on number could involve using social pressure: this is one way of bringing about growth, or of preventing reduction. This social pressure need not be painful, but could be a matter of making the community attractive, something one desires to be a member of, for instance since there are already many other people there. This pressure is a means one makes use of. In doing so, however, a risk is involved: the means could get the upper hand, and ideological focusing is needed to come to terms with this, which, in its turn, risks confining the community to itself.

The focus on number could also involve a demand for ideological renewal. To the community, it is important that this renewal is understood as continuous with what has preceded it, of course. However, notice that what is continuous and what is not is an open question; what is important is not that the community really makes explicit what this continuity consists of, only that it believes that this could be done. Here it becomes evident that the ideology does not always have the role it might seem to have, when the community is looked at superficially, or the role the ideology is said to have by the community itself. In fact, it could be the community itself one believes in. Vice versa, the focus on ideology can have many forms. Exclusion is not only a matter of excluding someone actively, but also of someone getting the feeling that she does not belong there. That this person "does not belong there" can be made evident to this person in a very subtle way, so subtle that those who make this evident are not themselves clear about doing so. Furthermore, since a group could have an unclear and shifting status – sometimes, and in certain respects, a togetherness, otherwise a community – this feeling of not belonging there need not be clear and evident.

Since the unity of the community is kept up by something, being the member of a community is often chosen. One's ideological opinions need not be chosen; in that sense, ideological agreement is not chosen. However, it is different when joining a community; here a kind of judgment is made. As I said, the ideology could be secondary; what one believes in could be the community itself. What is primary for me could be me wanting to be a member of some community and I look for some community which fits me more or less, and choose to join it on such grounds. The features which for me are the reasons for choosing this community need not be ideological in the strict sense, but could be aesthetical (ritual forms) or a matter of what I think of those who are already members of it, and so forth. If such a choosing and judging attitude exists, this will affect those that do not have it too: such a person may become, or be, one who does not fit in, one who "ought to choose" something different, irrespective of whether this person herself understands the situation in those terms or not.

Consequently, the same apparent paradox arises once again here: the community is collectivistic (the unity of the community, its feeling for itself) *and* individualistic-atomistic (the choice and how the members are included/excluded).[10] The latter way of characterizing it cannot be rejected by saying that whatever happens, I will remain faithful to the group I have chosen, I will try to avoid relating to it on the basis of what fits me. This is not a rejection of such a characterization, for even though faithfulness of that kind is possible, it does not change anything essentially. By being a member of the community, I still make use of the categories inside/outside, belongs/does not belong, fits in/does not fit in. If I really reject this way of thinking, then I do not think of other persons as members, or not members, of a community I am a member of. Togetherness, on the other hand, is different; here there is no "whatever happens", since if I relate to others in the spirit of togetherness, nothing can change this but me.

Having come this far, it is time to make the difference between the community and the togetherness more explicit. The togetherness does not count numbers, since this is not possible and intelligible here: there is no boundary, there is no "unity" to keep up, which means that there are no criteria used to exclude and include.[11] That I relate to someone in the spirit of love does not mean that she fulfills some criteria, making her belong to this group, but is to reject thinking in terms of criteria: it is her I relate to, not a set of properties. Since there are no criteria here, there is no "whatever happens": I could fall from love, and it could be or become unrequited, but there is no question of the relation between a possible change and some criteria. A problem in togetherness is not about what to do when ideological changes occur – deviations, criteria not fulfilled – but about my own possible difficulties of relating to someone in this spirit and her possible difficulties of relating to me in this spirit: a problem between us, which has obvious connections to our difficulties with everyone else.

To say that something is or is not the same religion or denomination as one's own, need not necessarily be a rejection of togetherness. The issue concerns how "same" is understood here. One possibility is that saying so is a matter of recognizing some familiar phrases and some familiar ritual forms, and that the question whether *God* (a God of love) is really worshipped (loved) here or not is not asked at all. The similarity of phrases and ritual forms guarantees essential similarity, dissimilarity guarantees essential dissimilarity. If the belief is essentially these phrases and these ritual forms, this is quite right, but if the belief is love of a God of love, this is not so. This does not mean that love of a God of love is inclusivistic (with respect to religious diversity) – or ecumenical – since such a categorization is still on an organizational and ideological level. In relation to organizations – *all* organizations – love of a God of love is not obviously open, but rather skeptical, only in relation to *persons*. It is with them one wishes to be together in love.

But how are problems and subjects for rejoicing possible without ideology and criteria, someone might ask. To answer this question, it is not necessary to take a stand on every possible example. It suffices to bring out one example of a problem or a subject for rejoicing which is not mediated by an ideology to show that this is possible. An example is the joy at the presence of another human being. If this joy were mediated by an ideology – and saying so need not be saying that this is the result of a decision; the idea could be that this happens spontaneously – then the absence of this joy would be a consequence of me not having adopted this ideology or of me not being able to live up to this ideology. But in that case, the problem would simply concern my relation to this ideology, and not my relation to this human being. My relation to her is not an ideology (but my problems with her could have an ideological background, and my relation to her could give me problems with an ideology). Consequently, anything cannot be a problem or a subject for rejoicing had together; saying that something is had in togetherness is not a formal determination. On the contrary, it should be evident, from what I said in Chapter 4, that what is had in togetherness has always to do with love.[12]

Whereas the community is both collectivistic and individualistic-atomistic, the togetherness is neither. It is not collectivistic, since the togetherness is not mediated by anything, is not something I need to submit to or join. On the contrary, the community is a place of refuge from the personal, as love, or, with a possibly more positive way of characterizing it, something I resort to in order to organize things for want of faith.[13] Nor is it individualistic-atomistic, since what is central here is something *between* you and me.

Here two clarifications are needed. First, it might seem as if I say that the togetherness is better than the community. For the one who loves a God of love, it will be, but not always. For instance, when it comes to politics, to being member of a political party, it would be wrong not to choose political affiliation on ideological grounds, it would be wrong to remain being a member of the party whatever happens. This does not mean that the political party must become a community, but it shows that there is no place for togetherness here. (Or rather, to the extent that there is place for togetherness here, the party is not merely a party.) The togetherness is in this context what determines politics as politics from the very start: that I have a responsibility for, say, the city I live in, however rotten I find its politics to be. That I have such a "place" is not a matter of ideology, about exclusion and inclusion. The philosophical question as to religion is then whether faith is more like a party within the sphere of politics or more like the sphere of politics as such.

The second clarification concerns different transitions, between community and community, between togetherness and togetherness, between community and togetherness. Of course, the transition to a community is made on ideological grounds, in the wide sense of the word: what fits one. This includes different forms of social pressure. Speaking about a transition from one togetherness to another is misleading, since a togetherness is not the kind of separate entity presupposed in the term "transition". But since togetherness exists, to the extent it exists, between me and those I encounter, it is possible to talk about different togethernesses in the sense that I encounter different persons in different contexts and at different times of my life; the transition from one togetherness to another is then not an important question. Where the clarification is needed is with respect to the transition from community to togetherness. It could refer to a transformation of the relation, where the persons are the same as before, but it is not that case I would like to discuss. The case I would like to discuss is when the transition is a transition to a relation to *other* persons, and this transition is not accidental, comparable to the transition from one togetherness to another. It might appear as if I deny the possibility of such a transition. The transition cannot be done on ideological grounds, on the ground of what fits me. And if the transition is not accidental either, what is it then? To give up hope about someone – to say that togetherness with her is impossible – is never a simple statement of fact, but expresses *my own* way of relating to her and thus means that *I*, too, reject togetherness.[14] To reject a community with one person (or several persons) for a togetherness with someone else (or several others) need not be an expression of having given up hope about someone, however. Since togetherness is not the kind of "thing" one can bring about by means of some technique – as the community is, where there are different methods, with their respective degree of efficiency, of attracting a greater number – remaining in community with this person (or these persons) need not at all be facilitating with respect to a future togetherness. This does not mean that the transition to (a possible) togetherness with other persons will necessarily facilitate the togetherness with the previous one (or ones); it is not possible to draw a conclusion in either direction. The point is simply that everything having an organizational aspect is of a provisional character: it is not more than that, but not less either. The latter is also important to bear in mind.

Let me conclude this section by quoting Simone Weil, not as a summary, but as an expression of one of the themes we have been discussing:

> If we could be egoistical it would be very pleasant. It would be a rest. But liter- ally we cannot … Only one thing [on this earth] can be taken as an end, for in relation to the human person it possesses a kind of transcendence: this is the collective. The collective is the object of all idolatry, this it is which chains us to the earth. In the case of avarice: gold is of the social order. In the case of ambition: power is of the social order … And love? Love is more or less of an exception: this is why we can go to God through love, not through avarice or ambition … A society like the Church, which claims to be divine, is per- haps more dangerous on account of the *ersatz* good which it contains than on account of the evil which sullies it.[15]

III. *Reductionism*

In Chapter 7, I will say a few words about reductionism; here this issue enters for the first time. Emile Durkheim writes:

> Society in general, simply by its effect on men's minds, undoubtedly has all that is required to arouse the sensation of the divine. A society is to its members what a god is to its faithful.[16]
>
> If the true function of the cult is to arouse in the faithful a certain state of soul, are of moral strength and confidence, and if the various effects imputed to the rites are only due to secondary and variable causes of this fundamental state, then it is not surprising that the same rite should seem to

> produce multiple effects while keeping the same components and structure. In every case, those mental dispositions that its permanent function is to bring about remain the same; they depend on the fact that the group is assembled, not on the particular reasons why the group is assembled ... the apparent efficiency will seem to change, even though the real efficiency remains unchanging; and the rite will seem to fulfill disparate functions even though in fact it has only one, which is always the same.[17]

As should be evident by now, on the one hand I agree with what Durkheim is saying here, yet on the other hand I do not agree with him at all. What Durkheim has done is having given a description of the religious community. A member of such a community might protest and say that the description is erroneous, but this does not change anything (supposing she is really a member of a community): here we have an example of something she shuts her eyes to. But Durkheim has forgotten another possibility – being together in love of a God of love – and here his description is fundamentally erroneous. One of my purposes in describing the difference between the community and the togetherness was to make the one-sidedness of descriptions of Durkheim's kind obvious: without denying that there is a point to them in some cases, showing another possibility.

That the member of the religious community might protest against such a description shows something important, however. This shows that she is not a wholehearted member of the community. The reductionist knows this: in order for the reduction to have a critical edge, it is necessary that the member does not want to see things in the way the reductionist does. In other words, a doubleness becomes visible here. This is important to bear in mind as soon as the reduction is taken to be a part of a *general* criticism of religious belief, since the generality presupposes that one of the sides in this doubleness is not noticed. Furthermore, such a general criticism is only attentive to what is de facto existing and disregards what is possible; it is, simply put, an expression of lack of imagination.

This doubleness is not noticed by D. Z. Phillips either. He is right in pointing out the difference between what can be understood in terms of social pressure and what cannot, but other things he says are highly misleading: "[T]he common bonds are only intelligible in terms of the common ideas and beliefs people share ... solidarity is not achieved by people sticking together for the sake of solidarity ... but by their common regard for certain values, beliefs, standards, etc."[18] This is misleading, for if there is self-deception here, that means that the ideas, beliefs and values will have a double character: they will be held up to constitute the focus, but they will be held up in order to hide what really is the focus, thereby being a means to a hidden end. The point, however, is that what is here hidden, what they deceive themselves about, is hidden for a reason. This means that although the ideas, beliefs and values are, in a sense, not the focus, they are actually more than a mask: they have a real importance, otherwise the people would not hide behind *them*.[19]

IV. *Conclusion*

In brief, the organizations have not the sole right to what religious belief is and could be. What makes the organizations what they are is a belief logically primary to them, a belief they are, at the most, an expression of; what makes the organization a *religious* organization is that we see it as something we were already able to recognize. This is one of the senses in which togetherness is primary to the community: to the extent that the latter is hidden, does not want to be acknowledged and has features intelligible independently of itself, this depends on the fact that it is already from the start dependent on togetherness. That the organizations have not the sole right to religion is not necessarily a criticism of them, even if their organizational aspect is their character of community. Rather, the question is what loving a God of love in togetherness means, and this is what I have tried to say something about in this chapter.

CHAPTER 7

THE MIRACULOUS

The discussion in the philosophy of religion about miracles – the standard question concerns whether miracles are possible – often starts, explicitly or implicitly, from examples of miracles held to be paradigmatic: the sick are healed, the dead are raised.[1] This can be understood in two ways. Either the question is whether such paradigmatic examples, in case they happen, could, or should, be regarded, within the framework of a given religious belief, as a miracle. "Miracle" is then an intrareligious category, the application of which takes place within a religious life which is already there. As far as I can see, the concept miracle, understood in this way, is not generally problematic.[2] Or the concept miracle is regarded as independent of religious belief, and the question is then whether there could be miracles or not, whether there could be "objective" miracles or not. It is the concept miracle understood in this latter way I will discuss here.

In the background of the standard discussion, there is the idea that a miracle, if one occurred, would lead to religious belief.[3] What is it about miracles that makes them into reasons, if they happen? It is, one thinks, their being inexplicable, that such happenings make it necessary to postulate the existence of God in order for us to be able to account for them.[4] But what one does not pay attention to when arguing in such a way is that the inexplicable, a concept which will be examined in what follows, only becomes a reason against the background of one particular way of considering it, of one particular attitude to it. Even though this attitude, for historical and other reasons, has been common, it is not an attitude one should philosophically presuppose as evidently given. Hence, the focus of my discussion will primarily be that attitude which a particular way of asking the question is already from the start an expression of, not the question whether miracles are possible or not. An important point – the meaning of which it remains to account for – is that belief and miracles are, in one sense, mutually dependent. The way one understands miracles expresses already from the start a specific way of relating oneself to religious belief; and, vice versa, the way one understands miracles is one aspect of the way one relates one-self to religious belief. A specific spiritual orientation hides behind the standard way of seeing miracles in the philosophy of religion. It will not do to say that this is only a way of asking the question about miracles – as if asking a question is innocent and neutral and only the answer possibly wrong, misguided or misleading – since asking in this way is still an emphasis which is far from a matter of course. Thus, the decisive issue is not what understanding of the question we should "choose" nor what the answer is when we have chosen, but to become clear about how one's way of understanding the question shows a specific spiritual orientation already on the philosophical level. This attitude need not be clear for one; it may be a result of the fact that one has taken over the standard way of asking the question without deliberation. But having taken over this way of asking the question, one has at the same time taken over that attitude which this question is an expression of; and simply taking over the standard question because it is the standard one also expresses a specific attitude.

In other words, by the way in which one asks the question one has already settled what answers, or what kind of answers, one will accept. The one who feels the inclination to ask the question "Are miracles possible?" must then at least see the importance of asking a prior question: "What is a miracle, what does the concept miracle mean?" If there is any kind of lack of clarity with regard to the latter question, asking, and even more answering, the former one will not be of philosophical value. The course of my discussion will be another one, however. I will start negatively, trying to become clear about what miracles are taken to be in the standard discussion and what kind of spiritual orientation this expresses. By means of this, another way of understanding the issue will become clearer as we go on.

I begin (section I), by making some comments on the standard discussion, especially on the relation between miracles and science. In section II, before continuing with my discussion, I make some methodological points, by saying a few words about reductionism. In the rest of the chapter (sections III–V), I discuss the concept miracle against the background of one understanding of religious belief, the understanding this book tries to investigate: as love of a God of love. Section III is the main part of that discussion, while section IV relates specifically to the concept power and its relations to the concept miracle and the concept God. In the last section (V), I return to a question already mentioned: is the concept miracle an intrareligious concept or a concept independent of religious belief? Thus, how should the line between what is said to be religious and that which is said not to be religious be drawn?

I. *The standard discussion*

One starting point for many discussions about miracles in the philosophy of religion is that there is some kind of tension between miracles and science. The idea is that science has showed, or one believes that it will show, that there are no miracles; or, in opposition to this, that there is really something scientifically inexplicable, that is, miracles. In other words, "miracle" is here taken to be a quasi-scientific concept, referring to what does not, even cannot, have a scientific explanation.[5] That this is so is evident in the second case, but it goes also for the first one: the reason for the dismissal is that the concept miracle is not scientifically explanatory, and since it is taken to be a (quasi-)explanatory concept, it is dismissed generally. Another example is when miracles are dismissed since the use of the concept is taken to presuppose that something spiritual, God, works by means of material causes, which is held to be impossible.[6] Ontologically understood, it is hard to see the point of identifying the causal and the material, an identification which this line of thought depends on. However, the argument seems to be another one. When one asks for causes, it always makes sense to ask for the cause of this cause, it is held. The cause of a miracle, on the other hand, is God, and here no more questions about causes can be asked. Therefore, explaining something by means of the concept miracle is only a pseudo-explanation, the argument goes.

At present, it is the presupposed understanding of science which needs to be commented upon. A more straightforward discussion of this (implicit) answer to the question "What is a miracle?" – that which does not have a scientific explanation – will have to wait a minute.

The idea here is that "There is nothing inexplicable / Everything is possible to explain" or "There is something inexplicable" are scientific statements which science could establish, corroborate or refute. The mere fact that "everything" in the first one is used in a completely vague way shows that it is not a matter of a scientific statement, but, rather, of an emphasized denial of the second one. But also the second one is strange. In what situation is such a statement established scientifically? In one sense, but in another than the one here intended, the statement is uncontroversial. There are always, at every stage of the scientific development, lots of things which are not possible to explain: the scientific practice is about finding answers to such questions. "There is something inexplicable" – when it does not refer to something temporarily inexplicable but to something definitely inexplicable – would then be possible to state in a situation when one knows that it is pointless to look for an explanation. And the question is what it

                    Love of a God of Love

would mean to know that. Saying that something is definitely inexplicable is not, as the advocates of this idea would like to give the impression of, to give a humble expression of the limitations of human knowledge; on the contrary, from the fact that *I* have not found an explanation, the conclusion drawn is that *no one* will; from the fact that *we* have not found an explanation, the conclusion drawn is that no one *ever* will.[7] (On the one hand, it does not take much for the person who draws such a conclusion to give up – "We have failed to find an explanation, so there is no point in trying" – yet, on the other hand, this person has a strong need for explanations – "Since we have not found an explanation, we must take God as the explanation; it is not alright to leave the issue open and unsettled".)[8] Thus, "There is nothing inexplicable / Everything is possible to explain" are not theoretical statements within science, not statements which the scientist establishes as true or false, but rather statements describing the character of science as *practice.*

Since science, especially asking for a scientific explanation, is a practice, there is a question about the place of it. In order for something to be explainable or inexplicable, there must be a place for asking for an explanation, some reason for doing so, and when there is such a reason, the kind of explanation there is a place for need not be a scientific explanation.[9] If something is a chemical phenomenon, the scientist tries to find a chemical explanation for it, if the phenomenon is of any interest. In other words, it is of the utmost importance to consider, scientifically, what is really a chemical phenomenon: to treat something which is not a chemical phenomenon as a chemical phenomenon only results in the phenomenon becoming distorted, in one explaining something else than what one believes oneself to be explaining. It is in relation to the kind of phenomenon something is, or in relation to the kind of phenomenon something for particular reasons is regarded as being, that it makes sense to ask for explanations, that the question what kinds of explanations it makes sense to ask for could be answered. Hence, the first question is not how to explain something, but what this something is and what it means to relate to it in this or that way.

Consequently, whether there is a tension between belief in miracles and being scientific depends on what type of phenomenon miracles are. If one identifies miracles and that which does not have a scientific explanation, a tension arises, but not because two contradictory theoretical statements are contrasted, but because one makes use of a practice without paying attention to what it means to make use of this very practice. To find something that one cannot, however much one tries to, find an explanation for, something that one cannot dismiss by claiming that it is more probable that

I have seen (heard, remembered) wrong than that it has really happened,[10] is then still not of any help, since science as a practice is still striving for an explanation.[11]

The idea behind this way of understanding what miracles are is, as far as I can judge, that if the concept miracle is not used as some kind of explanation of the inexplicable – if it would relate to something which already has, or to something one believes will get, a scientific explanation – it is redundant and meaningless. Although, or rather precisely because, miracles are here understood as the opposite of the scientifically explainable, redundant here means scientifically redundant, meaningless means scientifically meaningless. If there is a natural explanation for something, this something *cannot* be the work of God, it is held, since the work of God must be something other than that which "merely" happens, namely either a break of the causal chains or that which starts them off.[12] Even if one does not go this far and talk about redundancy and meaninglessness, one might have the idea that there must be something that makes it certain, that it must be something that makes it beyond all doubt, that what has happened is the work of God; and this certainty one gets if it is *necessary*, because of the inexplicability of the occurrence, that God is brought in. This is then what a miracle is supposed to be. The force of the spectacular is that it is able to destroy some kind of doubt or lethargy; it is spectacular only against this background and presupposes that perspective. The point of miracles, it is held, is that they make it necessary to postulate the existence of God – and so to believe, according to this line of thought – on pain of us otherwise not being able to explain them.[13]

Having come this far, it is wise to halt and try to get some perspective on these kinds of discussions. The discussion about miracles, as it is normally pursued in the philosophy of religion, is characteristically compulsive: it is pursued as if it were not even possible to think in other terms than those used in the debate. The standard discussion is not based on a preceding discussion of what miracles are, a discussion which has already been concluded. However, the task is then not only to find an alternative, as if the standard discussion was still the standard. Instead, one should try to understand what it means to ask the question in the way it is usually done. One characteristic feature of the standard way of asking the question is the way in which it emphasizes some contrasts. Miracles are the scientifically inexplicable, in contrast to that which is scientifically explained; miracles are what is in that sense improbable, in contrast to the well-known and the familiar; miracles are in that sense spectacular, in contrast to the everyday; and all this means that miracles could be graded, from the not so miraculous to the very miraculous.[14]

However, one should note that the relation between miracles and the familiar is not a stable one on this account; miracles are here both improbable and probable. What has been said thus far is only one side of the coin. The other one is that an attempt is made to show, philosophically, that miracles are, after all, credible. Miracles are on the one hand spectacular, on the other hand something to take for granted. It is only without the postulation of the existence of God that the miracles are really miraculous. When the existence of God has been postulated, on the other hand, miracles are something to count upon: that is the reason for the postulation.[15]

A relation connected to the relation between miracles and science is the one between religion and technology more generally. There is a story often told about how religion is born out of the dependency of human beings on nature and how religion dies when technology makes us independent of it:[16] whereas we formerly hoped for a miracle to happen, we nowadays visit the physician, it is said. No doubt there is much confusion in this line of thought – the one easiest to recognize is the idea that technology brings about independence; in fact, the difference technology makes is to be found at specific points and is furthermore at most relative[17] – but what I am here going to focus on is something in this line of thought which is really an insight. The point is then not a historical one, but this: if one understands miracles in a technological way – as a way in which some goals of mine are achieved – the difference between miracles and technology is only, as has already been pointed out, one of explanation; since I am not able to explain them scientifically, I cannot employ them technologically. In other words, the question is not whether miracles, so understood, do happen or not, or whether they could happen or not. Instead, the point is that with this understanding of miracles, it is only a coincidence that technology has not taken the place of miracles, if it has not already done so. Consequently, even if miracles would be something to count upon – in particular when – it is important to ask the question about whether miracles are, or could be, something else, whether there is a non-calculative understanding of miracles.[18]

II. *Reductionism*

Before beginning to try to describe such an understanding of miracles, I want to make some methodological remarks. When I talk about different understandings of miracles, from where do I take them? Is what I do a matter of contrasting a philosophical picture of what miracles must be (the one discussed in the section above) with the understanding of miracles which shows itself in the practice of religious believers?

Such an investigation could be of interest, but it is not one of that type which I will pursue here. In fact, what I will say is not dependent on anyone having had the understanding which I will try to describe, least of all is it dependent on whether I embrace that understanding or not. To explain this, let me illustrate by a discussion of reductionism.

A reductionist claim about religion – say, "religion is wish fulfillment"[19] – is not simply wrong. If it did not apply to some cases or in some sense, it would be strange that such an idea ever struck anyone. However, the reductionist wants, precisely as reductionist, to say something more than that this goes for some or many cases: her claim is that this is the only possibility. But that this is the only possibility, if it is, could never be established by means of the gathering of empirical evidence, would not be established even if the theory would de facto accord with every hitherto known case. (And if the reductionist says that every counter-example is an example of something other than religion, one could answer, "Alright, you do not have to call it religion if you do not want to, but do not shut your eyes to the similarities".)

When it is really a matter of reductionism, "religion is wish fulfillment" is said to be a disclosure. Here the point is not to regard something in a certain way for specific purposes, but to say something about the nature of the subject in question, that is, religion. That something is a disclosure means that this nature has previously been hidden and that there is resistance against disclosing it. The resistance has to do with the critical character of reductionism: something is said not to be what people generally claim and want it to be. However, that it is a criticism says something important about the way in which reductionism works. It may be the case that the reduction is de facto correct with regard to every hitherto existing case. But that it is a criticism – and not just a simple statement of a fact – shows that there is here already a direction toward something else; that is, that even in the one to whom the reductionist's analysis applies, there is a rudiment of something else, in so far as this person understands what the reductionist is saying as criticism. That this is so is something which the reductionist systematically shuts her eyes to.[20]

Another example is when Freud says that religion is a matter of consolation,[21] which is supposed to be a disclosure, not a simple statement of a fact. Thus, Freud's way of using this remark has as background the fact that the religious believer does not see her belief in that way; if the religious believer feels stricken by the remark, this means that Freud is, on the one hand, right, since the belief has had this function for this believer, but, on the other hand, wrong, since the believer sees this as a problem, something that calls for a deepening of her relation to faith and God.

The only answer which the reductionist might be able to give is that there is no alternative, that all other alternatives are a priori excluded.[22] In other words, reductionism, when it is consistent, is not an empirical claim, but a philosophical one. However, the reductionist's basis is commonly taken to be of an empirical kind.

However well that understanding which I discussed in section I might accord with what religious believers take themselves to believe, the question is, consequently, whether there is another possibility.[23]

III. *Miracles and love of a God of love*

I have now described some aspects of the attitude of which the standard way of asking the question is already from the start an expression. Thereby, I have at the same time described what I meant when I said that belief and miracles are, in one sense, mutually dependent, that the way one understands miracles already from the start expresses a specific way of relating oneself to religious belief, and that, vice versa, the way one understands miracles is one aspect of the way one relates oneself to religious belief. In other words, the basic point is that we should not primarily try to answer the question asked, but try to understand what asking it means, what attitude the very asking of this question is an expression of. Hence, what I try to do is not bring hidden theoretical presuppositions to the fore, but to understand what that *act* of asking expresses. Since what miracles are is an expression of a spiritual orientation, I will in the remainder of the chapter work with one way of relating oneself to religious belief – the understanding this book tries to investigate: when it is understood as love of a God of love – and try to see what form the question then takes. In a way, this means that I will understand the concept miracle as an intrareligious concept. However, what is important right now is not whether the place of it is inside or outside of religion, but the way in which this understanding of the concept miracle *contrasts* with the one in section I; in that respect, they are not on completely different planes. In the final section, I will return to the question about how the line between what is said to be religious and that which is said not to be religious is drawn. Moreover, this understanding of religious belief – that it is love of a God of love – is not a hypothesis, an assumption, or the like. Instead, our question is: *if* one understands religious belief in this way, what does this mean with regard to miracles? But starting out from this understanding is not arbitrary: as I said and as we will see, this understanding creates a good contrast to the standard discussion. (That it is a contrast does not mean that these two possibilities are exhaustive. But, of course, what I will say in what follows is relevant also for those who would like to find some third or fourth possibility.)

However, saying what I have just said may make it sound as if the two understandings of miracles are on a par. But our previous discussion points in another direction. The tension between miracles and science takes place within the framework of a specific attitude, an attitude which could be described as a-scientific (the "reasons" or motives for it are philosophical, existential, not scientific) or unscientific (when the one whose attitude this is claims that it is of a scientific kind, thereby misusing science). When this attitude is one of a religious believer, it may nevertheless be combined with rhetorical outbursts against scientism, but that does not change anything: de facto everything is seen from an explanatory perspective which is simply taken for granted as self-evident. The criticism of the concept miracle as an intrareligious category, a criticism which I touched upon at the outset, should be understood against this background. The idea is that the concept miracle could not mean anything other than an "objective" attempt at explaining something; the concept miracle as something intrareligious is then no more than an illegitimate attempt at explanation. However, as an intrareligious concept, the question is not what the *explanation* of some happening is, but what its religious *meaning* is. To the religious believer who shares the above attitude – which means that she affirms the possibility of the kind of explanation which the non-believer denies – the predilection for explanation in contrast to meaning may have its ground in fear of immanence: the explanation takes us outside of the world, whereas meaning is by necessity stuck in the world, one believes.[24]

However, to believe that the difference is simply a difference between different persons would be a simplification, as if each one of us exclusively emphasizes the one or the other. No, for my part, and I do not believe that this is just a personal idiosyncrasy, I can see a doubleness – a doubleness not necessarily dependent on an explicit religious confession – between wonder *about* something on the one hand, and wonder *at* something on the other hand (using, as a verb, a word kindred to "miracle"). What follows, when we start out from religious belief as love of a God of love, is one way of making this doubleness clear.[25]

When it comes to love of a God of love, the contrast to the explanation perspective widens, in two respects. First, using the concept miracle as the way to account for that which is scientifically inexplicable, means that no fundamental difference between good and evil is made: if something is scientifically inexplicable, it does not matter what further characteristics it has.[26] Second, the need which I have mentioned above – to make certain that what has happened is the work of God, which can only be done if it is necessary, because of the inexplicability of the occurrence, that God is brought in – arises only against the background of a doubt: we cannot be sure that this miraculously good thing is really the work of God. But for the one who loves a God of love the relation to God is not a hypothetical one – since the relation is one of love – which means that there is no further step to take beyond the immediate wonder at the good.

Also in this context, one could say that miracles are improbable. But this should not be understood as a contrast to something else: the familiar, the well-known. What is miraculous is not some particular thing as opposed to others. Rather, seeing that something is miraculous has its home in a new way of seeing everything. Another way of expressing the point is that in the case of explanations, what the character of the occurrence is, is clear; the question regards how one should account for its possibility, what must be postulated in order for it to go together with what we already know. But, in contrast to this, seeing the miraculousness of something could be to see it in a new light, to really see it for the first time although it might be something extremely familiar. Here what I come to see is not something additional to this; this thing does not get its importance from its making it possible for me to draw some conclusion. But what I come to see is nevertheless new to me; what I see is the relation between this thing and God, a relation inherent in this thing.[27]

Whereas the direction in the former case goes from the improbable to the familiar – upon seeing something spectacular, one tries to account for it by saying that it is a miracle, thereby seeing to it that it goes together with what we already know – the direction in the latter case goes from the familiar to the improbable. In that sense, both of them are orientations with regard to the world in its generality; to emphasize the spectacular in contrast to the familiar, as the former one does, is an attitude to both of them. When it comes to the latter one, however, miracles are not contrasted with something non-miraculous: in the end, nothing is to be counted upon (as probable), everything is seen as a miracle (as dependent on God).[28]

However, what I have just said is not right as it stands. What has been forgotten is that the understanding of religious belief we are working with is as love of a God of love. Love is then not *improbable*. Having such an attitude would rather indicate a lack of faith. Loving a God of love means seeing love as fantastic, as something to rejoice at, without seeing it as strange or bewildering. Furthermore, not counting upon anything, not taking anything for granted, is typical for the hard-boiled person, the one who, in order not to be disappointed, has "freed" herself of every expectation. But there is an important difference between, on the one hand, trying to foresee what is going to happen (and such an attempt may take religious forms) in order to be able to use the opportunities that arise, in order to take appropriate precautions, and so forth, and, on the other hand, the hopes and expectations which the loving person's defenselessness expresses. In the latter case, the expectation is not a hypothesis. Expressed differently, for the religious believer the concept miracle is intimately related to joy; it is this that creates room for talking about miracles. For the believer it is not the case that there is first a question about whether something is the work of God or not, on which a question about joy accidentally follows. No, it is the question of joy which makes it possible to talk about something as the work of God or not; within belief, there is no room for an indifferent attitude to it. That something is a work of God means for the believer that it is something to rejoice at. Instead of "joy" one could say "gratitude": to some, the latter word is held to be more obviously religious. The problem with "gratitude" is that it may be a matter of distancing oneself: instead of one's immediate relation to that which one is grateful for, questions about how to express this gratitude arises, but that is not the case with joy. (However, when it comes to third-person accounts – saying "she rejoices at x" or "she is grateful for x" – there are, in this context, no relevant differences.)

An example of the intimate relation between joy and the concept miracle is when the birth of a child is said to be a miracle. Two things need to be pointed out here, however. First, saying that the birth of a child is a miracle should not be understood as a contrast, as if the existence of the child would be the less a source of joy the older it grows, as if the miracle would be the "innocence of childhood". Second, saying that the birth of a child is a miracle should not be understood as a matter of shutting one's eyes to the problems this birth may give rise to, that the child may be an additional mouth to feed. On the contrary, that this is a real problem in such a case, and not just something to shrug one's shoulders at and not care a bit about, underlines one aspect of what the one who says that this is a miracle means by saying so.

As I said, that something is a work of God means for the believer that it is something to rejoice at. This puts limits on what could be a work of God: only that which it is possible to rejoice at is a work of God. The emphasis on the possible is here important. It is one thing to see that something is of God, another to actually rejoice at it. When something thwarts my egoistic plans, I hardly feel joy at it, even though I see, reluctantly, that this something is good – and seeing this includes coming to see that my plans were egoistic – which means that a *question* about joy is addressed to me.[29] The question about the works of God will for the believer be a question about considering what it is really possible to rejoice at, and, conversely, what it is, in a sense, necessary to rejoice at, although I may not actually rejoice at it; and that I do not immediately rejoice at what it is necessary to rejoice at is one thing to consider. (That does not mean that joy is chosen, thought out, or the result of a decision or of exertion. I may become broken and lose my faith, through what I in Chapter 9 will call "negative miracles", and then there is no joy there for me. In such a situation, what is needed is not exertion. However, what we are considering here is not the limits of a perspective, but its meaning.) What one rejoices at, and what one sees as a miracle, is expressive of who one is. To rejoice at what is evil, is evil. The one who takes the spectacular to be the prime example of the miraculous, is existentially focused on the spectacular. For the one who loves a God of love, everything is not miraculous: what is miraculous is first and foremost love. For her, nothing hangs on whether or not something spectacular – like the breaking of a causal chain – happened on the way; she need not affirm *or* deny a claim about something spectacular having happened. As Simone Weil says: "Hitler could die and rise again fifty times, but I would still not regard him as the Son of God."[30]

IV. *Power and miracles*

The emphasis on the spectacular is connected to a specific emphasis on, and understanding of, power. The more spectacular, the more powerful God; the power simply shows itself in the inexplicable. (There is a difficulty here which I will not discuss: it is not clear what it means to say that it is difficult, requires power, to do the inexplicable. If I in some way can relate to the means used, there is a point in saying that something is more or less difficult to do, but here every such relation is excluded.) Thus, the ground for talking about the power of God is here the fact that there is no explanation. The idea is that this way of talking about the works of God, in contrast to every other way, does not result in a limitation of the power of God: the spectacular is seen as no more than an extension of the familiar, in the sense that if one has said that it is God who has made the spectacular, one has ascribed a power to God which includes the ability to make that which is easier, namely the familiar.

The contrast to this idea is, as has already been said, the work of God understood only as a matter of goodness. The one who emphasizes the spectacular therefore probably asks: does this not mean that the power of God is limited? There are two simple ways of rejecting that question. First, to the one who loves a God of love, the question makes no difference: to her, the question about power is not at all central, so she does not care about having or not having limited the power of God. Second, the question can be rejected by pointing out that if love of a God of love is putting a limit to the power of God, not limiting it would be rejecting love of a God of love. (This does not mean that God is judged by means of some sort of principle; such an idea presupposes that love is a principle and not a person, which is the opposite of what love of a God of love means.)[31] The one who emphasizes the importance of not limiting the power, simply has a spiritual orientation of her own. Hence, one cannot object to the one who loves a God of love by claiming that she makes power (or miracles) into something which is not worthy of as much reverence, that God (or miracles) are "smaller" to her than they are to the one who emphasizes the spectacular, that religious belief to her is not as serious, that her God is not as worthy of worship. For saying this is to give expression to precisely that attitude which the one who loves a God of love turns her back on; the objection is based on one particular way of relating to power and miracles. To hang on firmly to that attitude and try to force others to decide on it on its own terms, is not to ask a philosophical question in a neutral manner.[32]

However, both of these rejections – which are important, of course – risk accepting a simplified understanding of the concept power. It is not the case that we have religious belief in isolation, here understood as love of a God of love, and that this later on is related to other things, as if religious belief and these other things were originally unrelated. No, *what* these other things are – how they should be understood – is intimately related to how religious belief is understood. That this is so we have already seen when it comes to the concept miracle. Thus, it is not the case that what power is, is clear, and that the question is only about relating to it in some way or other.

Consequently, what one should avoid philosophically is a routine affirmation or denial of omnipotence. There are questions that precede every such emphasis or denial, namely: "What does 'omnipotence' mean?" and, above all, "What could 'omnipotence' mean?" Without an answer to these questions there is nothing to emphasize or deny. In other words, the question is not about "omni-" but about "-potence". (That God is omnipotent with regard to that kind of power it is relevant to say that God has, could be said to be a grammatical point.) Our discussion of these questions is here brought about by the discussion about miracles, more generally speaking by the discussion about the work of God, and in addition by the understanding of religious belief as love of a God of love. It is in relation to this context we ask the question.

That asking whether something is in someone's power, whether she has the power to do this something, is a question which depends on a relevant contrast – and hence that "power" is not something one simply has without further specifications – could be seen already in cases in which God is not involved. If I claim, say, that running 100 meters will take me no more than 12 seconds – that I have the power to run that fast – and I fail when proving it, does this show that I do not have this power? Not necessarily. Someone might say that it is in my power, what I must do is only to train harder; what "having" means is hence not absolutely determined. Say that I train harder, but do not succeed. Does this show that it was never within my power? The question is indefinite, and could be answered in both ways; someone might say that it was within my power, that I would have succeeded if I had only had a tiny bit of luck. Furthermore, and focusing on a question nearer to the philosophy of religion, if one person says that she would never be able to kill another human being however much money someone would pay her for it, another person could say that he is not that sure, that he is afraid that he might become corrupted in such a situation. Here we see that not being able to do something may be a matter of strength, being able to do something a matter of weakness. (Imagine a Mafia boss who precisely because he is able to do to other human beings as he pleases feels himself imprisoned in a life he has come to see is a lie, whose power is impotence.)[33] The primary question is about whether one has the power to do something, when that action is, in a specific sense, described in its entirety: whether one could kill someone or not. Hence, to say about someone that she is in fact able to kill – because she has the requisite physical strength – and claim that her insistence that she could never do it is no more than a philosophically or scientifically misleading phrase, is confused. Secondarily, one could, for specific, in some context relevant, purposes, abstract from certain features of the action – not describe it in its entirety – in order to become clear about why someone says that she could not kill someone else: one could contrast the one who is a good shot with the one who is not. But concentrating on these secondary questions should not make one believe that one could account for the "could not" by referring to, say, a psychological inability (as if the "could not" did not concern the person as such) or a choice on her part (as if killing or not killing were an open question for her). Thus, for the person who loves a God of love it is not possible to account for God's not being able to kill for money – comparing God to the first person in our above example – by referring to a choice on God's part: that would trivialize the question. Instead, what one could say is that God's inability to kill for money – or doing evil generally – is as fundamental as can be, or that there is no application for "killing for money" – or "doing evil" – here at all: it would be like asking whether a stone has the power to think.

Consequently, the question about the omnipotence of God cannot be correctly understood until it is made clear what is meant by freedom generally – an abstract conception of freedom of choice on the one hand is contrasted with the freedom in love and the impotence of evil on the other hand – a question which is far from well understood. This question about freedom will not here receive a discussion to the extent which it deserves, and I hope to be able to return to it in another context. Right now, it suffices to clarify something we have already caught a glimpse of, a way it is *possible* to understand the omnipotence of love, and thus the omnipotence of a God of love. The power of love is that love does not set limits on who should be loved, whereas the hateful person will *always* see herself as surrounded by opponents and is consequently in that sense impotent.[34] This could also be seen if one tries to understand what cultivating the image of God as pure power would mean. If one removes every limitation, what one will get, what will remain – and this is supposed to be God – is a pure will, which is not limited by anything, someone might argue. But if one thinks this over, one will see that not even this will remain. God as pure will is unmoveable, callous. Furthermore, such a God would be incapable of making any decisions – it would be unclear what willing here would be – since everything is supposed to be subjected to God as a question of God's decision, and one thing would then be as good as another for God.[35] Thus, what remains is not a will, but the pure arbitrariness or, rather, the mere chance.[36] Further away from a personal God it is hardly possible to get; what remains is, at the most, a philosophical pantheism. The power of love is, on the other hand, one that is not in contrast to dependency – love is not voluntary (nor involuntary) or optional, the sense in which love has to do with power and freedom is not one of will or choice – and the one who loves is fundamentally dependent on the loved one.

We have here approached the question about the power of God by focusing on the concept God; another way is to focus on the concept of belief. What we then come to see is that *love* of a God of love means a belief in the omnipotence, and omnipresence, of love. No limits to the reach of God are set: if there is love, God is there – this is what it means to talk about the work of God – so there is no preceding question about the reach of God which must be answered before one is able to tell whether God is in *this* love or not. In other words, joy is joy at *everything* good.

V. *Is "the miraculous" a religious concept?*

If it is the case, as I have tried to show, that that line of thought which tries to make miracles into an argument for the existence of God – the existence of God must be postulated for us to be able to account for the inexplicable – already from the start expresses a specific attitude, this means that miracles are only an argument against the background of that attitude, and only against the background of that attitude is the question about whether the argument is good or bad applicable. But also the other understanding, the one I have tried to describe in the last two sections, can, but does not have to, be seen as such an intermediation. In that case, it is an intermediation in a very different sense: the point is simply that this understanding of miracles has its home both within and outside an explicitly religious belief. That I have approached it by starting out from religious belief as love of a God of love does not mean that this belief must play a role for anyone who speaks about miracles in the same spirit. This does not mean that the concept miracle remains even when the framework which made it an intelligible one has been abandoned.[37] No, in *one* sense the concept miracle is primary to religion: it is not the case that not until one has come to embrace a religious belief is one able to see what is meant by "the work of God". Rather, already in saying that something is miraculous – insofar as this saying relates to joy at the good – there could be something which makes it possible for one to understand what is meant by "the work of God". If someone who says that she is not a believer sees something as miraculous, does this then show that she is after all a believer? There is a tendency to answer definitely in the negative to such a question, by referring to the fact that she does not use the word God or simply feels that such a label is uncomfortable. But that is a bad point, since if the weight is put on the word God or on a way of labeling oneself, it would be unclear what religious belief would be in such cases in which they are really found. And, furthermore, the possibility that someone is a believer even though she says she is not should not be excluded by means of definition. Conversely, those who call themselves religious believers cannot claim their ownership of the concept; if it means something to them, it can mean something to others too. Therefore, to answer definitely in the affirmative would not make anything clearer either. Rather, what I would like to say is that it is pointless, philosophically, to try to draw a definite line – and in that way making "religion" into a heavy term – instead of simply trying to understand what it means, existentially, to say that something is a miracle. Hopefully, what I have done here is a contribution to that endeavor.

CHAPTER 8

NATURE

In Chapter 4, I said that it is not at all strange to say that the inorganic nature has a soul, for example, that a mountain has a soul. And in the last chapter, I wrote about the concept miracle, which, to some degree at least, is connected to nature. In view of this, one might get the impression that I connect love of a God of love to nature, in some sense or other, even though this is obviously not the only thing it is connected to. Saying so is not at all misguided, but it invites too many misunderstandings to be left without comment, hence the subject of this chapter.

I will discuss three ways of relating religious belief to nature: nature as reflecting God's will and being (section I), human beings' sense of dependence on nature as the basis of religious belief (section II), and religious belief as providing a foundation for caring about nature (section III).

I. *Nature as reflecting God's will and being*

A common religious idea is that nature reflects God's will and being. Things temporal (which are not man) – nature – are closer to the eternal one (which is not man) – God – than man himself is. By studying nature, one could get knowledge of who God is. And since God is good, it is possible to gather morals from nature: the study of nature becomes a source of moral knowledge and what is natural becomes synonymous with the morally good.

To be sure, this idea is often balanced by insisting on the transcendence of God, on the distinction between the creator and the creation, on ideas about a Fall which affects nature too. Nonetheless, this idea still has some role, despite this modification.

The problem with this idea is not that it is impossible to say that nature is good, is not that connecting nature and God necessarily means saying that God is not love. Rather, the problem is that it is unclear what saying this and making this connection mean, the problem is that the supposed relation has another character than it is then taken to have. It is easiest to get hold of the problem if we start with the idea that it is possible to gather morals from nature, that the study of nature is a source of moral knowledge. For imagine a thoroughly selfish person, a person who is completely calculating;[1] what could she learn by studying nature? She could learn to calculate in a better way: through her study of nature, she discovers more efficient ways of obtaining what she wants to have. She could learn that something she wants to have is not, practically speaking, possible to get, however hard she exerts herself. But this is all; what would it mean to say that studying nature could teach someone that this calculating attitude should be rejected? However, what is possible to imagine is that nature, or something in nature, is seen as an immediate address – not as external information – comparable to, for example, an appeal. (I am about to hit someone, he says "don't hit me", and I change my mind.) But notice that acknowledging something as an appeal – not seeing it as information, as something additional to take into account – is already not to be thoroughly selfish and completely calculating. Thus what is most essential is something which nature does not teach me, but which is a presupposition for it being possible to learn something at all from nature, morally speaking. Differently put, how I see nature, what in it I see as good or not, is an expression of my moral standing. Nature is not an extramoral source of morality, but how I relate to it is already a moral question. I cannot start in some sort of extramoral study of nature from which moral conclusions are supposed to follow, as if nature was a bridge between what is extramoral and what is moral, as if there were an extramoral question about what is natural which can then be used to draw conclusions about what is good. Rather, it is the other way around: to the extent "the natural" can be used as a moral concept, moral clear-sightedness is already needed for it to be possible to see what is natural in this moral sense. The same thing goes for the description of nature as good: in the same way as every human being is good in the moral sense that she is someone I can sin against, that she is not an insignificant piece I can do whatever occurs to me to – a moral use of "good" which does not refer to behavior (in which sense it is clear that she is not always good) but to being – nature is good not because everything which happens in nature is good (that is obviously not so) but because nature is something to care about.[2]

(Furthermore, the idea of nature as a source of moral knowledge is readily connected to an idea of harmony as the end of morality. But what is harmonious to man? Is it not that harmony of oppression where everyone is satisfied, even the oppressed one, and the one who enters and condemns this oppression is immediately driven away as a disturber of peace?)[3]

Things would be different if one understood morality aesthetically. One expression of such an understanding is a person who tries to become alike to nature – but what should be counted as being alike or not is not self-evident, of course – and studies nature in order to get to know what being alike to nature involves. Here it would be possible to derive rules from the study of nature. But adopting such an aesthetical understanding means shutting one's eyes to many things. First, anything which happens in nature is not good, as I have said – and in what sense is it possible to understand someone who claims the opposite? – so copying nature would, to say the least, not be good.[4] Second, placing morality in something solely external would be (an attempt at) escaping one's responsibility: "I'm sorry, I would like to act in another way, but now doing this happens to be what is right, and that I cannot do anything about, however much I wish that what is right would be something other than it is." Third, relating to another human being on the basis of aesthetics and rules is to relate to her in a mediated way, not directly, in love.[5]

The idea of nature as a religious and/or moral manual is often taken to be overthrown with Darwin. However, questioning this idea is not dependent on some specific discovery; it is not questioned on empirical grounds, but on moral ones. But if the idea is that with Darwin it is not possible to see nature as good at all – nature is simply the meaningless striving of the genetic material to reproduce itself – this idea should be questioned.

First, this idea has not much to do with Darwin, but that is not that important. Even though phrases like the one I use above – "the striving of the genetic material to reproduce itself" – is often used in descriptions of Darwinism, this is not at all a good description. If one apple tree gets ten times more fruit than another apple tree close to it, it is clear that the first tree gets more descendants than the second one, ceteris paribus. But this has nothing to do with some "striving", not to reproduce itself, not to anything else. The genetic material does not strive; the point is the simple one that there are more of those who get many "children" than of those who get fewer. This element of the theory of evolution is then nearly a tautology.[6] Of course, striving would be meaningless if the goal was futile, but what we have here is not a matter of striving at all. Consequently, the theory of evolution does not say anything about meaning and about what is meaningful.

Second, and this is more important, the picture of nature as a mechanism is simply a picture. (Sometimes it is said that this picture does not exist anymore, since one has now realized how complicated the connections are, how difficult it is to survey them. This is only a modification of the mechanistic picture, however; if one takes saying this to be having given it up, one is blind to many aspects of it). In some situations and for some purposes, this picture can be used in order to clarify something, but to believe that this outlook is the only outlook, the one who underlines all other possibilities, is metaphysics. On the contrary, it is an important philosophical task to consider what role some specific outlook has, and in that its limitations. What it means to see the movements of the bird outside my windows as reactions and what it means not to see them as that, what it means to see the bird as a specimen (a blackbird) and as this particular bird (as an "individual"), are not empirical questions. "Nature" is not defined as "that which science studies"; science has the meaning it has since nature is already something we relate to, in many different ways. Whereas the former outlook could get its point by making nature serve our purposes (but it could get its point in other ways too), the opposite is to see nature as nature, as life, as something different from me, as something which is not primarily related to my interests, as something I encounter. The idea of its usefulness has no place here, is inapplicable. The difficulty which the latter outlook points out – alienation from nature – does then not depend on inadequate knowledge of nature – epistemological inadequacy – but on the difficulty of not seeing, say, animals as nothing but the marionettes of some specific scientific theory, of not seeing an individual animal as nothing but a specimen (of, say, a species).

II. *Human beings' sense of dependence on nature as the basis of religious belief*

Another picture of the relation between religious belief and nature is that the basis of religious belief is human beings' sense of dependence on nature, their deserted position, their powerlessness when confronted with the powers of nature. In a way, this is not completely misguided. Religious belief understood as love of a God of love means awareness of the fact that I am not everything there is, and this love does not mean a way of relating to one object in contrast to other objects but a way of relating to everything. But the picture mentioned connects religious belief to my inability to carry through my plans. Of course, such an inability exists – what would an absolute ability of carrying through one's plans mean? – but what is the contrast to love of a God of love is not the absolute confidence in one's own ability of carrying through one's plans, but the very *attitude* of trying to carry through one's plans generally, irrespective of whether one succeeds in doing so or not. For this reason, it might be tempting to say that whereas the first way of understanding the relation makes belief vulnerable to technical development – the greater my ability of carrying through my plans are, the less belief – the second way of understanding the relation makes the possibility of belief independent of technical development – technology is simply a means and the question concerns if and in what way I should make use of this means. There is something to this, but it is a simplification. First, there is no such thing as a *pure* means: the means is never neutral, but already from the start connected to purposes, praxis, a way of being.[7] In the essay *Die Frage nach der Technik*,[8] Heidegger emphasizes that the fundamental question is not about the possible dangers of technology, since that still presupposes that technology is a means we make use of, a means which is good or bad. Instead, the fundamental question concerns the outlook which technology is, an outlook where everything is exclusively seen as resources. A river, say, is seen as a supplier of energy, or by the leisure industry as something the tourists watch for a few minutes. And when nothing concerns me but as a resource, I see myself exclusively as a utilizer of resources, that is, I am simply a resource too. The danger here is not that we see something as a resource, but that we do not see that this is simply one way of seeing things: other outlooks remain concealed. The task is then, according to Heidegger, even though he does not understand this in terms of moral responsibility, to disclose that which remains concealed or let that which remains concealed disclose itself. Second, technological development is not primarily a way of satisfying, or of satisfying in a better and simpler way, needs we had independently of this development, but is itself creating needs. This does not mean that I am deserted to this development, as if what I see as a need were not a moral question, only that my way of relating to the development is not a matter of relating to something which does not get a moral significance until it is applied.

This means that my way of relating to nature is not isolated from my way of relating to everything else, but reflects my general way of being. As I said above,[9] love is not a way of relating to one object in contrast to other objects but is a way of relating to everything. Morality does not consist of different ethical sectors – business ethics, medical ethics, and here, environmental ethics – where different and unrelated questions arise, sectors focused on different "objects", objects the importance of which first have to be proved. Is it not characteristic of the good person that she does not have any limits to her love? In other words: is it really possible to solve one problem here, taking this to be unrelated to problems in other "sectors"? The well-known chain beginning with the boss treating one of his employees badly, who goes home and beats his wife … ends with the child kicking the dog. The one who wants to build a hydroelectric dam and for whom the animal life there is indifferent is also the one who wants to drive away those who live there. When we repress what we know at heart about the effect of our consumption on people in other parts of the world and on the environment, this is one and the same attempt at forgetting. Is there not a parallel between hatred of wolves and racism: in both cases one sees nothing but an indefinite threat which has to be exterminated in order to restore the idyll. And the one who exploits a mountain by ruthless mining operations is the one who treats workers as – animals.

However, in one sense the relation to human beings is primary. My difficulties here are different (in addition to the ones I have generally, also in relation to nature): I might find a human being irritating in a way I do not find a mosquito irritating, say. And many of my difficulties in relation to nature are only intelligible against the background of a difficulty with human beings (and this goes for some of what I mentioned in the paragraph above): when I handle some object carelessly due to pretended nonchalance – and more examples could be given, of course: stress, nervousness – this has its intelligibility in the fact that this pretended nonchalance has its place in relations with other people. The point here is that one could, perhaps, say, that in so far as I solve my difficulties with human beings, all my moral difficulties will be solved: there seems not to be any difficulties specific to the relation to nature. Religious belief, understood as love of a God of love, is in *this* sense more closely related to the relation to other human beings than to the relation to nature: it is here my difficulty of really living this love shows itself. And, furthermore, this shows how dissimilar religious belief as love of a God of love is from a humanistic interpretation of religion: avoiding any deeper relations with an irritating person is what, humanly speaking, is self-evident and reasonable, but love of a God of love is something completely different.

That relations with human beings are, morally speaking, primary, shows itself in some ways of relating to nature too. Someone who lives lovingly in relation to other human beings but is ruthless in relation to nature, is hard to imagine: if her way of relating to nature should not be described as a result of lack of knowledge – not as ruthlessness, not as having a moral/ immoral character – it seems as if she acts out her difficulties with human beings in her ruthlessness to nature. That is, her love gets, in the light of her way of relating to nature, a forced character: she does not really live lovingly. On the other hand, it is not hard to imagine someone who is hateful in her relations with other human beings, but cares for animals. However, this description is somewhat misleading: obviously, this "caring" has a false character since it is something she takes refuge in, and the animals are not loved for what they are – are not loved as being themselves – but for what they are not: human beings. In the same way as the relation to nature can be something to take refuge in, religious belief can be such a refuge. However, if religious belief is understood as love of a God of love, this is not possible, since if one takes refuge from some love – for example, the love to and of this irritating person – one takes refuge *from* God, not *in*.

III. *Religious belief as providing a foundation for caring about nature*

A third way of relating religious belief to nature is to say that the belief provides a foundation for caring about nature: the picture of God as the creator makes it necessary, for the one who wants to turn to what is "higher", to turn to what is "lower". Without the belief, nature would not have any particular significance, but as a means for the fulfillment of my needs (which could include aesthetical needs and in that way make some form of nature conservation necessary). This way of relating religious belief to nature might seem to have a positive character: the belief contributes something important. But that we *are* able to see this as positive, as important, means that the contribution does not really have a function. We are not at all unaware of the fact that nature is something to care for, for its own sake. The idea seems to be that the belief gives the believer a foundation for caring about nature: previously, this has seemed to be gratuitous, something which cannot be explained, but now it has a theoretical justification. The belief becomes some sort of deep ecology. In what follows I will criticize the idea that a deep ecology – understood in this way – is needed. At the end, I will return to the question about the relations between religious belief, deep ecology and nature.

The paper I will start out from is the one where the phrase "deep ecology" was coined, "The Shallow and the Deep, Long-Range Ecology Movement" from 1973, by Arne Næss, the most well-known philosopher in this sphere.[10] The contrast Næss makes in the paper is, as is evident from its title, one between two different movements within the ecology movement. The shallow ecology movement focuses on pollution and the exhaustion of natural resources, that is, on environmental problems as they affect people in the rich part of the world. Phrasing it differently and more sharply, the aim of this movement is that people in the rich part of the world should be able to go on living more or less as they already do, that they should find a form of exploitation where the effects on themselves are minimal. Næss distances himself from such anthropocentric ways of thinking, and instead presents a movement which is more complex, and among other things has equality of man and nature on its program. But at the same time it is evident that deep ecology is not only a movement for Næss, but a theory, a philosophical foundation for ecological action. Whereas the shallow ecology movement can depict coming, predictable threats, can appeal to our calculative self-interest, the deep ecology movement seems to be in need of a theory which shows why I should care for that which is not me.

Næss uses scientific discoveries to show this: nature is a system where everything hangs together, where everything is mutually dependent, a system which human beings are a part of. But above all, showing why I should care for that which is not me is for Næss a philosophical task. His main work – *Økologi, samfunn og livsstil*[11] (partly translated into English as *Ecology, Community and Lifestyle*[12]) – is for that reason to a large extent a work in moral philosophy and metaethics, and the language Næss is using a standard analytic-philosophical one: he writes about value axioms, systems of value priorities, sets of sentences with deductive relations between them, and so forth. It might seem as if Næss distances himself from the analytical metaethics of the 1950s and 1960s when he writes, "Wisdom is … prescription, not only scientific description and prediction"[13], but the dissociation is made in its own language. Thus I would say that Næss's philosophy is not the solution to what is wrong in our thinking about nature, but an expression of the problems in that thinking.

The question is: is a theory at all needed? Are we really in need of a philosophical justification of the fact that nature is something to care about? The shallow "ecology" movement worries about nature only because of the consequences environmental problems might have for ourselves, but this is not to care about nature at all. All *ecological* action is an expression of awareness of nature as something not indifferent, as something with a significance of its own. The difficulty, which Næss's theory is supposed to bridge, concerns the possibility of passing from the one side of the gap to the other one: how is it possible to explain why something which is not me, here nature, is something to care about?

There are two alternatives here. Either one questions the idea of a gap – and then no theory is needed, since there is no gap to be bridged. Or there is really a gap, but what the theory then does, to the extent one finds the theory to be a good one, is simply hide for one the fact that one has passed from the one side of the gap to the other one. The theory tries to make passing from the one side of the gap to the other one into something "natural" by justifying it on grounds one already acknowledges before one has passed from the one side of the gap to the other one. But by doing so, the theory remains stuck on the first side. (The very technocratic character of Næss's discussion is no coincidence.) Passing from the one side of the gap to the other one, the theory cannot do for one. And even if we, for the sake of argument, assume that the theory could do this, this new relation to nature would only be a relation mediated theoretically, not that kind of awareness of the significance of something internal to love.

This significance is not something which needs to be proved. On the contrary, that something is a moral question means that it faces me with an issue of responsibility I cannot escape by saying that I did not know of it; this is something Næss, as well as many other philosophers, does not pay attention to. This is simply what something being a moral question means. However, I often try to transform this moral question into a theoretical question, in that way postponing taking my responsibility to the moment when the theoretical question has been solved, and it is possible, if one is simply skeptical enough, to postpone this indefinitely. This shows itself in that perseverance with which some people question the fact that our way of living is destructive: the question is here only apparently a scientific one, but at bottom concerns there being things one does not want to see.

What we need is not a proof or a philosophical argument. Instead, one could say that what we need to do is draw our own attention to the love we already have for nature,[14] let the experience of the significance of nature speak out. That our relation to nature is already "deep" is simply something we tend to forget, or tend to repress. Using the word "experience" is not necessarily an expression of anthropocentrism, since the experience is an experience of something *different*; saying that anthropocentrism is inevitable is as stupid as saying that morality is inevitably selfish. For the one who loves a God of love, the belief itself is something which draws one's attention to this love, something which lets the experience of the significance of nature speak out. The belief is not a foundation for this love, externally related to it; this love is, for the one who loves a God of love, an aspect of the belief.

However, there is more to Næss than attempts at finding a theoretical foundation. For example, he emphasizes the possibility of identifying oneself with more than oneself, in that way getting a self that is larger than oneself.[15] Caring for nature is then not caring for something which is outside oneself: ecological action as a kind of self-defense. Even though this is a possibility, the concept of identification leads one away from the important issues, I think. Næss seems to be stuck in a thinking which is still self-centered, instead of seeing another possibility: caring for something precisely as different, as not being me. This different being is not something I am a stranger to, of course, but describing the relation as identification makes the relation into, at the most, an inferior version of something which, better described, is love.[16]

Is there then anything religious belief, understood as love of a God of love, might contribute? As should be evident by now, this question is badly put. What kind of contribution has one in mind? That our way of relating to nature is something to think over, something which calls for consideration and action, is clear. What kind of consideration and action? The problem is not that I immediately give a clear-sighted answer to the question about what kind of contribution is needed but then do not know how to find this contribution, but that I am unclear as to what contribution is needed. For the one who loves a God of love, it is within the framework of this belief that the necessary consideration and self-examination will take place. The belief is then not something which delivers an external contribution – then it would not be a matter of *self*-examination – but is to *do* something.[17]

Chapter 9

The Negative Miracle

That love is relevant, in some sense or other, as to what philosophers of religion use to call "the problem of evil" is clear; one of the propositions which give rise to the alleged contradiction is "God is good", and the problem could be understood as making the belief in – the love of – a God of love difficult or impossible. At the same time, it is evident that this theme is not present in the discussion. Not only is the word "love" absent; many arguments in this discussion are based on a blindness to this theme. For example, see what Richard Swinburne writes in his theodicy:

> A particular natural evil such as pain makes possible felt compassion – one's sorrow, concern, and desire to help the sufferer. It is good that if pain exists, compassion exists, whether or not it can lead to action ... But of course, the objector will say, even if pain is better for the response of compassion, better still that there be no pain at all. Now obviously it would be crazy for God to multiply pains in order to multiply compassion. But I suggest that a world with some pain and some compassion is at least as good as a world with no pain. For it is good to have a deep concern for others; and the concern can be a deep and serious one only if things are bad with the sufferer. One cannot worry about someone's condition unless there is something bad or likely to be bad about it. If things always went well with someone, there would be no scope for anyone's deep concern.[1]

How is this to be understood? In what sense is compassion a good thing? Swinburne says that "the concern can be a deep and serious one only if things are bad with the sufferer". In other words, this compassion, this concern, is not the same thing as love; love can be deep irrespective of whether things are bad or good with the one I love. Swinburne's idea seems to be that what brings us together, what makes us feel for each other, are practical concerns. These practical concerns do not necessarily find a solution, but it is they that are central: if it were not for them, we would not need each other. Notice that Swinburne says, "whether or not it *can lead to action*"; compassion is a good thing, according to Swinburne, since compassion aims at supplying, by means of this action, what is lacking, at solving the practical problems, but there may be external obstacles which make it hard or impossible to bring about the necessary consequential action. However, if the focus was on love, things would be different. Love is not something one does, but something one is, to use a somewhat simplified phrase. Here there are no external obstacles. Loving someone is not to find some lack in the other which awakens my love and makes my want to supply what is lacking. Of course, love involves helping the one I love, but the point is simply that I, when loving someone, am affected by her life, however it turns out.

This does not mean that what Swinburne says is not at all related to love. On the contrary, his line of thought reminds us of problematic relationships: what he says has to do with my problems with love. Imagine someone who wishes for a fire to break out. Then he would get the chance to save the one he loves, then she would understand what he feels for her without him needing to tell her this, then her gratitude could transform itself into love, he thinks. Or imagine a man who now and then wishes that his wife would meet with an accident: then we would get close to each other again, he thinks. And vice versa: someone wants to meet with an accident, for he thinks that others, or some particular person, will feel pity for him then.

However, Swinburne's theodicy is not the theme here. This has simply been an example, showing how absent the concept of love is from these kinds of standard discussion of the problem of evil. I will return to this question about love in section III. Before that (in section I), I will try to show that the *philosophical* problem of evil does not exist at all. This might suggest that I support one of the sides in the debate – the theistic side – but that is not the case. If there is no philosophical problem, there is no philosophical solution. The philosophical atheist who emphasizes the problem of evil in order to argue for her own theory and against the theist theory opens for the possibility of a philosophical solution to the problem: her own emphasis on the problem as a philosophical problem presupposes that, even though she does not believe there to be one. In the second section of this chapter, I will sketch some of the forms the problem may take, but none of them are philosophical. The question is whether any of them should be called a "problem of evil" at all; as you see, I have instead chosen the title "The Negative Miracle" for this chapter, and I will explain what this is supposed to mean in the fourth section of this chapter, where I come back to the different forms of the problem.

I. *The philosophical problem of evil*

The problem of evil is described, in writings of philosophers of religion, as a conflict between three propositions: "God is omnipotent", "God is good", and "there is evil". These three propositions do not immediately result in a contradiction, however. The logical contradiction does not arise until these three propositions are combined with some additional premises, it is held.[2] Against this background, it is possible to sketch most of the contemporary discussion of the problem of evil in analytic philosophy of religion. The philosopher of religion critical of religion sticks to this way of phrasing the problem, and her task is then simply to criticize the attempted solutions. For the defender of what is usually called "theism" – a theory consisting of, among other things, the propositions "God is omnipotent" and "God is good" – there are some different possibilities. She could try to show that the proposed additional premises are not necessary truths, which would mean that it is possible that the three original propositions are compatible.[3] This discussion is often held to be closed, in favor of the theist.[4] Even if the additional premises are not necessary truths, it is possible that they are highly probable or credible, however.[5] For this reason, a new discussion arises, of the so-called evidential problem of evil. And here a kind of metadiscussion arises, about whether this problem only requires, as an answer, a defense showing the possible problematic and relative character of this kind of judgment of probability,[6] or if a fully developed theodicy must be constructed, a kind of explanation of why God allows evil to exist.[7]

As is evident, the concept of logical contradiction is absolutely central in this discussion. This also goes for the evidential problem of evil. *If* the additional premises are true, we have a logical contradiction; the question only concerns what to say about their possible truth. However – and it is this I will try to show – to say that there may be a logical contradiction here builds on a specific conception of logic which is simply presupposed. This conception of logic has been criticized in a discussion starting with Cora Diamond's paper "What Nonsense Might Be".[8] The points she there makes have been deepened and radicalized in the subsequent discussion.[9]

The criticism is directed at what has come to be called a substantial conception of nonsense. According to the criticized conception, something is nonsense because the contents (meanings) of some words are in contradiction; in other words, the parts of the sentence have content in themselves and are for that reason compatible or incompatible in a way which determines whether a sentence combining these parts is meaningful or not. The contrast to this – a contrast partly articulated already in Frege's context principle[10] – is then, to use Wittgenstein's way of putting it, "When a sentence is called senseless, it is not, as it were, its sense that is senseless. Rather, a combination of words is being excluded from the language, withdrawn from circulation."[11] Nonsense is not a matter of an erroneous combination of meaningful elements. If something is nonsense, it is nonsense in its entirety, that is, when it is not at all intelligible.

The criticism of the substantial conception of nonsense can, shortened and simplified, be described as directed at two features of this conception. First, the criticism points out that nonsense cannot be explained in terms of formal properties of sentences. The paradigm of a logical contradiction is, according to the substantial conception of nonsense, $p \wedge \neg p$. But that this is a logical contradiction follows directly from the logical forms of use: such an expression only describes the relation between formal signs; in other words, there is always a question about whether some linguistic expression should really be formalized as $p \wedge \neg p$. This means that simply because someone says something which, formally speaking, is "similar" to $p \wedge \neg p$, it should not be taken for granted that what has been said is really a logical contradiction. (In other words, a common picture of logic, according to which it is about some formal properties every expression has irrespective of content, is untenable. If something does not say anything, it does not do so due to its form, but since it is not intelligible.) But saying a thing like "it is raining and it isn't" can be really saying something, is not necessarily a logical contradiction:

> [T]he utterance "It's raining and it isn't" … may be a fully adequate characterization of the weather … Someone who says, "It's raining and it isn't" is not using the word "raining" in two different senses. He is not, as it were, giving separate responses to two different questions (he is not saying, "Well, if you use the word 'rain' in the sense …., it *is* raining, but if you use it in the sense …, it's *not*") … The contradictory form of words is a way for him to get across what the weather is like. It does not prevent him making a point, rather it helps him say what he is trying to say.[12]

The second aspect of the criticism of the substantial conception of logic has to do with how to understand the nonsensicality of something which is really nonsense. Take a trivial geometrical example, such as "this square is circular": according to the substantial conception of nonsense, the nonsensicality has to do with the meaning of the words "square" and "circular". However, the problem is that this is not a matter of the intrinsic properties of the signs "square" and "circular": these could just as well stand for something else, and, besides, it is not all difficult to imagine a case where saying "this square is circular" would not be nonsense, when I am talking about the city square, say. When "this square is circular" is a contradiction, this cannot be understood unless one understands how words like "square" and "circular" are used in geometry; a context of use is one of the necessary conditions for the possibility of contradictions. (Here it is important to not have a rigid understanding of "context of use"; if the context of use is supposed to provide another kind of determination, the same problem, as with the substantial conception of nonsense, would arise again.) In other words, it is against the background of a specific context of use that the transformation of "this square is circular" to "this figure has four sides and it is not the case that it has four sides" to $p \land \neg p$ is made. Since the supposed logical contradictions having interesting consequences – the problem of evil, say – do not have the second or the third form, the idea must be that it is possible to, taking one's starting point in religious uses of concepts such as "omnipotence", construct sentences such as "God is omniscient and God is not omniscient" and then transform this one to $p \land \neg p$. The starting point for the possibility of this transformation is the meaning of the expressions in question; the transformation is from one expression to another one having the same meaning. How is this to be understood?

This creates the following problem.[13] What does it mean to say that two expressions have the same meaning? How is it possible to show that a transformation of the above kind is possible? The problem is that the greater consequences the discovery of what is taken to be a logical contradiction are supposed to have, in that it is supposed to thwart a whole way of life, the more obvious it is that the concepts used to formulate the problem – "omnipotence", say – do not have the (religious) meaning they are taken to have by the critics. One way of seeing this is that from a logical contradiction, anything follows. However, it is evident that the supposed logical contradictions taken to have interesting consequences do not sprawl. A religious believer, say, does not draw any conclusion from her belief, that is, the problem of evil does not have the consequences a logical contradiction has.[14] In other words, the contradiction only arises if it is already clear beforehand what an expression like "God's omnipotence" means, if every logically possible consequence is already there hidden in the expression, before it is used in concrete situations.[15] If one does not think that, one must be attentive to what could be called the "limits" of use, in that way coming to an understanding of what the expression means by paying attention to what conclusions are *not* drawn. The philosophical task does not consist in constructing logical contradictions, but in describing the expressions supposed to result in a logical contradiction in a way that does justice to their use: in which contexts are they used and in which not, which conclusions are drawn and which not, and so forth. In our case, the task is to see how the expression "God's omnipotence" and related expressions are really used. Such an investigation would, among other things, point out the asymmetrical form characteristic of such religious expressions: gratitude for the good in life does not comparably correspond to a reproachful attitude as to the worse in life; the way in which prayers are seen to be answered does not comparably correspond to a way in which prayers are seen not to be answered.[16]

There is an objection which could be directed to this line of thought. It might seem as if I reject the possibility of nonsense *tout court.* If the use of expressions is what is primary, every use, even the nonsensical ones, will be on a par, someone could object: instead we must pay attention to the fact that there are uses of a given expression which are central and uses which are more peripheral, and that it is only the central uses which determine the meaning of the expression.[17] However, this objection is problematical. There is *something* to it, but one has got things backwards. It is not because there is a distinction between what is central and what is peripheral which is fixed independently of the context of use, as if there would be some kind of book to read in order to see where the limit is, that nonsense is possible; on the contrary, it is because I am unable to do anything with what is said, because I do not understand it, that I can make a distinction between what is central and what is peripheral in this case, if I want to. (It is not because $p \wedge \neg p$ is there already in the sentence, hidden, that I am unable to do anything with what is said; on the contrary, it is because I am unable to do anything with what is said that I am justified in transforming it to $p \wedge \neg p$.) There is nothing which settles in advance whether a new use contradicts an old one, or even whether the use is a new one and not simply a repetition of the old one: it is in connection to my understanding of what has been said, or my difficulty of making anything of it, that such distinctions are made. Or rather, to be more precise, when it is not possible to make anything with what is said, when it is not intelligible, there is no use at all, nothing at all is said. Compare this misleading formulation of Phillips's:

> It is important to distinguish between Wittgenstein's grammatical use of the term ["practice"], and what might be called its sociological use. In Wittgenstein's use "practice" does refer to a cluster of language games, and it makes no sense to speak of a confused practice. But the sociological use simply refers to whatever happens. In this latter context confusion is still practice. Wittgenstein recognizes confused practices in this latter context. In the sociological use of "practice", it makes sense to say that confusion could reign on a large scale.[18]

What is misleading in this formulation is that it is only possible to describe something as a practice – irrespective of whether the description is sociological or grammatical – if we are able to account for the sense and intelligibility the practice has.[19] If something is senseless and unintelligible, it is unclear what it would mean to describe it as a practice, also in a sociological sense. Furthermore, a contradiction like "this square is circular" exists in relation to the sense and intelligibility the practice has, which means that the practice itself, as soon as we have identified something as a practice, is not contradictory.[20]

One should distinguish between two different ways in which something could be a contradiction. First, we have the case where I am unable to do anything with what is said. Second, we have the use of the concept "contradiction" *within* a practice. Someone could try to trisect an angle using only an unmarked straight edge and a compass, and after having seen it mathematically proven that this is not generally possible, she realizes that the expression "it is always possible to trisect an angle using only an unmarked straight edge and a compass" is a contradiction. However, it is important to notice that it is not the mathematical proof, seen in isolation, which makes this a contradiction. The proof says something about the contradictory character of the expression only due to the relation between the expression and the fact that trisecting an angle by eye does not count as trisecting an angle in mathematics, however exact the trisection is. In other words, no ontological conclusion follows from the fact that this is a contradiction. If someone continues to claim that it is possible to trisect every angle using only an unmarked straight edge and a compass, nothing prevents her from claiming this; she has only diverged from the rules of a theoretical notation. To be sure, difficulties of communication may arise, but for those who hear her claim, the question simply concerns what intelligibility this has, what "trisect" and "using only an unmarked straight edge and a compass" stand for here, and so forth. However, if she claims, when I am trying to understand what she is saying, that she means exactly the same as I do when using these expressions, if she says that what she has done is having trisected a given angle but has evidently not done so, there is nonsense: I do not know what to do with what she has said, what has been said is not a use, she does not say anything.

Concerning the problem of evil, this means that if the problem is of the first kind – a contradiction within a practice – the discussion is empty. The atheist's criticism is then no more than insisting that a word like "omnipotence" should not be used here. No ontological conclusion can then be made. The dispute does not concern what there is, but what words should be used. (Here one takes recourse to a substantial conception of nonsense to give the discussion the appearance of having content, despite its emptiness.) However, it is evident that the problem is not of the second kind. If it were a problem of the second kind, the problem would simply be that we did not know what to do with what the believer says, we would see what she is saying as simply nothing. But the atheist's criticism is not of this kind. It is not because of an absence of sense that the atheist does not understand it – then what the believer says would simply be an enigma – but it is because of the sense it *has*, or, possibly, is taken to have, that the atheist does not understand how someone can say this. This becomes evident in the unarticulated pathos with which the criticism is expressed. How this problem should be understood I will return to in section II. My point here is that as long as the problem is understood as a theoretical problem, a problem concerning logical contradictions, the discussion is empty. The philosophical problem of evil, where the problem is understood in this way, is, at most, a trivialization of it.

What I have said about logic and meaning generally here means that the question about the meaning of an expression is not an empirical question. In a way, this should be obvious also to the one who lays stress on the issue of logical contradictions: if the question were strictly empirical, a contradiction would not arise. The contradiction would then be supposed to arise since some use contradicts some pattern the researcher has found in the uses she has studied, but taking this to be a logical contradiction would then be to declare this datum invalid instead of seeing it as an additional datum to take into account when formulating one's theory. Instead, the point is that it does not matter how often some expression is used: something does not become intelligible by being said again and again, and something is not unintelligible because it is seldom said. A philosophical clarification of the meaning of some expression means that I try to become attentive to such features of the use that I am, in a sense, already familiar with – if I am not at all familiar with them, it is not possible to say anything as to possible contradictions, since in that case it could just as well be this defect which makes me unable to do anything with what is said – but the importance of which, as to its meaning, are easily overlooked. Thus, the question is how what is said should be understood, and empirical findings do not settle this for me: that would simply be adding something which, and the relation between which and what is said, I need to come to an understanding of. The contradiction is here something purely negative: I cannot see how I could become able to do anything with what has been said; it appears to me as empty, as empty words, as something the saying of which is not a use. It is tempting, in a way, to see logic as a set of norms possible to apply to anything, thereby judging what it is applied to from an external position. The idea of philosophy as a scientific discipline with a sphere of its own, a sphere of truths to discover – metaphysical truths – partly builds on the idea that philosophy has some non-empirical tools by means of which it is possible to reach these truths. But as long as logic is seen as such a set of external norms, it will not have a special status, and is not even then able to judge in this way. If logic is brought in from outside, a question about its foundation arises, and as soon as we try to justify logic we take away its pretension of being foundational.[21] What we can do is show that it is already a foundation in what we are doing, that it is not an opinion, or the like, which enters externally to correct what it is we are doing, an opinion which then would stand in need of justification; what is possible to do is clarify the meaning of what we do, and this may be called clarifying the logic of concepts.[22] Logical notation and formalization can possibly, in some cases, make us aware of how we are already using language, but risks strengthening the idea that logic is external. In that sense logic – the logic of concepts, not formal logic – must take care of itself.[23]

II. *Some forms of the problem*

What then is the problem of evil about, if not about logical contradictions? Someone might point to something in the mainstream discussion of the problem which could be this "second understanding" of it: the discussion of the so-called existential problem of evil. Even though what I referred to as the partly unarticulated pathos in the discussion of the problem of evil gets some kind of articulation here, this is still a very defective articulation: either the existential problem is understood in purely psychological terms[24] or it is understood as an aspect of the problem which remains after the logical (and evidential) aspects have been solved.[25] Obviously, this characterization is dependent on the more common philosophical characterization, and is marred by the same problems. In saying this, I do not want to dismiss everything said in that discussion, only point out that there is still a fundamental lack of clarity as to what the problem is about.

The logical contradiction is a problem of understanding: what is said is something I cannot see that I could do anything with, something which appears to me as empty, as empty words, as something the saying of which is no use. But there is, as I hinted at a moment ago, another kind of problem of understanding: when what one does not understand is not what is said, but that someone says it. The lack of understanding is here not negative: it is not because of an absence of sense one does not understand it, but it is because of the sense it has that one does not understand how someone can say this. (Here it is not at all strange that I no longer understand what I once understood.) The lack of understanding is here not one that opens toward an explanation – the one who does not understand what is said could doubt the possibility of such an explanation, but this doubt has as its background the fact that if such an explanation would be given, this would give her understanding – but expresses the fact that giving such an explanation would implicate one all the more in that the saying of which is unintelligible. (However, this does not mean that it is impossible for such a lack of understanding to disappear, but this is not occasioned by the "question" "How is it possible to say this?" getting an answer, but by the asking of this "question" beginning to be questioned.)[26]

Here the problem does not concern an ontological question – should I say yes or no to some proposition – but what one could call a moral (or existential) one: is it possible to believe this in one's heart? The confusion the atheist accuses the believer of is not a logical confusion, but a moral one.

That the problem has this character is actually visible also in the usual description of it, even though it is hidden there. The problem is described as a conflict between three propositions: "God is omnipotent", "God is good", and "there is evil". However, saying that someone is good is not observing some indifferent property, in the way saying that someone weighs this or that is indifferent. Saying that someone is good is an expression of, for example, admiration or praise. Saying that God is good is not giving a report about some property, but is an expression of faith. Above I said that if the problem of evil is understood as an issue of a contradiction within a practice, the atheist's criticism is then no more than insisting that a word like "omnipotence" should not be used here. Now we see that this was a bit misleading. If one wants to replace a word like "good" with some other word or words, possibly more fitting, one has not gone from one rapport to another rapport, but from an expression of faith to something else. This does not mean that it is impossible to say that one believes in a God which one does not see as good – but it is not that obvious what saying this would mean[27] – or to say that one believes that there is a good God, a God one does not believe in – but in this case it is unclear to what extent one *means* what one *says*. The point, in the context of this chapter, is simply that the difficulty of saying and meaning "God is good", as this difficulty shows itself in the problem of evil, should be understood as a difficulty of believing something in one's heart. The difficulty is not about some abstract question of truth. It does not concern whether something is untrue, but whether it is false, in the moral sense of the word: something one cannot *believe in*. In other words, there is no theory – theism – which I hold to be true or not, a theory consisting of a set of propositions I hold to be true or not; one of the "propositions" taken to be included in that set is "God is good", and saying and meaning that is something more than and different from holding a proposition to be true. Atheism, *if* it is merely a repudiation of theism – a-theism – is consequently a confusion.

The repudiation of the problem of evil as a theoretical problem means that the problem only becomes relevant when it is actually a *problem*. If one's repudiation of religious belief is about something else, it is tempting to justify this repudiation, to oneself and others, using a moral pathos which is not deeply meant: one seeks out the problem of evil, as it were, without having a relation to the real problem. (If one justifies the repudiation to oneself in this way, it is hard for one to see that it is not deeply meant, of course: a form of self-deception.) The genuine form of the problem of evil is when one's own repudiation actually has to do with this; this may be a repudiation of a belief one once had or of the belief of others.

In other words, what is vital is that the problem is my problem. It is me who believes or does not believe; it is me who, in my life, encounters evil, directly or indirectly. Whatever is said philosophically about evil, it is important that this is something *I* am able to say. The discussion of the problem of evil as it is usually carried out – by the apologists on *both* sides – takes place on a level where all this disappears, since I am not there: looking down on the world in its entirety from a position outside it. What is there said about evil is something that I cannot say, on grounds of principle; what is said is not said by anyone. But it is always *me* who encounters evil, and the question is how I do that.

Thus, Irving Greenberg makes a good point when he writes, referring to the Holocaust: "No statement, theological or otherwise, should be made that would not be credible in the presence of the burning children."[28] The aim here is to try to get away from an abstract and empty idea of truth. Something that cannot be said is not even a *candidate* for truth. This means – if this has not been clear for a long time – that all attempts at theoretically compensating for evil, or theoretically balancing it, come to nothing. At the same time, it is important to see that there is a problem in the quotation from Greenberg. The thought of the burning children short-circuits *all* saying: *no* statement can be made anymore. Saying "life is wonderful" as a theoretical, totalizing statement is impossible here, of course, but the same goes for "life is wonderful" as an expression of joy at being with one's friends, a walk in the forest, the weather. A black hole opens here, sucking up all meaning. At the end, no more than pure desperation seems to be left. Even the position from which the suffering originally became visible as the terrible thing it is, here seems to dissolve, as no more than another expression of an incredible hope. Thus, what is important is to see that this second "life is wonderful", even though it cannot be said in the presence of the burning children, is still the contrast without which this presence would not be what it is. For this reason, it is important that "life is wonderful" is possible to say. Furthermore, it is not only the case that this suffering is something we now and then shut our eyes to. There are also examples of another kind: how the sight of this suffering may be seen as attractive,[29] partly because this is a convenient way of justifying a pessimism the roots of which are independent of this suffering, a way of justifying, to myself and others, my distrust and lack of love: I have seen the deepest truth as to man and existence, and all joy – an aspect of trust and love – is an expression of spiritual superficiality. Consequently, also "paying attention" to suffering may be an expression of moral insensitivity, when one, in the name of this attentiveness, exploits this suffering for one's own purposes.

The question concerns *how* and *what* I believe. And the problem of evil does not concern an abstract issue of truth, but the possibility of *belief*, in the sense of wholeheartedness, commitment, devotion. Am I able to believe? Asking this question means two things. First, a theory, a philosophical theory, say, is unable to settle this question for me. Believing that a body of doctrine – however consistent it is – could solve what I have called the genuine problem, is, frankly, stupid. Second, the commitment is not something which is simply given, as a feeling which "arises" and "disappears". The presence or absence of the commitment is something which *means* something and this meaning I could try to describe. For the meaning is not something automatically obvious. On the contrary, I could try to see what it is really about: is something hidden here, is there something I try to shut my eyes to, and so forth? In other words, there is a place for philosophical reflection here – philosophy as something one *does* – concerning my own way of being and living. Reflection of this kind would, even though it is personal, describe problems of a generally intelligible character: it concerns what things mean. This means that its official form does not at all need to be autobiographical. The question of real philosophical importance is *what* belief I repudiate, a question which is intimately connected to the *how* of belief.

Before entering upon the relation between the problem of evil and the theme of this book – religious belief understood as love of a God of love – I will discuss an example of the difference I hinted at a moment ago. Think of an expression – central in this context – such as "God is good". What could this mean? Say that a sign with this message hangs in a workhouse. What does this mean? It may obviously be an expression of oppression, when it means "… unlike you", or have an opiatic form, when it suggests that changing the present conditions is not important since everything turns out well in the end. But remember that Marx is ambiguous on this point. When he writes that religion is the opium of the people, he writes, at the same time, that religion is the protest against oppression.[30] The idea seems to be that religion, as a form of protest, is ineffective, since it is passive. However, this is not quite right, since there are also active forms, but Marx could object to this by saying that such forms are misleading since they do not realize what the question is really about and for that reason they are unable to say when to act and what the conditions for the success of the revolutionary action are.[31] However, nowadays it is clear, if it has not always been clear, that "scientific" socialism is not able to make such predictions either: neither Marx, nor Thomas Münzer, know when the time has come.[32] (Another idea would be to claim that the time will never come, that the moment of action is always in the future; but then we end up in the same passivity as Marx accuses religion of and the result is no more than a historical theodicy, as repellent as its religious siblings.) In other words, it is not clear how "God is good" is to be understood. It could be an expression of oppression, but the opposite is also possible: "God is good, and since what happens here is not good it is not an expression of God's will, but should be changed." What content "God is good" has is not immediately clear, which means that it is not immediately clear what it would mean to believe this – the "how" of belief – either. What goodness is, is a moral question and thus a question put to me. We get nowhere with the problem of evil as long as I try to relate to it externally, as long as I do not ask myself what is really possible for me to say.

III. *Love and evil*

When the question concerns belief understood as love of a God of love, it is obvious that the problem of evil, as it is usually understood, does not arise. Here the issue of God's omnipotence is already from the start subordinated to the issue of God's love. It is the latter which decides the meaning of the former; it is the latter which decides what power *is* in this context – the power of love or the power of force – a question preceding the question of the proportions of this power, omni- or not. I have already discussed this in Chapter 7.

What is decisive here are two different understandings of belief. For the one who believes instrumentally, the belief contains an element of prediction. The belief is something I stake on, expecting this will pay, in some way or other. If this result is not obtained or does not seem to be obtained, the belief loses its value. But as Kierkegaard stresses, believing in the good is not believing expecting this to pay, neither now nor later. Not now, since the good one never gets on well, Kierkegaard claims: if one expects something else, one should be advised against believing in this.[33] Not later, since believing in the good expecting an external payment is believing in the payment, not in the good.[34] "Sure, point taken, but is it not an imperfection that goodness does not pay, is it not conceivable that things were different and wouldn't that be better?" This objection is partly misleading, since here it again sounds as if what I am striving for, when I believe in the good, is something else. But the belief in the good is simply no solution to any problems, some kind of strategy for action. If I have a puncture on my bike and do not know how to fix it – a banal example – belief is not a strategy for achieving this, wished for by me, state. But this does not mean that we now have entered a sphere – the sphere of the practical – which is independent of the belief. Because the practical problem is a part of a life – is not a problem the solution of which has a purely "theoretical" interest – the question about what kind of part it is, is an aspect of how I live my life. However, the objection points to something important: it is in the light of love which the lack of love in the world shows itself. This could be called an imperfection, if one wants to, but it is an imperfection the discovery of which presupposes this very belief in the good.

Suffering is an expression of belief: *what* brings me suffering and *how* I suffer is an expression of what I believe in and how I believe. Consequently, that evil brings me suffering is an expression of my love of a God of love, if I have any, an *expression* of the belief, not something which counts against it, which should be explained away or which is unrelated to it. The intentionality of suffering means that it would be better if this terrible thing which has happened would not have happened, of course, but it also means that given what has happened it would not be better if there were no suffering: the latter possibility would mean that one does not see it as terrible, that one does no longer love a God of love. Deceiving oneself religiously, shutting one's eyes to a suffering, would not be to "save" one's belief, but to give it up.

There is also another kind of difficulty: when I do not shut my eyes to this suffering, the sight of it may result in me no longer being able to love a God of love, but not because what I see is "counterevidence", but rather due to something one could call an experience of hopelessness. What kind of difficulty is this?

IV. *The negative miracle*

I have now come to that which I have given as the title of the chapter: the negative miracle. Since the problem of evil based on (one understanding of) God's omnipotence is not relevant here, we will search for another form of the problem, starting out from those difficulties we have just now run into, and see what consequences they have for religious belief understood as love of a God of love. My point has also a further aim. This other form is part of that which gives the problem of evil the weight it has, even when it is discussed in very confused terms.

Imagine the following example: I miss the train, and, of course, this is something I wish had not happened. This wish could include the awareness of what consequences it would have had for the other passengers if the train had stood still one more minute and I had managed to catch it; there is not a great number of other passengers and for none of them would it have mattered if the train had become late. My wish may be a self-centered wish, but need not be so. But this badness – that I miss the train – does not result in a problem of evil. Or if it would, this would be absurd. This shows that the problem is not a logical one, in which case an occurrence such as this would be counter-evidence to "theism". For the same reason, the problem is not an evidential one, in which case this occurrence would not necessarily prove the falseness of "theism" but would nonetheless count against it, even though it may only be to a small degree. (That this would be absurd is also evident from the fact that the problem is called the problem of *evil*: evil is not a *quantitative* term, evil is not a *large amount* of badness.) What the phrase "the negative miracle" points to is that the problem, when it is really a problem and not a theoretical one, arises in a *situation.* Just as seeing the miraculousness of something is to see it in a new light, to really see it for the first time although it might be something extremely familiar, to see its inherent relation to God and God's love, the negative miracle is the experience of meaninglessness and hopelessness, of the absence of God.

Such a situation is always mine. To be sure, the philosophical idea that nobody is able, on grounds of principle, to understand me and feel what I feel is stupid, but there is *something* right in it. An experience is not some kind of thing possible to hand over, from one person to the next, a thing which then gets different significances due to the background and psychological constitution of the person in question. No, when I ask someone about what she has gone through, I do not do so in order to incorporate her experience into myself – as if what was in focus was this "experience" and she was unimportant – but since I am interested in what *she* has gone through. For the same reason, there is a point in emphasizing the difference between our experiences even when what we have gone through is the same.[35] I cannot bypass your experience by putting myself in the same place as you, taking part of your experience by turning my back on you, facing that which you face. The difference between our experiences I have in mind here is not one of background and psychological constitution: the difference is simply that it is to you as another person I turn, in order to talk about what you/we have gone through. The point is simply that I cannot get hold of your experience from an external, epistemological, third person, perspective, by studying you or the situation you are going through, but only by turning to you in a conversation.[36]

In this context, this is important to point out, since this makes totalizing conclusions impossible, conclusions starting out from a description of "the situation itself" or my own experience of it. The meaning of someone's experience of God's presence or absence in some situation cannot be determined by an external investigation of this situation or by a psychological investigation of her. It is the person having gone through some sufferings which is in the position of saying whether these sufferings are healed or not, but this does not mean that I have to take everything she says at her word, that it is impossible to be bewildered by the way she is affected by something (that she takes something as if it were nothing, that she takes something as if it were the end of the world, and so forth): it is things like these a conversation could be about. (I hardly need to point out that "healed" does not mean "compensated": rather, the question about whether it is healed or not is a question about the role of what is not possible to compensate for.)

Differing reactions to a situation – how something which for someone has the result that he loses his faith, for someone else strengthens her faith in what she holds to be of real importance – show what kind of problem we are dealing with here. How do I relate to this difference? If someone has gone through something really terrible – philosophers are usually fond of the Holocaust as an example – and says that he has lost his belief in life, it would be stupid to say that he is wrong, but as a friend I would, nevertheless, try to help him, without falsifying what he has gone through, to find some kind of joy, despite everything. If someone has gone through something really terrible and says that she still believes in life, it would be stupid to say that she is wrong, however difficult to understand I find her way of being to be.[37] In neither of these two cases do I relate as if to an intellectual mistake. But the difference between my two ways of relating shows an important asymmetry.

This asymmetry is often forgotten by philosophers. They try to make a show of being full of pathos by coming back, again and again, to what is terrible and by stressing meaninglessness. In some cases, this could have its importance, but often, I would say, it is false and dishonest: they try to look more affected than they are and even could be.[38] One should not forget that what torturers try to do is precisely to break someone's belief, in a wide sense of the word. So in a sense it is self-evident that this is possible to do, but then it is, to say the least, unclear if one should agree to what they do and claim that what they manage to show is the deepest truth about man and existence.[39] When it is important to question one form of satisfaction with life, this is, for example, for political reasons (when, say, criticizing the satisfaction of the rich one who shuts her eyes to how this wealth has come about). But such a questioning always occurs, or should always do so at least, against the background of a belief in the good, otherwise it would end in complete destructivity. (And it should not at all be denied that many, in theory liberating, movements end here when one is carried away, as it were, by desperation.) In other words, as far as I can see there is a belief in life, a belief in the good, or, as far as that goes, a love of a God of love, which nothing terrible is able to shake. This does not mean that I think that I, or someone else, would never lose the belief we possibly have, no matter what would happen; the point is simply that to the one who really *loses* something, this would be a *loss*, a loss of something which she still, in some sense, sees as important: "To say that the world is not worth anything, that this life is of no value and to give evil as the proof is absurd, for if these things are worthless what does evil take from us?"[40]

"But haven't you made things far too easy for yourself? You speak about some vague belief in life, but is it not belief in *God* we are discussing and are not the problems different in this case?" It is not completely clear how this difference should be understood – it is too easy to say that this belief in life is "vague", without taking the pains to really try to understand what it is about – but this is not what is important here. What is important is that the difficulties are of the same type in these cases, however similar or dissimilar they may be in other respects. The difficulty for the one who loves a God of love, when encountering suffering and evil, is not one of compatibility, as we have already seen, but one of her own difficulty of living this love. The difficulty is not a matter of some external obstacle – as if a wall, impossible to pass, suddenly stood in my way – but is my own difficulty of living the life which is mine. This difficulty is not unique to the one who loves a God of love, but affects me even if I do not do so. The objection, it seems to me, slides back to an understanding of belief as calculative, both as to content and act: here one could speak about intellectual mistakes, counter-evidence and external obstacles. The importance of this objection is then not what it says, but what it shows: that there is a deep-lying difficulty – a difficulty which is not primarily a philosophical one in the professional sense – of really taking religious belief, understood as love of a God of love, seriously. Consistently understanding religious belief non-calculatively seems to go against what I find self-evident.

If this book has shaken only a little of what I find self-evident, this is still much philosophically speaking.

Chapter 10

Arguing, Thinking

What have we arrived at? What does this book amount to? Have I tried to argue for one particular religious understanding, religious belief as love of a God of love? No, this is not at all the purpose of the book, nor do I believe that such an endeavor is even possible. What I have done is that I have *described* this religious understanding, so that we become clear about what it means. This is important both for the one who adopts it and for the one who repudiates it. In both cases it is central to become clear about *what* they adopt and repudiate respectively.

However, this is not as simple as that, even though it could serve as a first description of the aim of the book. As I tried to make clear in Chapter 4, it is not completely clear what it would mean to believe in this way, or not to do so. This could be said to be part of the description: loving a God of love is not something one definitely does or does not do. Furthermore, it is misleading to keep the description apart from one's own relation to that which the description is a description of. As is evident from Chapter 3, it is not the case that we first have the philosophical task of describing something and that when that is done a completely different task follows, to adopt some or other kind of "attitude" to that which has been described. The question about whether one believes in this way (that is, loves a God of love) or not is actually closely tied together with the question about how one describes this way of belief. It is clear from what I have said that it is hard, especially morally – but not necessarily religiously? – to deny the centrality of a concept such as love (as I pointed out at the end of Chapter 3). But argumentation would point in another direction: it would remove the personal side of the issue, and the belief (or the absence of belief) would become something one, on pain of being inconsistent, *has to* adopt or repudiate. The question is then not what *I* am ready to say (or not ready to say), for example religiously, but what *one* has to say. I will return to this.

The second aim of the book is to show how this understanding of religious belief transforms the discussions in the philosophy of religion.

Here one's own relation to the understanding is of less interest, as long as this understanding is a *possibility*. In that way it becomes evident how many more and different questions there are than those usually discussed, and that also the old ones could be approached in new ways.

A further aim, one I have not mentioned yet, has been to bring about a kind of freedom, a freedom in relation to the traditional, metaphysical language, not only in the sense that it is a way of talking which we do not have to remain bound to, but also in the sense that this way of talking *is* possible to use, in a more playful way perhaps, to the extent that it really connects with something. Take as an example what I said about transcendence and immanence in Chapter 2. Here we have a situation where this distinction really does connect to something – but in a very different way than in the metaphysical tradition: the concepts do not have a general relevance here but get their applicability in a specific situation, and furthermore they are not opposed but in many ways tied together (it is *in* life one experiences something transcendent). In that way one could say that it is the situation and the description which give content to the concepts, and not the other way around. The descriptions are placed side by side, one could say, are different ways of making the same point, not statements related deductively, as if we tried to "prove" anything, draw a conclusion, arrive at a thesis with a content determined in advance. As I said,[1] that the authority the Samaritan experiences is transcendent is not a hypothesis about its origin but a description of the character of this very experience. A critique of metaphysics should not be merely negative; it would be just as metaphysical to say that some concept must not be used as saying that it has to be used. What we must stay away from is every monist point of view, where everything should be reduced to some basic set of concepts, where one is striving to make use of as *few* concepts as possible. What makes religious belief as love of a God of love interesting is moreover how tied together those aspects are which in the metaphysical tradition have been separated: love is both how and what; what I believe in and how I believe are two sides of the same coin when it comes to love of a God of love, the way a belief is held (the act of belief) and the content of the belief are here intertwined. The transcendence I mentioned is certainly emotional, for example. Here it is neither possible to emphasize the one at the expense of the other, nor keep them strictly separated. The relevant objection would be that some description, and the concepts used, does not catch what the issue is about; but when it does, it could be phrased in different ways, of course, and one is free to express oneself in other, possibly more familiar, terms.

In this concluding chapter I will explain in more detail how this repudiation of argumentative philosophy is to be understood. Since the repudiation does not exclusively concern philosophy of *religion*, the examples will be of many kinds. This will be a way of shedding light on the discussions in this book from another angle.

I. *Arguing and thinking*

That many philosophers see their task as consisting of producing arguments bewilders me. Both what they say they do, and what they in fact do strikes me as strange, when someone, say, constructs a new argument for moral realism. What I will discuss here is "arguing". I will contrast arguing to something else, which one may be inclined to believe must be a form of arguing: thinking. Philosophy is about thinking. Philosophy is not about arguing. What follows is an attempt at clarifying what this means.

Someone might raise objections to my distinction between arguing and thinking, by saying that the word "argument" could be used and is used in many different ways, which would mean that my contrast is pointless. That the word could be used in many ways is no doubt true, and I do not want to forbid some use of it; if one wants to use this word when trying to characterize what philosophy is about, one is free to do so. But such an objection misunderstands what I want to do. The task is not one of conceptual analysis, determining the necessary and sufficient conditions for the use of some concept. That the concept "arguing" could be used in other ways than the one I describe here is no objection; the question is whether the contrast I want to make – between what I *call* arguing and what I *call* thinking – exists and is important.

Another background to this question is a specific picture of what philosophy is, common both among persons who do not do philosophy (or do not take themselves to be doing philosophy) and among philosophers: philosophy is a matter of arguing, of arguing for or against some answer to the philosophical question. And, to stress the *philosophical* (or "scientific") character of this argumentation, it is said to be a matter of logic. This is especially evident as to ideas about what moral philosophy is, when it is understood as a more rigorous way, as compared to how we usually answer them, of arguing for or against specific answers to moral questions.

Here in section I I have introduced the subject. In the next section (II) I discuss the idea, expressed in the last paragraph, of a purely logical way of answering a question. In section III I discuss another idea of how a question might be answered: as a matter of the purely empirical. These two ways – the logical and the empirical – are ideas about how questions should be answered generally; the question may be of a philosophical or of some other kind. Since I reject these two ideas, I must discuss how it is at all possible that there is something other than these two. This is done in the next section (IV), where I explain what I mean by "thinking". In section V the question about argumentation comes back; I try to show the unfruitfulness of argumentation by means of two philosophical examples. Section VI brings up the question about argumentation in morals, section VII in politics. Section VIII brings the chapter to an end.

II. *The purely logical*

The first question I would like to investigate is then this: is there a purely logical way of answering a question, a philosophical question, say? Should philosophy be described as *essentially* a logical activity? Let me begin by quoting Wittgenstein's *Philosophical Investigations*:

> Disputes do not break out (among mathematicians, say) over the question of whether or not a rule has been followed. People don't come to blows over it, for example. That belongs to the scaffolding from which our language operates (for example, yields descriptions). "So you are saying that human agreement decides what is true and what is false?" – What is true or false is what human beings *say*; and it is in their *language* that human beings agree. This is agreement not in opinions, but rather in form of life. It is not only agreement in definitions, but also (odd as it may sound) agreement in judgements that is required for communication by means of language. This seems to abolish logic, but does not do so.[2]

These paragraphs are very dense, and there is much to discuss in them. I will only seize upon one thing, however. What Wittgenstein wants to point out is that rules – for example, definitions – are not the foundational elements in language. What determines whether something which has been said is true or false is not a formal agreement with some rule, as if the rule were a mediating link between reality and what has been said. Mathematics and logic, which are often seen as spheres where the argumentation is particularly irresistible, are not about noticing how axioms by themselves result in new conclusions.

These points lead back to earlier paragraphs, where Wittgenstein discusses questions about rules and interpretation of rules. He writes:

> That there is a misunderstanding here is shown by the mere fact that in this chain of reasoning we place one interpretation behind another, as if each

one contented us at least for a moment, until we thought of yet another lying behind it. For what we thereby show is that there is a way of grasping a rule which is *not* an interpretation, but which, from case to case of application, is exhibited in what we call "following the rule" and "going against it" ... That's why "following a rule" is a practice. And to *think* one is following a rule is not to follow a rule.[3]

The point is not that the agreement, the form of life, is another kind of criterion; such an idea would only create the same problem once again. The point is that no criterion is able to give us what we want, that the search for such a foundational rule – or whatever is taken to have the same function – is illusory. As to conceptual connections, there is nothing more foundational than that this is what the concept *means*, that this is what this phenomenon *is*.

The same point is made by Peter Winch in *The Idea of a Social Science*.[4] Achilles and the Tortoise[5] are discussing three propositions, A, B and Z, where Z follows logically from A and B. The Tortoise says that he accepts A and B as true, and asks Achilles to show why he is forced, logically, to accept Z as true. Achilles says that if A and B are true, Z must be true, since it follows logically from A and B. "Okay," the Tortoise says, "but this rule I want you to write down; let us call it C (if A and B are true, Z must be true). Now show me that if I accept A and B and C as true, I am forced, logically, to accept Z as true." How the story goes on is not hard to see: the same problem comes up again, and we get a new rule, D, and so forth. Winch concludes the discussion by saying:

> The moral of this, if I may be boring enough to point it, is that the actual process of drawing an inference, which is after all the heart of logic, is something which cannot be represented as a logical formula; that, moreover, a sufficient justification for inferring a conclusion from a set of premises is to see that the conclusion does in fact follow. To insist on any further justification is not to be extra cautious; it is to display a misunderstanding of what inference is. Learning to infer is not just a matter of being taught about explicit logical relations between propositions; it is learning *to do* something.[6]

Winch's point may be underestimated – if one takes it to concern inference in logic exclusively – but in fact it concerns inference, argumentation, and so forth, on the whole. It is easy to believe that in logic, the conclusion follows by itself; that $p \land \neg p$ is a contradiction follows from the logical forms of use (which one has to learn, of course). The real work, where the matter is settled, is then not the work with the logical symbolism, but the formalization;

the central question is *if*, and *how*, a specific expression is possible to formalize. This question can only be answered by seizing upon what the expression means. One example[7] of this is that "It is raining and it isn't" may be a fully adequate characterization of the weather, but not since the word "raining" is used in two different senses; on the contrary, it is *precisely* the contradictory form of words which, in some situation, makes the description a good one. (Other examples – of another kind – are "I both want to and do not want to" or "I both love and hate her".)[8] The same thing – that it is the meaning of the expression which is central – goes for inference, argumentation, and so forth, on the whole: whether it is possible to draw some specific conclusion or not is dependent on the meaning of what one has said, or, expressed in other words, on the nature of the phenomenon one is discussing.[9]

III. *The purely empirical*

In this situation, when logic has turned out not to be some special, external tool we can make use of to make the argumentation more rigorous, there is another picture of what answering a question – a philosophical question, say – at bottom must be which easily makes itself felt. The idea is that we must find something to hold on to in our inquiries, something capable of guaranteeing its correctness, something which forces us to the right answer, something which stops our own whims from being decisive. This something is here taken to be the empirical. This is what I will discuss in this section.

Of course, it is possible to come to see that something one has said or wanted to say is incorrect, in some sense or other: if I made a prediction and what I predicted does not happen, I could be said to be corrected by the empirical. I do not see what I expected to see (and this is connected to the question about logical contradictions). The problem with the above idea is the specific role one wants to give to the empirical. By itself, nothing follows from a fact. In the case of the prediction where I say that it will rain tomorrow, my prediction is incorrect to the extent that what happens tomorrow cannot be described as "raining". Only against the background of there being a concept such as "rain" is it meaningful to describe what happens as showing that my prediction was wrong. In other words: if I do not see that my prediction was wrong, this shows that I do not understand what "rain" means, which means that I do not understand what the prediction I made means. And this no fact can alter.

One thing I just said is somewhat misleading, however. If one says that by itself, nothing follows from a fact, it is unclear what is meant by "fact". If one believes that what is needed is a fact plus an interpretation it is unclear how the fact and the interpretation are connected, if the fact "in itself" is without meaning. Here the problem Wittgenstein is discussing in §§ 201–02 returns. Instead, the fact is already meaningful to begin with, without any interpretation. The point is rather that we are not always clear about how we should describe something, that we are not always clear about what a description we have given means. Then one must think the issue over, and this thinking is not a matter of more, or more careful, logical inferences or of more empirical findings. To talk with someone about the issue is, among other things, to try to call the other's (or one's own) attention to circumstances that, for one reason or other, are easily overlooked. In other words, overlooking something is not only, or primarily, a matter of directing one's gaze in the wrong direction; there is no definitive amount of how much it is possible to say about some situation.

The idea that knowledge is always possible to analyze exclusively in terms of logic and the empirical has been expressed most radically in terms of logical construction from sense-data.[10] This is not the place for an extensive discussion of this idea. I would only like to mention one thing, and this is hardly the decisive difficulty, but of interest in the context of my discussion: how do the logical constructions connect to sense-data? A definition is only applicable if what it is applied to already has a description. From where comes the description? Not from the logical constructions. From the sense-data themselves? But only if I have learnt a word like "red" or a phrase like "is in this and that point in a system of coordinates" am I able to use them; sense-data do not by themselves give rise to such expressions. In other words, the idea that it is always possible to analyze knowledge into two parts, into contributions from perception (the source of the "purely empirical") and logic, is in fact unintelligible. These cannot teach us anything, cannot make us see that something is this or that.[11]

IV. *Thinking*

"But isn't this very obscure? How is it possible to be forced by something other than logic and the empirical? What would this third term be?"

It is tempting to dismiss these questions by saying that it is that line of "thought" which makes this appear obscure that is obscure. But let us go a little deeper than that. This is the topic for section IV, and I will here try to say something more about what I mean by "thinking".

The way of understanding the empirical we have run into above is in one sense not at all strange; or, it is not at all strange to have this strange idea. When things go their normal course, when one day is like the other, then the way of settling an issue is by looking and seeing. (There is a moral aspect to this, which I will come back to in section VI.) In this situation, it seems as if the only possible difficulty – apart from technical difficulties, that I do not have the technical resources to settle some issue – is the difficulty of mastering some vocabulary, that I do not know the definitions of some terms, that if only all the definitions were made explicit, what would be needed is simply looking and seeing. The problem with this idea is its way of (mis)understanding language. An object of comparison to illustrate the confusion could be my (lack of) knowledge of Italian. My knowledge of Italian consists exclusively of my ability to relate some Italian words and phrases to words and phrases in other languages. And my lack of knowledge consists in my being unable to do this with respect to many other words and phrases. That is, there are lots of things I am unable to say in *Italian*, although I am able to say it, and when someone speaks to me in Italian I mostly do not understand what she is saying, although what she says is something I, so to speak, ought to understand. For this reason, it would be very misleading to describe my (defective) linguistic capacity by comparing it to the (defective) linguistic capacity of an Italian child, as if I was on the same level as a child of this or that age. My defective capacity consists in me not mastering one system of expressions; the child does not lack the resources to say something definite. Now it is clear why the way of settling an issue is not always to look and see. If one asks a question such as "Is the mind and the brain the same thing?" – and I will return to this question in a moment – I must know what the question is about to be able to answer it, I must know what "mind" is. This is not a question about the *English* word "mind": it is possible to ask more or less similar questions in other languages too. The difficulty is that my ability to use the word "mind" is not the knowledge of a definition. Therefore, it is not at all strange that a word – the word "mind", say – which I have no trouble using, may be one I run into all kinds of philosophical confusions about as soon as I try to give an account of it. This lack of clarity is decisive when a question like "Is the mind and the brain the same thing?" is asked.

In this situation, one may be attracted by the activity of empirical science, seen as a sphere where this difficulty does not exist (or does not seem to exist), which for that reason constitutes the paradigm for sound thinking, characterized by one kind of linguistic transparency: one tries to define the scientific concepts explicitly and unambiguously. However, it is important to stress the word "one" in "one kind of linguistic transparency". To be sure, there is no such thing as *absolute* explicitness and *absolute* unambiguity – what one tries to do is simply avoid problems which have arisen or seem to be able to arise, problems which must be seen as *problems* – and however clear one makes the concepts one uses, it is not possible to make the phenomenon one tries to explain by means of these concepts neither more nor less clear, neither more nor less uniform, than it in fact is. Every attempt at achieving *that* kind of clarity only results in the phenomenon one tries to understand becoming distorted; that is, one does the opposite of explaining it. Therefore, what is needed is something other than "seeing and looking": thinking. One example of a situation where it is not enough, if one wants to answer the question, to do one empirical investigation after the other, is the question mentioned above: "Is the mind and the brain the same thing?" One more empirical investigation makes no difference: to the one who has seen some difficulty in this way of posing the question they are irrelevant, since the difficulty is precisely what character these investigations in fact have. What one may succeed in doing is show some correlation between some phenomena, what one may succeed in doing is create methods for causing some phenomena. But how these phenomena should be described and what relations they have to what we call "mind" do not become any clearer by simply doing another empirical investigation. And it is of no use trying to define the concept "mind" more precisely, since what we then would be investigating is not the phenomenon as it exists. Nor is employing logic as some sort of external instrument of any use, since what we are unclear about is the logic of the concept "mind". What is needed is thinking.

That answering a question correctly means to "say it as it is" means that I should not approach the phenomenon with some ready-made schema for thought, but, so to speak, extract the concepts from the things themselves, let them speak. But the thing only speaks if I approach it with a question; the point is simply that I should not decide beforehand what I will, and will not, accept as an answer, and that I should be open to the possibility that my question is a bad question. The answer to the question is never more exact than the phenomenon itself; to approach it with an ideal of exactness is not to be rigorous, but to distort the phenomenon one says that one wants to investigate: this is what an *ideal* means. And phenomenon and concept are here, in a sense, inseparable: the phenomenon of x is not something one approaches independent of the concept of x. So a question arises about what exactness means in this context, since a concept is not exact as such but exact relative to, say, some practice or other. In other words, there is no such thing as an "absolutely" exact concept. What kind of exactness is relevant is simply the kind which fits the phenomenon. The most difficult difficulty is not the evident subjectivism, but that kind of subjectivism which hides behind an ideal of exactness; a mathematical-technical schema of thought may seem to be the paradigm of objectivity, but precisely in being a schema it is a demand, made upon the phenomena, which one has taken a fancy to, that is, a subjectivism.

"But how could there be such a thing as 'thinking'? What prevents one from saying anything here? As to the empirical there is something which limits me – if I make a prediction and what I predicted does not happen I am wrong – but what is it that limits me here?" This is only an apparent contrast. What is the connection between what has happened and what I have predicted? Even though it is natural to say that this is a connection I simply *see*, this is not in contrast to saying that it is a connection I think. The question which may be asked is how what I see should be described, or, differently put, saying that what I see means that my prediction was wrong *is* to describe it. So if there were no limitations for thinking, nothing would be limited.[12] However, the limitations for thinking are not possible to put in a formula. The question about what is connected to what and the question about what does not agree with what – examples of questions one has to think about – are questions which arise when something is unclear to me. Referring to a formula, a rule, or the like, is then pointless, since it is that kind of connection my question is about, the connection between what one could call a "formula" and some phenomenon. In other words, when a philosophical problem has struck me, referring to what *one* means by some concept is of no use, since I must see what *I* could mean by it in order for the question of meaning to have any bearing on the problem I have.[13]

V. *The unfruitfulness of argumentation*

Perhaps it might seem as if I have digressed from the theme I stated in the beginning: argumentation and its relation to what I have called thinking. Now is the time to return to it. In this section I will make use, as examples, of two philosophical discussions, in order to show the unfruitfulness of argumentation. This does not mean that argumentation is always bad, only that when it is good, this depends on the fact that something which is not a matter of argumentation plays a decisive role in the argumentation. (I will explain what this means later on.) Notice that the unfruitfulness of argumentation is nearly connected to what I said in previous sections (II–IV):

if there were such a thing as a purely logical way of answering a question, argumentation could be something fruitful. Differently put, the question in this section is about what makes an argumentation a good one: if it is the case that thinking, as I have described it in section IV, has an essential role here, should this thinking be understood as a form of argumentation? If not, good argumentation is based on something of another nature.

Philosophy is often described as "critical thinking", and, in general, critical thinking is taken to be important. This may be so, but if one reads books about critical thinking, one typically finds different methods described: logic, argumentation theory, and the like.[14] The point here is not that such methods are of *no* use at all. But if one tries to understand what critical thinking is, or what philosophy is, such an account is very insufficient. Let me give two examples. The first one is about the limited point of logical objections. Often they have no more than a rhetorical function: "Look at that idiot, he cannot think correctly!"[15] In that way, someone can try to catch the opponent in a political debate being mistaken in order to dismiss everything she has said. The limited value of such an objection is (which does not mean that it is never of importance) that the objection is uninteresting, peripheral, and it fails to notice possibly more serious and central problems. When Carnap[16] criticizes Heidegger's text *Was ist Metaphysik?*[17] his criticism is that Heidegger's sentences are pseudo-sentences: meaningless, logically incorrect, sequences of words. However, it is clear that Heidegger formulates himself in the way he does not unknowing of the fact that his wording is paradoxical or in spite of the fact that it is, but precisely *because* it is paradoxical.[18] For that reason Carnap's objection is uninteresting; instead, the question one should ask oneself is: what is Heidegger trying to say? And if one asks this question, one will be able to discover more central problems: is anxiety really fundamental to scientific research, as Heidegger claims it is?[19] Of course, research can be done for many and mixed motives – just like every other human activity – but is it possible to understand the desire to find out how it is, love of truth as a motive power, if it were isolated from a love of the reality one investigates? Consider what Simone Weil writes: "To desire truth is to desire direct contact with a piece of reality. To desire contact with a piece of reality is to love ... We desire to know the truth about what we love."[20] (Heidegger's line of thought seems to be that of a common and shady kind: anxiety is something negative, what is negative is serious, what is serious is true.)[21] I will not enter into a discussion of these questions, so the question whether this possible criticism of Heidegger is more than possible is left open; the point is simply that if one approaches the text in the way Carnap does, these problems will not become visible.

(There is a weaker form of Carnap's objection, when someone claims that some philosopher has produced too *few* arguments for her thesis. In some situations, this objection is to the point, but I would express it in another way. One such case is when there is a lack of clarity as to the exact nature of the difference between what I say and what others have said with regard to some question: then there still remains descriptive work to be done. In that case, my point is not clear, and something is missing, but what is missing is not an argument. In other cases, however, the objection is often pointless, since it is formulated against the background of the idea that philosophy is about theoretical generalizations. If one is unconvinced as to one such theoretical generalization and asks for more arguments for the theory, one fails to notice what is essential. The task is simply to point out the cases which get lost in the process of generalization, and in that case no additional argument can save the theoretical generalization. My description of philosophy – as a matter of thinking – could also be formulated in this way: philosophy is a matter of observation, of attentiveness, not of generalization. Either one has actually observed something of importance, or one has not.)

My second example is about the limited usefulness of arguments for a specific opinion. When one is arguing, the aim is to convince others: an unconvincing argument is by definition a bad argument. Clarifying something philosophically and arguing are different in that sense: if something has really become clear for me it does not matter whether it has become clear for others. Since the aim of argumentation is to convince others, that the argumentation is correct is not an end in itself. That this is no end in itself does not mean that the one who argues must be tactical or deceitful. Rather, the point is that the one who argues has some opinion she tries to get others to embrace, but why she has this opinion, from where it comes, is a question which is not asked in the argumentation, which means that argumentation is a far cry from rethinking the issue. This does not mean that someone who tries to argue – tries to convince – is unable to come to see that the opinion she tries to argue for is wrong. The point is simply that this seeing cannot be understood in terms of argumentation. The limit of argument is the limit of imagination; if one is skilled, one can go on arguing indefinitely. "But is it not obvious that going on arguing may be absurd?!" Yes, but the argumentation does not tell one when going on arguing would be absurd: this is my point.

To illustrate this, let us look at Socrates' discussion with Polus and Callicles in *Gorgias*. As is well known, Socrates there says that doing what is unjust is worse than suffering what is unjust.[22] Socrates tries to argue for this, with "arguments of iron and adamant",[23] as he himself says, but his opponents are not particularly impressed: Polus finds himself forced to agree with what Socrates says even though he is far from convinced,[24] and Callicles says that what Socrates is doing is trying to ensnare his opponents by means of arguments.[25] If one looks closer at what Socrates says one sees that it consists of two things, apart from argumentation: partly an attempt at clarifying what it means to say that doing what is unjust is worse than suffering what is unjust, by making the connections between some concepts clear, among other things punishment, justice, goodness;[26] partly an attempt at showing that Callicles' thesis about the right of the superior one[27] is not seriously meant since Callicles expresses himself in a quasi-moral way.[28] But it is obvious that Socrates cannot "prove", in a general way, that doing what is unjust is worse than suffering what is unjust. If someone did not care at all about others, it would be unintelligible to her how doing what is unjust could be something bad, comparable to suffering what is unjust or hurting oneself.[29] On the other hand, what would it mean to try to refute – try to find a "counter-argument" against – Socrates' point of view? Obviously, what he says is a very important insight as to the nature of morality, the constitutive role of personal responsibility. This does not mean that there is not much to be said concerning this issue – his way of phrasing the idea should perhaps not be accepted, say – but this is not a matter of argumentation.

VI. *Argumentation in morals*

As you can see, I have now passed on to a question about morality, as I promised (section IV). I said that there is a moral aspect to the fact that the way of settling an issue, when things go their normal course, is by looking and seeing, without thinking. It is this aspect, and the issue of moral argumentation, that I will discuss in this section.

That the way of settling an issue when things go their normal course is by looking and seeing, without thinking, is not only connected to what I mentioned there – how language is to be understood – but is also a result of a thoughtlessness which is morally convenient, in one sense wanted. In this normal, morally thoughtless, course, morality is a way of helping me decide on questions "everybody" finds hard. When I see things in this way, I forget, however, or shut my eyes to, the fact that how I understand the problem, and that I see it as a problem at all, is not self-evident, is not necessarily morally innocent: it is not the case that the fact that I see something as a problem has nothing to do with me, as I try to convince myself when I say that "everybody" find this situation hard. In addition, I shut my eyes to the fact that I cannot hand over my problem to "morality" for it to solve it for me and free me from all responsibility, as if what I subsequently do has nothing to do with me. (In that sense, "morality" really does help me with what I want – to get rid of the problem – but does not help me *morally*.) In this normal course, I presuppose that my life, generally speaking, is good, that the problems are simply hitches: this picture should not be questioned. Consequently, there is a fundamental dislike of seeing what things mean here, of thinking, and it is then not at all strange that language is being automated. In that respect, philosophical thought is not at all generally "helpful" but could just as well, to say the least, be seen as a threat.

To moral philosophy, this observation is of special importance, of course – but also to that kind of moral reflection which does not see itself as philosophical – particularly when it understands itself as an argumentative activity. For if moral philosophy is a matter of arguing for or against different opinions or theses, it will never provide us with moral insights. The argumentative technique is never better than those ideas one carries with one into the technique; what it does is, at the most, give these a more systematic form (against the background of *one* presupposed idea about what systematic form means). If moral philosophy should be about something essentially moral, about the good, it must be directed by something else, something not given by the argumentation. (For one could ask this question, "How could a contradiction be *evil?*" And since an argumentative conclusion by some considered a reductio ad absurdum-argument against a specific way of thinking in moral philosophy, is by others considered an insight derived from this way of thinking, the decisive question in such a situation is not about whether the argumentation is correct or not, but about something else.)[30] Thinking is here – in contrast to arguing – connected to rebuking oneself, examining oneself, trying to thwart one's own endeavor to keep things from sight.

This becomes especially evident in a case of moral disagreement. One person may be very skilled in arguing, whereas the other one does not possess such a skill at all. It may be obvious to the latter that she has lost the argumentation, the debate. And despite this, it may be her who is trying to defend the good. (One example of this is discussions about feminism. My experience is that chauvinists are often very skilled debaters, and seen from a purely technical point of view, they often win the debates; but that does not "prove" anything as to the substantial issue.) This does not mean that the one who tries to defend the good has landed up on the right side simply by accident, as if it were a coincidence that her position agrees with the one of the perfect, but as yet non-existing, argumentation, as if she were like the broken watch which tells the right time twice in twenty-four hours. No, we compare the argumentation with what she sees, not the other way round.

(As you can see, this implies a critique of applied ethics. This discipline wants to justify our decisions, thereby making them more likable; it is basically an aesthetic activity, I would say. If it really were about morality, about thinking, it would not accept the problems as they are presented to it or the framework within which the specific problem is formed. It would essentially be a critical activity. Discussing a problem in medical ethics – about when some treatment should be terminated, say – would then not be about laying down criteria for when something should be done or not done, but would involve questions about what makes one understand this problem in this way, questions the asking of which means not shutting one's eyes to one's own responsibility for the fact that the problem has originated: this includes political questions about the place of health care in society, its economical conditions, and so forth. To be sure, it is not possible to put everything right on your own. It is possible that one is really practically incapable of doing something about these larger questions. But in such a situation, one must remember two things. First, it is very convenient, (im)morally speaking, to underestimate one's possibilities, so a critical question should be put concerning one's own feeling of hopelessness. Second, it is of utmost importance to be clear about the tragic character of this situation – and clarifying this is a philosophical task – so that one does not administrate the situation as straightforwardly given. This clarifying task of philosophy is then a matter of counteracting the tendency of making a virtue of necessity. Questions of this kind – about what makes one understand the problem in this way, about one's own responsibility for the fact that the problem has originated – will certainly be dismissed by some as irrelevant. However, one should notice that if one wants to corrupt people, one way would be to stick to what is (held to be) relevant, to what is customary to bring up in the discussion, and never remind anyone of something other than this;[31] this does not mean that the kind of moral philosophy that sticks to what is "relevant" is by necessity corrupting, since it may perfectly agree with that moral outlook which is already dominating in society.)[32]

As I have stressed above, the philosophical problem is mine. For that reason, referring to what *one* means by some concept is not relevant as to the philosophical work of conceptual clarification, since I must see what *I* could mean by the concept in order for the question of meaning to have any bearing on the problem I have. Now we have seen how the philosophical problem is essentially mine in another sense too: thinking is here connected to self-examination. What I could mean by some concept is an existential question:

what could I, honestly, mean by this concept? When arguing, this aspect vanishes. When I try to present my actions as the outcome of a chain of arguments, I am in a sense not myself: that it is I who act is here almost a coincidence, is simply a consequence of the fact that the properties of the person mentioned in the argumentative conclusion agree with mine. And it is precisely for that reason that prevarications have an argumentative structure.

That it is a problem I have means that I cannot make it disappear by means of a decision. In the case of moral problems this is especially evident: when I examine myself I face a responsibility I have no power over. That the problems are mine means that it is I who turn toward others, as one "I" to other "Is". Writing philosophy is to turn toward others, and what I try to do is point out things that you, perhaps, have not noticed and thought about. However, this is not to (try to) convince. It is precisely this idea – that the word "convince" covers everything that has to do with bringing someone else to an insight – I turn against.

VII. *Argumentation in politics*

Even though morality, as I said, is basically not about argumentation, one might be inclined to say that politics must be about argumentation, since it is about convincing others, not about turning toward another person as another "I", but rather about groups.[33] This question I will discuss in this section.

Thus, politics is taken to be an essentially argumentative activity. However, even if it were the case that no moral questions were discussed in politics – if there were a prevalent consensus about how society should be, what we want, and so forth – politics would still not be an essentially argumentative activity, since there would still exist a question about whether what we have achieved is really what we wanted to achieve, and this is a question which concerns thinking, not arguing, as I said in section III. However, it is true that the argumentative side of politics would get a stronger emphasis in such a situation, partly as the way of treating the questions which arise, partly as the form the struggle for positions then takes. But if this is one's *general* picture of politics, one forgets that there is such a thing as (what in a Marxist tradition[34] is called) antagonistic conditions, where prevalent relations of power are questioned, where new ways of thinking about society come forth, where real contradictions are revealed. In the light of such antagonistic conditions, the argumentative debate is a pseudo-struggle, a struggle in which the questions discussed – despite, or precisely because of, the fact that the different sides in this struggle are on the same side as to the decisive questions of power – become charged in a way that hides their relatively marginal role. (To be sure, some contradictions may appear within this consensus, but here they are not more serious than that they can be solved by means of negotiations and compromise.) An antagonistic condition, a real contradiction, has no argumentative solution, however, and it is this which Engels is talking about when he writes:

> Whoever declares that the capitalist mode of production, the "iron laws" of the present bourgeois society, are inviolable and yet wants to abolish its displeasing but necessary consequences, has no choice but to deliver moral sermons to the capitalists, moral sermons whose moving effect immediately once more evaporates by the private interest and if necessary by the competition.[35]

To be sure, Engels is here talking about "moral sermons", but his point is not dependent on this: we could read "argumentation" instead.[36] However, morality is not a matter of argumentation, as we have seen.[37] That an antagonistic condition does not have an argumentative solution means that the solution is either moral – a matter of thinking, insight, self-examination – or a struggle for power: political power grows out of the barrel of a gun, as Mao writes.[38] By mentioning this – "barrel of a gun" – and not something else, Mao romanticizes violence, but there are other possibilities. A struggle for power can take many forms, not all of which are violent: strike, occupation and sabotage are some. Furthermore, the two questions – the moral one and the one about power – are not symmetrical. When I, in practice – as opposed to what I say, how I present myself to others and to myself – dismiss the moral question, I offer but one solution to the problem to the other party: a struggle for power. But when the other party dismisses the moral solution, both of them still stand open for me. In that respect, politics could be the way of thinking together, of discussing the life we live together, even though it often is not.

VIII. *Conclusion*

By way of conclusion, I would like to point out that what I have said here entails a repudiation of the question of the usefulness of thinking, of the question of the usefulness of philosophy. If one tries to achieve something, thoughtfulness may be seen as a threat, as I have said. In such a situation, thoughtfulness may be an obstacle – if questions are asked about what that which one tries to achieve means, about what the methods one resorts to mean – to the effectiveness of these methods. (To be sure, this does not mean that intelligence, of some form, is not needed for making these plans and putting them into practice.) But even in that case, thinking cannot be completely shut out, since the question about the relation between what one wanted to achieve and the result one has achieved is not a question about methods. Even in this situation, a thoughtfulness which is not of use for anything – is not a means of any kind – would be needed; that there are questions one wants to shut out, questions thoughtfulness may arouse, is another matter. In that sense, philosophy is neutral – even though this concept is often used misleadingly – since it is not the means for achieving something specific. But that does not mean that it is not important: questions about what things mean are at the bottom of questions about means, as I have just said, and in that respect of a qualitatively different, and greater, kind of importance than them. To sum this chapter up in a short phrase: argumentation presupposes meaning, so asking a question about meaning, and trying to answer it, is not a matter of argumentation; thinking, on the other hand, is a matter of trying to direct one's attention to meaning.

Earlier I said that the fact that one could use the word "argument" in other ways than the one in which I am using it here is no objection, but that the question concerns whether the distinction I want to make – between argumentation and something else – exists and is important. This means that what I have done here – provided I have really done what I think I have done, a question one has to think about – is not to have argued. What I have done is to have tried to point out something, tried to clarify this. And whether I have succeeded in doing this or not is not a question you can argue for or against; it is a question you have to think through. And the same thing goes for this book in its entirety.

NOTES

INTRODUCTION

1 G. E. M. Anscombe, *Faith in a Hard Ground: Essays on Religion, Philosophy and Ethics*, ed. Mary Geach and Luke Gormally (Exeter: Imprint Academic, 2008), p. 59.

2 And even when "love" is initially said to be central, the discussion often turns out strangely vague and abstract. Jean-Luc Marion, *God without Being: Hors-Texte*, trans. Thomas A. Carlson (Chicago: University of Chicago Press, 1991), is a good example of that tendency, but that does not mean that he does not make any good points at all (see, e.g., p. 47). See also Michel Henry, *I Am the Truth: Toward a Philosophy of Christianity*, trans. Susan Emanuel (Stanford: Stanford University Press, 2003), pp. 186–87. And although Grace Jantzen (in *Becoming Divine: Towards a Feminist Philosophy of Religion* (Bloomington: Indiana University Press, 1999)) often opens the chapters with highly suggestive quotations about love (see esp. p. 204), it is not a topic which is central to her discussion, and the little she does say is not at all helpful (see, e.g., pp. 152–53).
The same goes for Henri Bergson: love is connected to the central distinctions between open and closed societies, between static and dynamic religions, but it is not that side to them he develops. See *Les deux sources de la morale et de la religion* (Paris: Librairie Félix Alcan, 1932).

CHAPTER 1

1 "Negativism", as I use the term, is related to, but not identical to, what Frederik Stjernfelt calls "negative edification" in his "Overskridelsens vulgærmetafysik: Den negative æstetiks erstatningskriterier", in *Kritik af den negative opbyggelighed: 7 essays af Frederik Stjernfelt og Søren Ulrik Thomsen*, 2nd ed. (Copenhagen: Vindrose, 2008), pp. 9–31.

2 R. M. Hare, *Freedom and Reason* (Oxford: Oxford University Press, 1963).

3 Ibid., p. 113.

4 Ibid., p. 105.

5 Ibid., p. 114.

6 Ibid., p. 167. Or this one (ibid., p. 169): "Most of us, even if we had an ideal of a society without Jews, would let this ideal be overridden by the normal moral principles which forbid such measures as the Nazis took to realize their ideal."

7 Hare, *Freedom and Reason*, p. 155.

8 Ibid., pp. 104–05, 178–79.

9 Ibid., p. 177.

10 See ibid., pp. 176–77.

11 But whether it in his case is so meant or not is not clear. In a strange way, his exclusive focus on the fanaticism of Nazism becomes almost a defense of that which according to Hare is possible to isolate from its first side: the ideal of Nazism, its content, what it means.

12 Cf. G. W. F. Hegel, *Phänomenologie des Geistes*, Werke, ed. Eva Moldenhauer and Karl Markus Michel, vol. 3 (Frankfurt am Main: Suhrkamp, 1986), pp. 431–41. Hegel's point is, generally speaking, that a merely negative freedom will always suppress every attempt at making use of this freedom, since it sees every such positive use as a threat against freedom. It is a tolerance which tolerates nothing but tolerance itself. Cf. also Hegel, *Grundlinien der Philosophie des Rechts; oder, Naturrecht und Staatswissenschaft im Grundrisse*, Werke, ed. Eva Moldenhauer and Karl Markus Michel, vol. 7 (Frankfurt am Main: Suhrkamp, 1986), pp. 50–52 (§ 5).

13 John Rawls, *A Theory of Justice* (Oxford: Oxford University Press, 1972), p. 12, 137.

14 Ibid., p. 11, 13, 118, 142.

15 Ibid., p. 142–44.

16 Ibid., p. 14, 119.

17 See, e.g., ch. 4.

18 As to this section, cf. Max Horkheimer, *Eclipse of Reason* (New York: Oxford University Press, 1947), ch. 1.

19 See, e.g., John D. Caputo, *On Religion* (London: Routledge, 2001), p. 22, 31, 34, 93.

20 Jean-François Lyotard, *The Postmodern Condition: A Report on Knowledge*, trans. Geoff Bennington and Brian Massumi (Minneapolis: University of Minnesota Press, 1984), p. 82.

21 Richard Rorty, *Philosophy as Cultural Politics: Philosophical Papers, Volume 4* (Cambridge: Cambridge University Press, 2007), 34. In another place, he writes (*Objectivity, Relativism, and Truth: Philosophical Papers, Volume 1* (Cambridge: Cambridge University Press, 1991), p. 175):

> Citizens of a Jeffersonian democracy can be as religious or irreligious as they please as long as they are not "fanatical." That is, they must abandon or modify opinions on matters of ultimate importance ... if these opinions entail public actions that cannot be justified to most of their fellow citizens.

Thus, standing up against the crowd, trying to prevent its violence against a single human being, is fanaticism. This is a typical example of what I talk about below: what Rorty is saying depends on him thinking only of *some* cases, being oblivious of other cases.

22 Thomas Hobbes, *Leviathan*, ed. C. B. Macpherson (London: Penguin Books, 1968), ch. 43, is a good example of how a philosopher, in order to maintain the political status quo, emphasizes weak (in contrast to strong) belief, and inner (in contrast to outer, active) belief.

23 One example of such a rare case is the ordinary, orderly German who did what was expected of him during the Nazi era. Is the question about the German guilt, apart from everything else the question is about, also an expression of the trauma inherent in the realization that decency is not the way to the good (or away from evil)? If so, by emphasizing the specific *German* character of the guilt, one tries to hide

from oneself the fact that it is possible that one would have done the same thing, or, if that is not possible, that this impossibility has nothing to do with nationality.

24 Caputo, *On Religion*, p. 108; see also p. 100. Gianni Vattimo is another example of someone who argues in this way. See *Beyond Interpretation: The Meaning of Hermeneutics for Philosophy*, trans. David Webb (Stanford: Stanford University Press, 1997), Chs 3–4; *Belief*, trans. Luca D'Isanto and David Webb (Cambridge: Polity Press, 1999).

25 For the line of thought in this paragraph, cf. John T. Edelman, *An Audience for Moral Philosophy?* (Basingstoke: Macmillan, 1990), p. 111.

26 Caputo, *On Religion*, p. 125.

27 Ibid., p. 34; see also p. 31.

28 See ibid., esp. ch. 4.

CHAPTER 2

1 John Macquarrie, *Principles of Christian Theology*, 2nd ed. (New York: Charles Scribner's Sons, 1977), pp. 4–18.

2 I will come back to this at the end of this chapter, and, especially, in ch. 10 (there is a tension in the concept of reason, between reason as argumentation and reason as thinking).

3 Hobbes, *Leviathan*, p. 397.

4 This question will be discussed in ch. 4.

5 Here a problem arises, about in what sense such a question could be asked honestly. I will discuss it extensively in ch. 4.

6 This latter question should here not be understood as a question about information, of course. It should be understood as a question about whether the originator of this something is the authoritative one, to the extent we find the authoritative to be a person – an authoritative *one* – not a principle.

7 That the answer to the second of the three questions is no is obvious also from the fact that what we are here discussing is theology, not religion. And religion is more than theology. This is important to remember, not the least since religion is a matter of doing and feeling and not exclusively of thinking, as theology. This means that the concept of "rightness" is not the same; compare Kant's Wogulite who lays the paw of a bear skin over his head with Kierkegaard's idol worshipper! (Immanuel Kant, *Die Religion innerhalb der Grenzen der bloßen Vernunft*, in *Schriften zur Ethik und Religionsphilosophie*, Werkausgabe, ed. Wilhelm Weischedel (Frankfurt am Main: Suhrkamp, 1968), 7–8:848; Søren Kierkegaard, *Afsluttende uvidenskabelig Efterskrift*, 2 vols, Samlede Værker 9–10 (Copenhagen: Gyldendal, 1963), 1:167–68.) However, as we will see (in sec. III–IV especially), the distinction between religion and theology, and between doing/feeling and thinking, is not at all as clear-cut as it may seem, to the further detriment of Kant.

8 See Hugo Strandberg, *Escaping My Responsibility: Investigations into the Nature of Morality* (Frankfurt am Main: Peter Lang, 2009), chs 1–3.

9 In the context of love, the expression "wronging someone" may be misleading: it may give the expression that the problem is that I break a rule (that I am *wronging* someone), not that I fall away from the good in respect of my relation to this person (that I am wronging *someone*.)

10 See Strandberg, *Escaping My Responsibility*, chs 1–2.

11 Luke 10:30-35. It should not really be necessary to point this out, but for the sake of clarity: The way I use this example is not different from how some other literary example could have been used; that this one happens to come from the Bible does not mean that one has to be a Christian to see the point.

12 John 4:9 (NRSV).

13 Cf. S. L. Frank, *The Unknowable: An Ontological Introduction to the Philosophy of Religion*, trans. Boris Jakim (Athens: Ohio University Press, 1983), pp. 128–29, pp. 232–33.

14 Walter Benjamin's concept of divine violence should, I believe, be understood along these "nonhumanist" lines (*Zur Kritik der Gewalt*, in vol. 2, bk. 1, of *Gesammelte Schriften*, ed. Rolf Tiedemann and Hermann Schweppenhäuser (Frankfurt am Main: Suhrkamp, 1977), pp. 179–203). It is also implicitly present in his theses on the philosophy of history, esp. theses 7, 8 and 17 (*Über den Begriff der Geschichte*, in vol. 1, bk. 2, of *Gesammelte Schriften*, ed. Rolf Tiedemann and Hermann Schweppenhäuser (Frankfurt am Main: Suhrkamp, 1974)). Moreover, cf. Slavoj Žižek, *The Fragile Absolute; or, Why Is the Christian Legacy Worth Fighting For?* (London: Verso, 2000), p. 121, 125.

15 Cf. Emmanuel Levinas, *Otherwise Than Being; or, Beyond Essence*, trans. Alphonso Lingis (Pittsburgh: Duquesne University Press, 1998), pp. 127–28:

> Modern antihumanism, which denies the primacy that the human person, free and for itself, would have for the signification of being, is true over and beyond the reasons it gives itself. It clears the place for subjectivity positing itself in abnegation, in sacrifice, in a substitution which precedes the will. [...] Humanism has to be denounced only because it is not sufficiently human.

Cf. also Emmanuel Levinas, *God, Death, and Time*, trans. Bettina Bergo (Stanford: Stanford University Press, 2000), p. 182.

16 Ch. 4 is relevant here.

17 Simone Weil, *Attente de Dieu* (Paris: La Colombe, 1950), pp. 145–61.

18 Gotthold Ephraim Lessing, *Die Erziehung des Menschengeschlechts*, in *Die Erziehung des Menschengeschlechts, und andere Schriften* (Stuttgart: Reclam, 1965), p. 8.

19 Gotthold Ephraim Lessing, *Über den Beweis des Geistes und der Kraft*, in *Die Erziehung des Menschengeschlechts, und andere Schriften* (Stuttgart: Reclam, 1965), p. 34 (my translation).

20 As Lessing seems to imply: Lessing, *Die Erziehung des Menschengeschlechts*, p. 24.

21 Of course, there are many ways in which we talk about knowledge, as being a matter of skill is just one. So one could say that an existential insight is a matter of knowledge; the point is simply that one should pay attention to what knowledge might mean in this context.

22 See, e.g., Lessing, *Die Erziehung des Menschengeschlechts*, p. 24.

23 Cf. Ludwig Feuerbach, *Das Wesen des Christentums* (Stuttgart: Reclam, 1969), p.74.

24 Johann Gottlieb Fichte, *Versuch einer Kritik aller Offenbarung*, in vol. 5 of *Fichtes Werke*, ed. Immanuel Hermann Fichte (Berlin: Walter de Gruyter, 1971), pp. 65–66, pp. 117–22.

25 Ibid., pp. 52–53, pp. 117–22.

26 Ibid., p. 80, pp. 117–22.

27 Ibid., pp. 54–56, esp. 88, 94, 106, 123, 125–26, 157.

28 Ibid., § 8.

29 In *Die Bestimmung des Menschen*, in vol. 2 of *Fichtes Werke*, ed. Immanuel Hermann Fichte (Berlin: Walter de Gruyter, 1971), pp. 255–60, however, Fichte gives an important role to conscience, and ends up with something which is partly, but only partly, close to the understanding of revelation I have been trying to express here.

30 Cf. Hegel, *Phänomenologie des Geistes*, pp. 76–80.

31 The fear of the idiosyncratic is based on the idea that the truth is in the many, in the group, in the multitude. But asking the question about authority is precisely to ask a question about one's relation to the many, so such an idea cannot be presupposed here.

32 Cf. Jacques Derrida, *Margins of Philosophy*, trans. Alan Bass (Chicago: University of Chicago Press, 1982), 329: "There is no metaphysical concept in and of itself. There is a work – metaphysical or not – on conceptual systems."

33 As J. L. Mackie does (*Ethics: Inventing Right and Wrong* (Harmondsworth: Penguin Books, 1977), pp. 38–39). However, Mackie's target of criticism, moral objectivism, is something I am critical of too (see Strandberg, *Escaping My Responsibility*, ch. 5).

34 The same goes for the saying that there is something good in that use of the concept of reason which was prevalent in the context of the Enlightenment, when one contrasted the reason of the individual as an authority to the alleged authority of the church. As we have seen here, the church has not an authority of its own, but, if it has any at all, a derived one, so nothing has to be contrasted to it. Rather, the question was about the church as a power of (physical or psychical) force – not as possibly authoritative – and what is the contrast to that is not reason but love. See chs 3–5.

35 For the answer to this objection, Cf. ch. 10.

CHAPTER 3

1 This question, about the attitude of calculation, we have already run into in ch. 2.

2 D. Z. Phillips, *Religion and Friendly Fire: Examining Assumptions in Contemporary Philosophy of Religion* (Aldershot: Ashgate, 2004).

3 Ibid., pp. 127–28.

4 D. Z. Phillips, "Ethics and Humanistic Ethics: A Reply to Dilman", in *Commonality and Particularity in Ethics*, ed. Lilli Alanen, Sara Heinämää, and Thomas Wallgren (Basingstoke: Macmillan, 1997). See esp. p. 164 and 171.

5 Making clear what role they play may show that they are *never* used for something entirely good, neither in a "heroic morality" nor somewhere else. I take it to be pretty obvious that this is the case with regard to "authenticity", but I will not pursue that question any further at this point; nothing I say here depends on this question.

6 I will come back to this later on in this chapter and explain it in more detail.

7 Phillips, *Religion and Friendly Fire*, ch. 8.

8 Søren Kierkegaard, *Purity of Heart, Is to Will One Thing: Spiritual Preparation for the Office of Confession*, trans. Douglas Steere (New York: Harper and Brothers, 1948).

9 See Phillips, "Ethics and Humanistic Ethics", p. 155, 160, 171–72, 175. In this paper, Phillips discusses and criticizes a paper by Ilham Dilman ("Psychoanalysis and Ethics: Some Reflections on the Self in Its Relationships to Good and Evil," in *Commonality and Particularity in Ethics*, ed. Lilli Alanen, Sara Heinämää, and Thomas Wallgren (Basingstoke: Macmillan, 1997)). I am not at all happy with everything Dilman says there, but the questions he discusses – about self-deception – are important, and, if I am right in what I say in this chapter, he has seen the philosophical importance of something which Phillips does not pay attention to.

10 Does not Kierkegaard belong to the same formalist camp? When contrasting an idol worshipper with a conformist, but dogmatically orthodox, believer (*Afsluttende uvidenskabelig Efterskrift*, 1:167–68), is not Kierkegaard contrasting the how and the what and saying that the how is all-important? This may be so, but this is not important for my purposes. However, if one wants to discuss this question, one should pay attention to the fact that Kierkegaard (p. 168) continues that discussion with a discussion about love, and not just as an "attitude"; the discussion in the rest of that chapter is also relevant. See also, and especially, Kierkegaard, *Afsluttende uvidenskabelig Efterskrift*, 2:272.

11 See Kierkegaard, *Purity of Heart*, above all pp. 73–78.

12 Phillips, *Religion and Friendly Fire*, p. 147 (italics added).

13 Søren Kierkegaard, *Opbyggelige Taler i forskjellig Aand*, Samlede Værker 11 (Copenhagen: Gyldendal, 1963), 29 (my translation, based on the translation in Kierkegaard, *Purity of Heart*, 45). See also Kierkegaard, *Afsluttende uvidenskabelig Efterskrift*, 1:249.

14 For example, Phillips fails to notice the irony in the quote from Tennessee Williams (Phillips, *Religion and Friendly Fire*, pp. 148–49). Big Daddy thinks that he has liberated himself from other people's judgment and that he is now able to act completely shamelessly, but he expresses this realization in terms which suggests the exact opposite, for example, when he says, and likes when his son says, that what he does is admirable.

15 See Luke 10:30-35. The parable has been much discussed in Wittgensteinian moral philosopy; Phillips's contribution to the discussion is D. Z. Phillips, *Interventions in Ethics* (Albany: State University of New York Press, 1992), ch. 17.

16 I use "the priest" as shorthand for "the priest and the Levite" throughout.

17 Hence, saying what I have been saying does not mean saying that one should always help the beaten man. Rather, the point is that even if a person is, for some reason, unable to do so, seeing the tragedy in this means seeing something which is not a matter of moral argumentation. Cf. ch. 10.

18 The criticism of Phillips's moral philosophy in this paragraph could be compared to other Wittgensteinian criticisms of Phillips in this regard. For "pity as normative for our descriptions of the forms of our indifference to suffering", as he phrases it, see Raimond Gaita, critical notice of *Interventions in Ethics*, by D. Z. Phillips, *Philosophical Investigations* 17 (1994): 616 (which is explicitly directed at Phillips); Gaita, *Good and Evil: An Absolute Conception*, 2nd ed. (London: Routledge, 2004), pp. 177–78; Gaita, *A Common Humanity: Thinking about Love and Truth and Justice* (London: Routledge, 2000), 267. For love as morally fundamental, see Rodger Beehler, *Moral Life* (Oxford: Basil Blackwell, 1978), ch. 1 and 6.

19 For a much lengthier discussion of much of what I have said in this section, see Strandberg, *Escaping My Responsibility*, esp. chs 1–2.

20 See Kierkegaard, *Purity of Heart*, above all pp. 73–78.

21 E.g., Phillips, *Religion and Friendly Fire*, ch. 6.

22 E.g., D. Z. Phillips, *Recovering Religious Concepts: Closing Epistemic Divides* (Basingstoke: Macmillan, 2000), pp. 3–6.

23 This is not just a rhetorical "if". As I said in ch. 2, using the concept of authority can be very misleading in this context. This qualification should be born in mind also in this chapter.

24 Kierkegaard did not pay attention to this when he talked about God as a middle term in love (*Works of Love: Some Christian Reflections in the Form of Discourses*, trans. Howard Hong and Edna Hong (New York: Harper and Row, 1962), pp. 112–13).

25 See Kierkegaard, *Purity of Heart*, above all pp. 73–78.

26 However, there is a question about to which extent that which is wanted is intelligible in isolation from the religious belief.

27 When considering these questions, what I say in sec. II above is relevant, of course.

28 The distinction between the calculating and the noncalculating religious belief shows that it is not possible to separate act and content: on the contrary, what it is to believe and what one believes are interdependent. What the distinction shows is that religious belief – when it is a matter of doing what one sees as the will of God – is sometimes a judgment (when it is a strategy for getting something else) and sometimes something to which the word "judgment" does not really fit (when it is not a part of a plan). This is a central difference. When we pay attention to it, we see that "strong belief" comes to very different things in these two cases. In the first case, one is convinced that this leads to that; in the other case "strong belief" comes to a commitment to that which is important. (Of course, this is still only a sketch of the difference; working it out is what the following is about. So this is not the place to start worrying about all the "cognitive" aspects of belief being possibly overlooked in the second case.)

29 See, e.g., D. Z. Phillips, *Philosophy's Cool Place* (Ithaca: Cornell University Press, 1999), p. 100; D. Z. Phillips, *Religion and the Hermeneutics of Contemplation* (Cambridge: Cambridge University Press, 2001), p. 325.

30 See, e.g., Phillips, *Philosophy's Cool Place*, p. 19; Phillips, *Religion and the Hermeneutics of Contemplation*, pp. 324–25.

31 Phillips, *Philosophy's Cool Place*, p. 19. However, see Phillips, *Religion and Friendly Fire*, p. 99.

32 Phillips, *Religion and the Hermeneutics of Contemplation*, p. 325.

33 Ibid., p. 324.

34 Ibid., p. 325.

35 See, e.g., ibid., p. 5.

36 Simone Weil, *Gravity and Grace*, trans. Emma Craufurd (London: ARK Paperbacks, 1987), p. 107.

37 For my part, even though I have criticized some parts of his philosophy in this chapter, this observation sheds some light upon the reception of Phillips's work in the analytical mainstream of the philosophy of religion.

38 Phillips, *Religion and the Hermeneutics of Contemplation*, p. 324.

39 Ludwig Wittgenstein, *Philosophische Untersuchungen; Philosophical Investigations,* 4th ed., trans. G. E. M. Anscombe, P. M. S. Hacker, and Joachim Schulte (Chichester: Wiley-Blackwell, 2009), § 129.

40 Wittgenstein, *Philosophical Investigations,* § 89. See also § 127; and Wittgenstein, *Philosophie; Philosophy,* trans. C. G. Luckhardt and M. A. E. Aue, in *Philosophical Occasions,* 1912–1951, ed. James Klagge and Alfred Nordmann (Indianapolis: Hackett, 1993), p. 161:

> What makes a subject difficult to understand – if it is significant, important – is not that some special instruction about abstruse things is necessary to understand it. Rather it is the contrast between the understanding of the subject and what most people *want* to see. Because of this the very things that are most obvious can become the most difficult to understand. What has to be overcome is not a difficulty of the intellect, but of the will.

41 Wittgenstein, *Philosophical Investigations,* p. 4e.

42 See Pl., *Phdr.* 229e–230a, 275abd; *La.* 188b; *Prt.* 329a, 347e–348a; *Grg.* 474ab; *Epist.* 341cde. The dialogue form in general is also an expression of this, I think. Even though it is not always hard to guess what Plato's own philosophical views were, it is significant that he does not present anything as his own view; instead, Plato gives us something, by placing it in the mouth of different characters, to think through on our own.

43 Phillips, *Philosophy's Cool Place,* p. 154.

Chapter 4

1 Most often, the atheist is content with criticizing some, but possibly common, forms of what she takes to be religious belief. (Hence, one could say, using a phrase of Iris Murdoch's (*Existentialists and Mystics: Writings on Philosophy and Literature,* ed. Peter Conradi (Harmondsworth: Penguin Books, 1997), 364), that this atheist is only discussing "mediocre" belief, does not mind paying attention to the inherent tensions in historically existing forms of religious belief, tensions that show a dependence on forms which are then in fact seen as superior.) How ever correct that criticism may be, the atheist must nonetheless – if she really wants to deny every *possible* form of religious belief, which is most often the way the atheist understands her atheism – try to find the *best* form of religious belief, in order to be able to repudiate it. But what its best form is, is, of course, an existential question.

2 This question will be touched upon in subsection III.b.

3 Cf. Martin Buber, *I and Thou,* trans. R. G. Smith (Edinburgh: T&T Clark, 1957), p. 107.

4 To be sure, concepts such as "afterlife" and "paradise" have many more sides to them then the ones I connect to here. I use them as a means of shedding light on the present topic; removing that one-sidedness would be a different task.

5 Pace Gareth Moore, *Believing in God: A Philosophical Essay* (Edinburgh: T&T Clark, 1988), 170 (despite the fact that what Moore says is in other respects close

to what I am saying – see, e.g., p. 198). Furthermore, cf. Jean-Louis Chrétien, "The Wounded Word: The Phenomenology of Prayer," trans. Jeffrey L. Kosky, in *Phenomenology and the "Theological Turn": The French Debate* (New York: Fordham University Press, 2000), pp. 156–58.

6 Cf. ch. 3.

7 Kierkegaard, *Opbyggelige Taler i forskjellig Aand*, 40–60 (*Purity of Heart*, pp. 60–86).

8 See Strandberg, *Escaping My Responsibility*, ch. 1.

9 However, there is something obviously strange about such a description, of the good as a result of social pressure. When someone protests against the society in which she lives – in the name of the good, pointing out the evil things which are made in the society in which she lives – in what sense is that a result of a social pressure? What she is protesting *against* is precisely the social pressure. And the social pressure against such a protest may be almost overwhelming.

10 Of course, this does not mean that I cannot be clear about that fact that most people would not have done it.

11 There may seem to be a tension between what I say here and what I said above about the good as without force. However, the distinction above is still valid: what one must do is noticing the difference between force and attraction. (Attraction can only be fought against by means of repression. Fighting against a force is always a matter of calculation: how likely is it that the fight will succeed, is the amount of work I have to put in on the fight in order to win worth it, and so forth.)

12 However, there is some kind of confusion inherent in this calculating form of belief which makes it impossible to state clearly. The meaning of that which is to be judged here comes from religion itself, and cannot be judged independently of it, which means that it is fundamentally unclear what it would mean to relate oneself to it in a completely external way.

13 What I try to do is clarifying what this means. That does not imply that the difficulties discussed in the first part of this chapter have vanished. To clarify what it means to love a God of love is to clarify *what* these difficulties are. One cannot get around the issue discussed in this section by claiming that the issue never becomes topical, because of the fact that really loving a God of love is still impossible. Saying this means saying that the difficulties are external to me, have not anything to do with me. That I de facto do not love a God of love does not mean that this love of a God of love is necessarily something alien to me.

14 The qualifications with regard to the concept of authority I mentioned in ch. 2 should here, and in what follows, be remembered: this "authority" is an "authority" above authority.

15 Another possibility is that that which is authoritative is not God – not even for the believer – but a principle, which God, *if* God exists, instantiates. I will come to this possibility in a moment.

16 This shows why it may be tempting to regard it as an open question, why it may be tempting to emphasize arguments for or against the existence of God. The one who emphasizes arguments may want to keep love of a God of love at a distance, since she feels that she, in a sense, cannot drop it, at the same time as she, for calculating reasons, wants to drop it. The arguments could then be used to make love of a God of love into something doubtful, into an open question, or

into something she must disregard since there is another form of religious belief which has been proved, she tells herself. But for the wholehearted believer, love of a God of love has a certainty which transcends the arguments, and it is this which makes it possible to mistake it for fanaticism (see ch. 1).

17 However, the question is whether there is really such a thing as not at all loving a God of love. We will return to this question later.

18 One whose line of thought is near to this objection – one who believes that love is a principle and not a person – is Feuerbach. See Feuerbach, *Das Wesen des Christentums*, pp. 60, 65, 105–06, 392, 401–05.

19 Cora Diamond, "Wittgenstein on Religious Belief: The Gulfs between Us", in *Religion and Wittgenstein's Legacy*, ed. D. Z. Phillips and Mario von der Ruhr (Aldershot: Ashgate, 2005), p. 125.

20 Ibid., 136. However, Diamond's example is strange. What does it mean to say that a human being is "beautiful"? Does it mean that she is subject to a purely aesthetical judgment? Or does it mean that one is attracted to someone, wants to be with her, does feel the opposite of disgust, does not hide one's face from her? In that case the relation is one the possibility of which is there in all cases, which the discussion in sec. I shows: one could say that the concept of love which we are here working with is one in which "beautiful" is not a distinguishing concept, not a concept of judgment. However, it is clear that meeting George Eliot could make one see how shady one's previous aesthetical way of relating to others was. And, furthermore, the opposite case is all too obvious: one turns away from someone by calling him or her – it may be George Eliot or someone else – ugly and repellant, and this seemingly purely aesthetical concept is used in order to place the problem outside of oneself, in something with an alleged general validity.

21 Ludwig Wittgenstein, *Culture and Value*, ed. G. H. von Wright, trans. Peter Winch (Chicago: University of Chicago Press, 1980), p. 86.

22 This is a point made by Blaise Pascal, even though the word "know" is misleading, intimating that the question is still of an epistemological kind (*Great Shorter Works*, trans. Emile Cailliet and John C. Blankenagel (Westport: Greenwood Press, 1974), p. 203):

> [W]hen speaking of things human, we say that we should know them before loving them – a saying which has become proverbial. Yet the saints, on the contrary, when speaking of things divine, say that we should love them in order to know them, and that we enter into truth only through love.

Simone Weil expresses the point better (*Gravity and Grace*, pp. 56–57): "Belief in the existence of other human beings as such is *love*. The mind, is not forced to believe in the existence of anything … That is why the only organ of contact with existence is acceptance, love." Marion makes the same point as Pascal, but formulates himself in a more misleading way: "[T]he love of Love constitutes an epistemological condition of theology as *theology*" (*God without Being*, 225). "Only the saintly person knows whereof he speaks in theology" (ibid., p. 155).

23 Hence, what follows is *not* some queer argument for the existence of God.

24 See Strandberg, *Escaping My Responsibility*, ch. 1.

25 Cf. ch. 3.

26 Furthermore, and for obvious reasons, the concept of the soul has not the concept of the body as its contrast.

27 To think that, would be to think that the relation between the existential/religious and the moral is external, that one of them must be brought into the other.

28 I will come back to this in ch. 8.

29 Cf. Francis Hutcheson, *An Inquiry into the Original of Our Ideas of Beauty and Virtue*, 2nd ed. (London, 1726), pp. 119–20:

> Our Senses of *natural Good* and *Evil* would make us receive, with equal Serenity and Composure, an *Assault*, a *Buffet*, an *Affront* from a *Neighbour*, a *Cheat* from a *Partner*, or *Trustee*, as we would an equal Damage from the Fall of a *Beam*, a *Tile*, or a *Tempest*; and we should have the same Affections and Sentiments of both. *Villany*, *Treachery*, *Cruelty*, would be as meekly resented as a *Blast*, or *Mildew*, or an *overflowing Stream*. But I fancy every one is very differently affected on these Occasions, tho there may be equal *natural Evil* in both. Nay, Actions no way detrimental, may occasion the strongest Anger, and Indignation, if they evidence only impotent Hatred, or Contempt.

30 Cf. ch. 3.

31 Cf. Emmanuel Levinas, "The Ego and the Totality", in *Collected Philosophical Papers*, trans. Alphonso Lingis (Pittsburgh: Duquesne University Press, 1998), p. 33.

Chapter 5

1 Martin Luther, *On the Bondage of the Will*, trans. Philip S. Watson, in *Luther and Erasmus: Free Will and Salvation*, ed. E. Gordon Rupp and Philip S. Watson (Philadelphia: Westminster Press, 1969), p. 157. This contrasts sharply with Erasmus's line of thought (which is what *On the Bondage of the Will* in its entirety directly turns against) which is manifestly moralistic, that is, not driven by the criterionlessness of love. See Erasmus of Rotterdam, *On the Freedom of the Will: A Diatribe or Discourse*, trans. E. Gordon Rupp, in *Luther and Erasmus: Free Will and Salvation*, ed. E. Gordon Rupp and Philip S. Watson (Philadelphia: Westminster Press, 1969), esp. p. 96.

2 Luther, *On the Bondage of the Will*, p. 157.

3 Ibid., p. 210.

4 Ibid., p. 212.

5 See ibid., pp. 211–13.

6 Ibid., p. 213.

7 Ibid., p. 211.

8 Ibid., p. 212.

9 What I have said here entails a criticism of Anders Nygren's influential account of love in terms of eros and agape. There is an ambiguity in his account. On the one hand (see Anders Nygren, *Den kristna kärlekstanken genom tiderna: Eros och agape*, vol. 1, 2nd ed. (Stockholm: Svenska kyrkans diakonistyrelses bokförlag, 1938), e.g., pp. 179–80), he says that the difference between agape and eros is that in the first one, the togetherness is theocentric, is brought about by God, whereas in the second one, the togetherness is egocentric, is brought about by man.

On the other hand (p. 175), he says that the self-centeredness of eros means that there is no real togetherness with God there. The first side of the ambiguity is more emphasized, but it is the other side which is the better point. That self-centeredness means that there is no real togetherness, means that togetherness cannot be brought about, cannot be brought about by, say, one of the "parties", or by the "parties" in "cooperation". This is what togetherness being a relation means.

10 Luther, *On the Bondage of the Will*, pp. 139–40.

11 Compare Luther's distinction between free choice with respect to what is beneath one and free choice with respect to what is above one (ibid., 143). It is the latter he denies, the one that concerns the determination of the more fundamental will (in contrast to the less fundamental, that is, the one that is beneath one).

12 Presupposed here is that the change from being evil to being good, or vice versa, if it were a matter of some doing, would have a moral character (good or evil).

13 Luther, *On the Bondage of the Will*, p. 122.

14 Ibid., p. 214.

15 In this context, it is important to notice that his problem should not be described as a matter of "lack of feeling", if this is supposed to mean that he is the same as before "intellectually", but now lack what he does not control – his feelings – in contrast to what he has control over – his intellectual attitude. The contrast feeling/intellect may in *some* context be enlightening, but generally speaking the idea of pure intellectuality should be questioned: what does it mean to mean something intellectually if one is emotionally numb? does one then really mean what one says one means? Besides, one should notice that feelings and the lack of them are not something that simply strikes one, as if they had not anything to do with one: one's callous or spiteful way of relating to others is such a thing one has a bad conscience for.

16 "Awaken" and "kindle" are metaphors, of course, and could, if they are understood in the wrong way, mislead: literally speaking, both "awake" and "kindle" refer to something causal – pushing the right buttons, so to speak – and my point is about something different.

17 The word "gratitude" would be misleading here, I think, but I will not enter into a discussion of that issue.

18 For this idea, see, e.g., William James, *The Will to Believe, and Other Essays in Popular Philosophy* (New York: Longmans, Green and Co., 1903), pp. 1–31.

19 "The heart has its reasons of which reason knows nothing ... It is the heart which perceives God and not the reason. That is what faith is: God perceived by the heart, not by the reason" (Blaise Pascal, *Pensées*, trans. A. J. Krailsheimer, rev. ed. (London: Penguin Books, 1995), §§ 423–24).

20 Ibid., e.g., §§ 7, 110, 380.

21 Ibid., e.g., §§ 3, 131, 444–46.

22 Luther, *On the Bondage of the Will*, p. 137.

23 Ibid., p. 149.

24 To object that Luther again and again stresses that "neither the divine nor the human will does what it does, whether good or evil, under any compulsion ... and yet the will of God is immutable and infallible, and it governs our mutable will" (ibid., p. 120) is no objection: the issue I am discussing here is another one.

25 Ibid., p. 180.

26 Kant, *Die Religion innerhalb der Grenzen der bloßen Vernunft*, pp. 667–68, 671–72, 692–94; F. W. J. Schelling, *Über das Wesen der menschlichen Freiheit, und die damit*

zusammenhängenden Gegenstände, ed. Thomas Buchheim (Hamburg: Felix Meiner, 1997), pp. 43–44, 57–61.

27 Luther, *On the Bondage of the Will,* p. 141.
28 Ibid., p. 200.
29 Ibid., pp. 236–37.
30 See, e.g., ibid., pp. 163–64, 295.
31 Rather, one could describe evil as an issue of self-deception (see ch. 3): rational consideration is one of the most important forms of self-deception and self-deception is not chosen (at least not in the usual sense of the word). Luther emphasizes this in his own way (ibid., p. 193): "Satan knows that if men were aware of their misery, he would not be able to retain a single one of them in his kingdom ... it is Satan's work to prevent men from recognizing their plight and to keep them presuming that they can do everything they are told."
32 Ibid., p. 121.
33 Cf. Alexandre Kojève, *Introduction to the Reading of Hegel,* ed. Allan Bloom, trans. James H. Nichols (Ithaca: Cornell University Press, 1980), p. 120.
34 Cf. Jean-Paul Sartre, *Being and Nothingness: An Essay on Phenomenological Ontology,* trans. Hazel E. Barnes (New York: Philosophical Library, 1956), pp. lxv, 40, 66–67.
35 Luther, *On the Bondage of the Will,* p. 118.
36 Ibid., 241. Here Luther approvingly quotes Erasmus (*On the Freedom of the Will,* p. 66).
37 Luther, *On the Bondage of the Will,* p. 119.
38 Ibid., p. 140.
39 Ibid., p. 240. See also these quotes:

> That remnant of nature, therefore, as we call it, in the ungodly man and Satan, as being the creature and work of God, is no less subject to divine omnipotence and activity than all other creatures and works of God. Since, then, God moves and actuates all in all, he necessarily moves and acts also in Satan and ungodly man. But he acts in them as they are and as he finds them ... It is the fault, therefore, of the instruments, which God does not allow to be idle, that evil things are done, with God himself setting them in motion. (ibid., pp. 232–33)
>
> But why does he not at the same time change the evil wills that he moves? This belongs to the secrets of his majesty, where his judgments are incomprehensible ... The same must be said to those who ask why he permitted Adam to fall, and why he creates us all infected with the same sin, when he could either have preserved him or created us from another stock or from a seed which he had first purged. (ibid., p. 236)

40 Ibid., p. 201.
41 Ibid., p. 121.
42 Frank, *The Unknowable,* p. 91.
43 Frank, *The Unknowable,* pp. 127–28. Cf. Hannah Arendt, *The Human Condition,* 2nd ed. (Chicago: University of Chicago Press, 1998), pp. 181–82, 241–42.
44 See, e.g., Luther, *On the Bondage of the Will,* 205ff.
45 Ibid., pp. 244–45.
46 Erasmus, *On the Freedom of the Will,* p. 50.

47 Immanuel Kant, *Kritik der reinen Vernunft*, Werkausgabe, ed. Wilhelm Weischedel, vols 3–4 (Frankfurt am Main: Suhrkamp, 1968), 25–26 (B xvii).

48 Cf. Immanuel Kant, *Kritik der praktischen Vernunft*, in *Schriften zur Ethik und Religionsphilosophie*, Werkausgabe, ed. Wilhelm Weischedel (Frankfurt am Main: Suhrkamp, 1968), 7–8:139: through being conscious of the moral law, I become conscious of my freedom.

49 See Kant, *Kritik der reinen Vernunft*, esp. pp. 31, 157–58, 231–32, 490–94, 501 (B xxvii–xxviii, B 165–67, A 195–96 / B 240–41, A 536–41 / B 564–69, A 551 / B 579).

50 See Immanuel Kant, *Grundlegung zur Metaphysik der Sitten*, in *Schriften zur Ethik und Religionsphilosophie*, Werkausgabe, ed. Wilhelm Weischedel (Frankfurt am Main: Suhrkamp, 1968), 7–8:41–51.

51 I have not explained how the good will comes in, but the line of thought, simplified and shortened, could be said to be this. Since whether I succeed in reaching an end is always a matter of skill, morality should not be understood as a matter of reaching certain ends: if I fail in fixing a bike I may simply say that I am not good at fixing bikes, but if I have treated someone badly saying that I am not good at being good is simply a lame attempt at exculpating myself. Here I cannot refer to some kind of lack of skill. Hence, Kant says (ibid., 18), the only thing that could be considered good without limitation is a good will. Since we must distinguish between actions in conformity with duty but done for some other motive than duty and actions in conformity with duty done from duty (for an example, see ibid., 23), the truly good will means the latter. And if we try to understand what it means to do one's duty from duty, to obey the moral law since it is the moral law: what is the formal property of a law – what is left of a law when we have removed all the ends it may serve – except its generality, universality? (ibid., p. 28)

52 Ibid., p. 55.

53 See esp. ibid., pp. 64–66, 81–82.

54 Ibid., pp. 59–60.

55 Ibid., p. 61; Immanuel Kant, *Practical Philosophy*, trans. and ed. Mary J. Gregor (Cambridge: Cambridge University Press, 1996), p. 80.

56 Kant, *Grundlegung zur Metaphysik der Sitten*, p. 60.

57 Ibid., pp. 25–26; Kant, *Kritik der praktischen Vernunft*, 205; Immanuel Kant, *Die Metaphysik der Sitten*, in *Schriften zur Ethik und Religionsphilosophie*, Werkausgabe, ed. Wilhelm Weischedel (Frankfurt am Main: Suhrkamp, 1968), 7–8:532–34, 585.

58 Here I will not enter into a discussion about how widespread this may be. One should simply pay attention to the fact that the possibility that one has hardened one's heart gives rise to problems for the one who lays great stress upon the fact that feelings cannot be commanded. What this person presupposes is that the starting point is some kind of emotional neutrality. However, if what is fundamental is a love, which later on might be repressed when one hardens one's heart, then the issue is different.

59 Hegel, *Grundlinien der Philosophie des Rechts*, § 135. A similar line of thought can be found in Hegel, *Über die wissenschaftlichen Behandlungsarten des Naturrechts, seine Stelle in der praktischen Philosophie und sein Verhältnis zu den positiven Rechtswissenschaften*, in *Jenaer Schriften, 1801–1807*, Werke, ed. Eva Moldenhauer and Karl Markus Michel (Frankfurt am Main: Suhrkamp, 1986), 2:461–66.

60 See esp. Kant, *Grundlegung zur Metaphysik der Sitten*, p. 70.

61 Ibid., p. 54.

62 Kant, *Die Metaphysik der Sitten*, pp. 518, 524–25.

63 See ch. 1 and 2.

64 This omission is not something unique to Kant, on the contrary. In fact, this is a decisive defect in moral philosophy as a whole as long as it sees *rules* as morally central; it starts too late and does not give room for that which makes what it investigates into a *moral* issue, for that which makes the rules into *moral* rules, in contrast to rules of some other character, for example, practical. In Kant this problem is simply less hidden than it usually is.
Strangely enough, Heidegger is on the brink of realizing this, when he criticizes the focus on rules and the concept of value in (traditional) moral philosophy (see Martin Heidegger, *Brief über den "Humanismus"*, in *Wegmarken*, Gesamtausgabe 9, 3rd ed. (Frankfurt am Main: Vittorio Klostermann, 2004)). But he takes that as a pretext for abstaining from doing moral philosophy, when it could and should be a reason for really doing it. What Heidegger and those he criticizes have in common is this picture of what moral philosophy must be. In that respect, his criticism is only half-baked.

65 In "Auf die Frage: Was ist deutsch" Adorno mentions (in *Stichworte: Kritische Modelle 2*, in vol. 10, bk. 2, of *Gesammelte Schriften*, ed. Rolf Tiedemann (Frankfurt am Main: Suhrkamp, 1977, p. 693) "… die berühmteste Formel des deutschen kollektiven Narzißmus, die Wagnersche: deutsch sein heißt, eine Sache um ihrer selbst willen tun." But here one should notice that if one connects this to a national identity, one does not do it for its own sake, how ever much one takes one's own interest to have that character. The phrase "doing something for its own sake" is far more complicated than one might be tempted to believe.

66 For such an objection, see Hegel, *Phänomenologie des Geistes*, p. 314.

67 In some early writings, Hegel criticizes Kant's moral philosophy, starting out from love as morally central (see esp. Hegel, *Der Geist des Christentums und sein Schicksal*, in *Frühe Schriften*, Werke, ed. Eva Moldenhauer and Karl Markus Michel (Frankfurt am Main: Suhrkamp, 1986), 1:324–38, 362–63). (His criticism is not identical to mine, however.) Soon Hegel tones down its importance considerably (see *System der Sittlichkeit [Critik des Fichteschen Naturrechts]*, ed. Horst D. Brandt (Hamburg: Felix Meiner, 2002), 13). In *Grundlinien der Philosophie des Rechts* (§ 158), Hegel writes that the place of love is the family and that it has no wider moral bearing. Kant gives love an important role in *Die Metaphysik der Sitten* (pp. 530–34), even though what he writes is ambiguous. But its role is subjective, which means that reason is, in principle, sufficient in itself, as the objective condition, an idea I have criticized here. One could compare this to what he says about affects and passions as provisional substitute for reason in morality (*Anthropologie in pragmatischer Hinsicht*, in *Schriften zur Anthropologie, Geschichtsphilosophie, Politik und Pädagogik*, Werkausgabe, ed. Wilhelm Weischedel (Frankfurt am Main: Suhrkamp, 1968), 11–12:582–84, 601–2).

68 The same thing could be said about another concept which plays an ambiguous role in Kant's moral philosophy: happiness. On the one hand, Kant stresses its importance (see, e.g., *Grundlegung zur Metaphysik der Sitten*, pp. 62–63); on the other hand he understands it as something purely psychological (see, e.g.,

Die Religion innerhalb der Grenzen der bloßen Vernunft, 650). But what he then fails to notice is that the question about whether I am happy or not is itself a moral question, and not simply a psychological-empirical one. Deceiving oneself about one's own happiness is a typical example of self-deception. (Hence, it is not possible to inquire into whether people are happy or not by simply asking them.)

CHAPTER 6

1 As William James does. See *Pragmatism, a New Name for Some Old Ways of Thinking: Popular Lectures of Philosophy* (New York: Longmans, Green and Co., 1907), pp. 243–44, 258.
2 Cf. Hobbes, *Leviathan*, p. 397.
3 In the act of intuiting, or painting, a wall, the wall is the intentional objects of these acts. But intuiting or painting is something *I* do, and love is in that sense essentially different. That Husserl has such a problematic individualistic bent is well known; in this context, *Logische Untersuchungen*, vol. 2, *Untersuchungen zur Phänomenologie und Theorie der Erkenntnis*, pt. 1, 2nd ed. (Halle an der Saale: Max Niemeyer, 1913), pp. 366–67 and *Ideen zu einer reinen Phänomenologie und phän-omenologischen Philosophie*, bk. 1, *Allgemeine Einführung in die reine Phänomenologie*, ed. Walter Biemel, Husserliana 3 (Haag: Martinus Nijhoff, 1950), pp. 82–83, 204, 298, are good examples. Even though there are important tendencies in other directions too, the same tendency is there also in Heidegger. This is not the place for an attempt at showing this, but if I would do that, I would take Heidegger's introduction of *Sorge* and *Fürsorge* as my starting point (*Sein und Zeit*, 18th ed. (Tübingen: Max Niemeyer, 2001), p. 121). Love should be seen neither as a theoretical phenomenon, nor as a practical phenomenon, as Hegel says (*Entwürfe über Religion und Liebe*, in *Frühe Schriften*, Werke, ed. Eva Moldenhauer and Karl Markus Michel (Frankfurt am Main: Suhrkamp, 1986), 1:242).
This is important to point out, not the least in relation to interpretations of religion in terms of emotion and feeling (see, e.g., Axel Hägerström, *Religionsfilosofi* (Stockholm: Natur och Kultur, 1949), pp. 48, 179–81, 192). Emotions are far more complex than philosophers often acknowledge; first one can point out that they are intentional, second that, in the case of love, even this point is misleading. An emotion should not be considered in isolation, since it is, in different senses, relational.
4 However, one question is what problems and what subjects for rejoicing it is possible to have in togetherness. I will come back to this issue.
5 This includes self-examination, of course. It is not self-evident that the happiness and the sorrow are pure; they may contain calculative elements – they may be fake or may be a result of a successful/unsuccessful calculation – which would then mean that my belief is not a belief had in togetherness.
6 For this distinction, see R. G. Collingwood, *The Principles of Art* (Oxford: Oxford University Press, 1938), p. 111.
7 "Simply happens" is a simplification. Since expressive possibilities are handed down to me through the culture, in a wide sense of the word, I belong to, it is no coincidence that the expression may be easily recognizable, even when it is a pure expression.

8 This is not necessarily so. I will come back to this.

9 Jean-Paul Sartre, *Critique of Dialectical Reason: Volume One, Theory of Practical Ensembles*, ed. Jonathan Rée, trans. Alan Sheridan-Smith (London: Verso, 2004), 440: "However, as can still be observed today in authoritarian parties, fraternity is the most immediate and constant form of Terror: traitors, in fact, are by definition the minority. ... no 'milieu' is *warmer* than an authoritarian party which is constantly subject to external threats."

10 Cf. Kierkegaard, *Opbyggelige Taler i forskjellig Aand*, 131 (my translation): "[A]ll concord is discord."

11 Pace Sigmund Freud, *Massenpsychologie und Ich-Analyse*, 2nd ed. (Leipzig: Internationaler psychoanalytischer Verlag, 1923), p. 49.

12 But is not one of the problems I discussed previously – the closing down of a factory – necessarily ideological? This problem may be mediated by an ideology, to be sure, but it does not have to be. As an individual problem it need not be mediated by an ideology; the problem could simply be that one will have difficulties to earn a living. When I relate to others who have the same problem as I have, the decisive question is in what spirit I relate to them. Do I make common cause with the others (the struggle will be more efficacious if we do not struggle individually, but the only problem I am really concerned with is my own)? Do I see the others as members of the same group as I belong to, since we have the same outlook on the issue (ideological community)? Or do I see their problems as mine (I care for the others as persons)? In the latter case, this has to do with love.

13 Cf. Kierkegaard, *Opbyggelige Taler i forskjellig Aand*, p. 117.

14 Søren Kierkegaard, *Kjerlighedens Gjerninger*, Samlede Værker 12 (Copenhagen: Gyldendal, 1962), pp. 11, 167, 226–27, 246.

15 Weil, *Gravity and Grace*, pp.144–45.

16 Emile Durkheim, *The Elementary Forms of Religious Life*, trans. Karen E. Fields (New York: Free Press, 1995), p. 208.

17 Ibid., p. 390.

18 Phillips, *Religion and the Hermeneutics of Contemplation*, pp. 240–41.

19 A background to Phillips's discussion is Winch's criticism of the idea "that the ideas of participants must be discounted as more likely than not to be misguided and confusing" (Peter Winch, *The Idea of a Social Science and its Relation to Philosophy*, 2nd ed. (London: Routledge, 1990), p. 95). But I agree with Winch on this point. On the contrary, as I see it, it is Phillips which does not take these ideas seriously enough. What must be done is paying close attention to the *use* of the ideas; besides, my emphasis on "doubleness" shows that the ideas cannot be discounted.

CHAPTER 7

1 When I here and below talk about the standard discussion, it is not possible to refer to one or a few texts. One or a few texts do not make up a tradition. Obviously, Hume is of vast importance, and I will refer to him now and then in what follows. But my points are not about Hume in the first place; rather, the focus is on how a specific way of thinking about these issues has been handed down. (And students are very often inclined to argue in ways very close to the standard

discussion, even before they know of it; basically, facts such as this are what make it standard.) If one wants to find examples of this, almost any anthology for the philosophy of religion will do. One example: In Michael Peterson et al., eds., *Philosophy of Religion: Selected Readings*, 2nd ed. (Oxford: Oxford University Press, 2001), there are three texts under the heading "Miracles," one by Hume, one by Swinburne, and one by Mackie. In other words, it does not matter whether the conclusion is positive with regard to miracles (Swinburne) or negative (Hume and Mackie): the way the issue is discussed is still the same.

2   Someone might say that there is something problematic in this case: the presupposition that God exists. For a discussion of that issue, see ch. 4. But in the context of this chapter it suffices to say that what is in that case problematic is that presupposition, not the concept miracle as such. For a discussion of the alleged difficulties of the concept miracle understood as an intrareligious category, see Hugo Strandberg, "Från död till liv: Om religionsfilosofins natur", *Svensk teologisk kvartalskrift* 83 (2007).

3   Hume (*An Enquiry concerning Human Understanding*, ed. Tom L. Beauchamp (Oxford: Oxford University Press, 1999), p. 184) talks about miracles as "a just foundation for any such system of religion."
One possibility with regard to that idea – Hegel is an example (*Vorlesungen über die Philosophie der Religion I*, Werke, ed. Eva Moldenhauer and Karl Markus Michel, vol. 16 (Frankfurt am Main: Suhrkamp, 1986), pp. 210–11; *Vorlesungen über die Philosophie der Religion II*, Werke, ed. Eva Moldenhauer and Karl Markus Michel, vol. 17 (Frankfurt am Main: Suhrkamp, 1986), pp. 196–97, 313–16) – is to deny that miracles are a foundation for anything, without rejecting the possibility of them or rejecting Hume's conception of them. Another possibility – Lessing is an example (*Über den Beweis des Geistes und der Kraft*, pp. 32–35) – is to deny that reports about miracles are a foundation for anything but at the same time claim that actually seeing a miracle would be a foundation for the belief in the authority of the one who performs one; according to Lessing, miracles occurred at the time of Jesus, but not nowadays (that is, in the 18th century). With regard to Lessing, Kierkegaard points out that whereas Lessing is right in emphasizing the impossibility of founding religious beliefs upon historical reports (Kierkegaard, *Afsluttende uvidenskabelig Efterskrift*, 1:82–84), one should not be too sure of one's reaction to Jesus had one lived then and there: the historical distance does not make it more difficult to believe, but perhaps too easy (Kierkegaard, *Philosophiske Smuler; eller, En Smule Philosophi*, in *Philosophiske Smuler; Begrebet Angest; Tre Taler ved tænkte Leiligheder*, Samlede Værker 6 (Copenhagen: Gyldendal, 1963), pp. 62–66; Kierkegaard, *Indøvelse i Christendom*, Samlede Værker 16 (Copenhagen: Gyldendal, 1963), pp. 97–98).

4   This is what the idea that miracles are violations of the laws of nature (Hume, *An Enquiry concerning Human Understanding*, 173) in the end comes to. But what is important to realize is that it does not matter whether one holds on to this idea or not; it is possible to reject this idea as being confused but still regard miracles as being something inexplicable which the postulation of the existence of God makes it possible to explain. It is this latter idea my discussion is about, not the idea as such that miracles are violations of the laws of nature. (One way of expressing the confusion, in the idea that miracles are violations of the laws of nature and in the idea of laws of nature on the whole, is this (Novalis, *Blütenstaub*, in *Gesammelte Werke*,

ed. Hans Jürgen Balmes (Frankfurt am Main: Fischer, 2008), § 12): "Wunder stehn mit naturgesetzlichen Wirkungen in Wechsel: sie beschränken einander gegenseitig und machen zusammen ein Ganzes aus. Sie sind vereinigt, indem sie sich gegenseitig aufheben. Kein Wunder ohne Naturbegebenheit und umgekehrt.")

5 That miracles are violations of the laws of nature is one form this idea might take.

6 Feuerbach (*Das Wesen des Christentums*, pp. 210–11) argues in this way, but uses another terminology.

7 Cf. Kant, *Die Religion innerhalb der Grenzen der bloßen Vernunft*, pp. 745–47; Fichte, *Versuch einer Kritik aller Offenbarung*, p. 74.

8 Feeling oneself forced to place a phenomenon on the axis between having an explanation and not having one, means forgetting that there is another issue: when the concept explanation is applicable and when it is not. I will come back to this below.

9 Consider this example (inspired by Aristotle, *Ph.* 195b–197a). If I happen to meet a friend of mine in the city square, I could explain why I am there right now, and she could explain why she is there right now. And so we meet each other, by coincidence. But there is no explanation of that coincidence (which does not mean that it is inexplicable, but that concepts such as these have no application here); if we had planned to meet each other then and there, that would be the explanation, but then it would not have been a coincidence. Furthermore, note that in all these cases, asking for an explanation is not to ask for a scientific explanation. It is, to say the least, hard to see what a *scientific* explanation would be here. (Cf. R. G. Collingwood, *Religion and Philosophy* (London: Macmillan, 1916), pp. 83–85; R. G. Collingwood, *An Essay on Metaphysics*, rev. ed. (Oxford: Oxford University Press, 1998), pp. 290–95.)

10 Cf. Hume, *An Enquiry concerning Human Understanding*, p. 174.

11 Ludwig Wittgenstein, "A Lecture on Ethics", in *Philosophical Occasions, 1912–1951*, ed. James Klagge and Alfred Nordmann (Indianapolis: Hackett, 1993), p. 43:

> Take the case that one of you suddenly grew a lion's head and began to roar. Certainly that would be as extraordinary a thing as I can imagine. Now whenever we should have recovered from our surprise, what I would suggest would be to fetch a doctor and have the case scientifically investigated and if it were not for hurting him I would have him vivisected. And where would the miracle have got to? For it is clear that when we look at it in this way everything miraculous has disappeared; unless what we mean by this term is merely that a fact has not yet been explained by science which again means that we have hitherto failed to group this fact with others in a scientific system. This shows that it is absurd to say "Science has proved that there are no miracles." The truth is that the scientific way of looking at a fact is not the way to look at it as a miracle.

Furthermore, cf. Ernst Jünger, *Annäherungen: Drogen und Rausch* (Stuttgart: Ernst Klett Verlag, 1970), § 50:

> In einem durchaus wunderbaren Universum ist es unnötig, daß auch noch Wunder geschehen. Daher hat die Heilige Stadt keinen Tempel,

> kein Heiligtum. Aus diesem Grunde sind im Neuen Testament die Wunder durchweg schwächer als die Gleichnisse. "Dein Sohn lebt!" – das ist kein Wunder, sondern ein Gleichnis, das auf ein Wunder weist. Würde ich es im Sinne des reinen Geschehens akzeptieren, das heißt, "an sich" als Wunder und nicht als Hinweis nehmen, so würde ich es innerhalb der Rangordnung für bedeutend halten, in der die Herztransplantation gelingt. Das Wort meint aber mehr. Es ist eine Bestätigung, die Tod und Leben übergreift. Der Jüngling zu Nain ist wie Blaiberg zum zweiten Mal gestorben, obgleich beide unsterblich sind.

12 This means that a confused idea about causal chains is at work here. Cf. Norwood Russell Hanson, *Patterns of Discovery: An Inquiry into the Conceptual Foundations of Science* (Cambridge: Cambridge University Press, 1965), ch. 3. This question I will not discuss here, however.

13 This is evident in Hume. His famous conclusion (*An Enquiry concerning Human Understanding*, pp. 173–74) – "The plain consequence is ... 'That no testimony is sufficient to establish a miracle, unless the testimony be of such a kind, that its falsehood would be more miraculous, than the fact, which it endeavours to establish: And even in that case, there is a mutual destruction of arguments, and the superior only gives us an assurance suitable to that degree of force, which remains, after deducting the inferior.'" – means that we can only conclude that something is a miracle if the opposite would be more "miraculous", that is, for Hume, since he identifies the two, incredible. In other words, the general a priori principle at work here is that we should always make the amount of miraculousness as small as possible.

14 Hume is very explicit on this point. The terms he uses for the miraculous (ibid., pp. 171–76) are such as the following: the extraordinary, the unusual, that which has seldom fallen under our observation, the incredible, the uncommon. And what he compares miracles to is of the same kind: take the example of the Indian prince who never has seen water freeze to ice (ibid., p. 172). For Hume, that miracles are uncommon is a priori.
See also Hobbes, *Leviathan*, pp. 469–70:

> By *Miracles* are signified the Admirable works of God: & therefore they are also called *Wonders* ... To understand therefore what is a Miracle, we must first understand what works they are, which men wonder at, and call Admirable. And there be but two things which make men wonder at any event: The one is, if it be strange, that is to say, such, as the like of it hath never, or very rarely been produced: The other is, if when it is produced, we cannot imagine it to have been done by naturall means, but onely by the immediate hand of God.

(Both criteria must be fulfilled.) And to Hobbes, miracles has an obviously instrumental, furthermore authoritarian, end (ibid., p. 471): "Again, it belongeth to the nature of a Miracle, that it be wrought for the procuring of credit to Gods Messengers, Ministers, and Prophets, that thereby men may ... be the better inclined to obey them."

15 Again, Hume's principle, that we should always make the amount of miracu-
    lousness as small as possible, is an example: that a miracle has occurred can only
    be established when the opposite is more incredible, which means that such a
    miracle would be, at least relatively, credible.
16 One example (Euan Cameron, *The European Reformation* (Oxford: Oxford
    University Press, 1991), p. 92):

> Obviously there were then [in the late middle ages], as at any other time,
> some people who were utterly apathetic to religion in any shape or form
> – though perhaps fewer than in modern industrial society, where the vital
> preconditions of human survival have been made much more controllable
> and predictable than in the late middle ages.

Max Weber is an important background here; for a short example, see
Wissenschaft als Beruf, in *Gesammelte Aufsätze zur Wissenschaftslehre,* 7th ed., ed.
Johannes Winckelmann (Tübingen: J. C. B. Mohr (Paul Siebeck), 1988),
594. (In a more philosophical context, cf. Max Horkheimer and Theodor W.
Adorno, *Dialektik der Aufklärung: Philosophische Fragmente,* 2nd ed. (Frankfurt am
Main: Suhrkamp, 1984), pp. 19–60.)

17 Moreover, there is always an ambiguity in talking about independence from,
    or mastery over, nature. Mastering nature means regarding it in a specific way,
    which means that other aspects of nature disappears from view; in that respect,
    mastery is impotence. (See Martin Heidegger, *Der Ursprung des Kunstwerkes,* in
    Holzwege, 8th ed. (Frankfurt am Main: Vittorio Klostermann, 2003), p. 33.) I will
    touch upon this question in sec. IV, but not with reference to nature.
18 It should be noticed that already the calculative understanding of miracles refers
    to something else. It is not anything which is counted as a miracle, even if it is
    not possible to explain. In other words, there is something noncalculative here:
    miracles as something good, as something to rejoice at. I will come back to this.
19 See Sigmund Freud, *Die Zukunft einer Illusion* (Leipzig: Internationaler psycho-
    analytischer Verlag, 1927), 47. In this context, it is not necessary to enter into a
    discussion about how Freud's claim should be understood.
20 For this doubleness, see ch. 6, sec. III.
21 Sigmund Freud, *Neue Folge der Vorlesungen zur Einführung in die Psychoanalyse,* in
    Vorlesungen zur Einführung in die Psychoanalyse, und Neue Folge, Studienausgabe,
    ed. Alexander Mitscherlich, Angela Richards, James Strachey (Frankfurt am
    Main: S. Fischer, 1969), 1:589.
22 But what should the reductionist do with someone like Kierkegaard, whose
    understanding of religious belief is far from consoling? Cf. Kierkegaard,
    Afsluttende uvidenskabelig Efterskrift, 1:64; Kierkegaard, *Opbyggelige Taler i forskjel-
    lig Aand,* part 3; Kierkegaard, *Dømmer selv!,* in *En opbyggelig Tale; To Taler ved
    Altergangen om Fredagen; Til Selvprøvelse, Samtiden anbefalet; Dømmer selv!* Samlede
    Værker 17 (Copenhagen: Gyldendal, 1964), pp. 211, 224.
23 Perhaps one might believe that Kant should be open to such different possi-
    bilities, since for him the theoretical one is not the only way of relating to the
    world. Of course, Kant denies claims to theoretical knowledge about miracles
    (*Die Religion innerhalb der Grenzen der bloßen Vernunft,* pp. 744–45), but the same

goes for the context of the practical: the belief in miracles is not a moral duty (ibid., pp. 740–41, 744–45). Hume's understanding of what miracles are, is simply never questioned by Kant (see Kant's definition, ibid., p. 743). The only indication of a different understanding appears in a note (ibid., p. 742), in which Kant in passing mentions the possibility that the work of God could be understood not as a matter of causation or magnitude but of the *form* of the event. And whether the event is natural or supernatural, "easy" or "difficult", does not matter then.

Moreover, what Kant says about the sublime could be interpreted as a different understanding of miracles; I will touch upon this in a later note. But Kant's official conclusion with regard to miracles is that they should not be denied since they could be of tactical use against Jews (ibid., pp. 741–42). In Fichte's words (*Versuch einer Kritik aller Offenbarung*, pp. 104–5): upon a person obsessed by the sensible, God must work through the sensible. What Kant has in mind is something along Fichte's lines.

24   I will not say anything about this line of thought here. Obviously, the very terms of it should be questioned. In that respect, some of what I say in ch. 2 and 4 is relevant.

25   The tension between miracles as explanations and miracles as meaning is discussed by Peter Winch ("Asking Too Many Questions", in *Philosophy and the Grammar of Religious Belief*, ed. Timothy Tessin and Mario von der Ruhr (New York: St. Martin's Press, 1995), p. 210).

26   That it does not matter what further characteristics this something has is evident in Hume (*An Enquiry concerning Human Understanding*, 173), when he says that miracles which are not discoverable are possible: "The raising of a feather, when the wind wants ever so little of a force requisite for that purpose, is as real a miracle, though not so sensible with regard to us."

27   It might be tempting to see Kant's discussion of the sublime as in line with this, but there are important differences. The apparent similarity is that the judgment about something as sublime is not a theoretical one although it is, in a sense, about something sensible (*Kritik der Urteilskraft*, Werkausgabe, ed. Wilhelm Weischedel, vol. 10 (Frankfurt am Main: Suhrkamp, 1974), pp. 164–65) and that Kant understands religion, in contrast to superstition, to be about the sublime (ibid., pp. 188–89). Saying that these are real similarities would mean to accept Kant's terminology, however. But most important right now is to notice the obvious differences. The sublime is nearly related to the spectacular: it is associated with quantity (ibid., pp. 165, 169). Furthermore, according to Kant nothing sensible is sublime (ibid., p. 166): seeing something as sublime is to see beyond it, this sensible something is simply that by means of which one becomes attentive to an idea of reason (ibid., pp. 166–67, 171–72, 180, 185–86). But what I talk about here is not something beyond that which is seen, but to really see this something for the first time. Cf. further John Stuart Mill, *Three Essays on Religion* (London: Longmans, Green, Reader, and Dyer, 1874), p. 26:

> A hurricane; a mountain precipice; the desert; the ocean, either agitated or at rest; the solar system, and the great cosmic forces that hold it together;

the boundless firmament, and to an educated mind any single star; excite feelings ... what makes these phenomena so impressive is simply their vastness. The enormous extension in space and time, or the enormous power they exemplify, constitutes their sublimity; a feeling in all cases, more allied to terror than to any moral emotion ... the feeling it inspires is of a totally different character from admiration of excellence. Those in whom awe produces admiration may be æsthetically developed, but they are morally uncultivated.

Consequently, Adorno fails to notice what is significant here when he writes (Theodor W. Adorno, *Ästhetische Theorie*, ed. Gretel Adorno and Rolf Tiedemann (Frankfurt am Main: Suhrkamp, 1970), p. 110 (see also p. 296)):

Auch die abstrakte Größe der Natur, die Kant noch bewunderte und dem Sittengesetz verglich, wird als Reflex des bürgerlichen Größenwahns, des Sinns für Rekord, der Quantifizierung, auch des bürgerlichen Heroenkults durchschschaut. Darüber entgleitet, daß jenes Moment in der Natur dem Betrachter auch ein ganz Verschiedenes zuwendet, etwas, woran menschliche Herrschaft ihre Grenze hat und was an die Ohnmacht des allmenschlichen Getriebes erinnert.

But in fact, megalomania and powerlessness are, in this context, merely two sides of the same worship of force; there is no necessary tension between them.

28 This is obviously related to Wittgenstein's wonder at the existence of the world, not wondering at the world being in this way as opposed to that way ("A Lecture on Ethics", 41–42); and "It is not *how* things are in the world that is mystical, but *that* it exists" (Ludwig Wittgenstein, *Logisch-philosophische Abhandlung; Tractatus Logico-Philosophicus*, trans. D. F. Pears and B. F. McGuinness (London: Routledge and Kegan Paul, 1961), § 6.44).
For another kind of emphasis on seeing everything as a miracle, cf. Friedrich Schleiermacher, *Über die Religion: Reden an die Gebildeten unter ihren Verächtern*, ed. Günter Meckenstock (Berlin: Walter de Gruyter, 2001), 108:

Das Streiten, welche Begebenheit eigentlich ein Wunder sei, und worin der Charakter deßelben eigentlich bestehe ... und das offenbare Bestreben, so viel sich mit Anstand und Rüksicht thun läßt, davon abzuleugnen und auf die Seite zu schaffen, in der thörichten Meinung der Philosophie und der Vernunft einen Dienst damit zu leisten, das ist eine von den kindischen Operationen der Metaphysiker und Moralisten in der Religion ... Wunder ist nur der religiöse Name für Begebenheit, jede, auch die allernatürlichste und gewöhnlichste, sobald sie sich dazu eignet, daß die religiöse Ansicht von ihr die herrschende sein kann, ist ein Wunder. Mir is alles Wunder ... Je religiöser Ihr wäret, desto mehr Wunder würdet Ihr überall sehen, und jedes Streiten hin und her über einzelne Begebenheiten, ob sie so zu heißen verdiene, giebt mir nur den schmerzhaften Eindruk wie arm und dürftig der religiöse Sinn der Streitenden ist.

29 That I may come to see something which thwarts my egoistic plans as a miracle is not paid attention to by Feuerbach. For him, belief in miracles and egoism are inseparable (see Feuerbach, *Das Wesen des Christentums*, 186, 297). But with regard to much philosophizing about miracles, what he says is to the point.
30 Simone Weil, *Lettre à un religieux* (Paris: Gallimard, 1951), 58 (my translation).
31 See ch. 2 and 4.
32 That the question about what to believe is a personal one – which does not mean that it is unrelated to philosophical questions, on the contrary – is systematically ignored in philosophical theology. That the question about what is "worthy of worship" – a heading popular in books of this type – is a question which has to do with the one who writes the book him- or herself, is almost never made explicit. One example, but not from philosophical theology as such: When John K. Roth ("Critique of David Ray Griffin", in *Encountering Evil: Live Options in Theodicy*, ed. Stephen T. Davis, 2nd ed. (Louisville: Westminster John Knox Press, 2001), p. 128) criticizes a specific conception of God for being "pathetic" and "too small", for inspiring "little awe, little sense of holiness", for not making "a difference that is decisive enough", for not deserving "much attention", he takes it for granted, since the issue is not discussed by him at all, that the problem is not in himself, that his way of making the distinction is morally innocent. This does not mean that I am an advocate of the conception he criticizes, but it is beyond my understanding how anyone can say, as Roth does, that God is pure will ("A Theodicy of Protest", in *Encountering Evil: Live Options in Theodicy*, ed. Stephen T. Davis, 2nd ed. (Louisville: Westminster John Knox Press, 2001), p. 13) – and thereby, in contrast to a God understood in moral terms, inspiring awe and a sense of holiness – without seeing how shady that general way of relating to the world which this understanding of God expresses is.
33 Cf. Strandberg, *Escaping My Responsibility*, ch. 4.
34 Cf. Martin Heidegger, *Was heißt Denken?* 5th ed. (Tübingen: Max Niemeyer, 1997), p. 43.
35 Cf. Hegel, *Grundlinien der Philosophie des Rechts*, § 15.
36 Cf. Lev Shestov, *Kierkegaard and the Existential Philosophy*, trans. Elinor Hewitt (Athens: Ohio University Press, 1969), p. 269.
37 That is, that there would be a similar relation between them as the one which Anscombe claims there is between moral obligation and religious belief (G. E. M. Anscombe, *Human Life, Action and Ethics*, ed. Mary Geach and Luke Gormally (Exeter: Imprint Academic, 2005), pp. 175–77).

Chapter 8

1 The possibility of such a person is far from clear. See ch. 3.
2 This shows the point of using a word like "soul": it is not an extramoral concept, and thereby does not give the impression of being such a bridge. (Of course, this concept is sometimes understood as a theoretical one and is then no better than other theoretical concepts, but as I said at the end of ch. 4, this is not how I use it.)

3 Cf. ch. 2.
4 Mill, *Three Essays on Religion*, 28:

> [N]ext to the greatness of these cosmic forces, the quality which most forcibly strikes every one who does not avert his eyes from it, is their perfect and absolute recklessness. They go straight to their end, without regarding what or whom they crush on the road.
>
> Killing, the most criminal act recognized by human laws, Nature does once to every being that lives; and in a large proportion of cases, after protracted tortures such as only the greatest monsters whom we read of ever purposely inflicted on their fellow-creatures. If, by an arbitrary reservation, we refuse to account anything murder but what abridges a certain term supposed to be allotted to human life, nature also does this to all but a small percentage of lives, and does it in all the modes, violent and insidious, in which the worst human beings take the lives of one another. Nature impales men, breaks them as if on the wheel, casts them to be devoured by wild beasts, burns them to death, crushes them with stones like the first christian martyr, starves them with hunger, freezes them with cold, poisons them by the quick or slow venom of her exhalations. (ibid., pp. 28–29)
>
> Supposing it is true that contrary to appearances these horrors when perpetrated by Nature, promote good ends, still as no one believes that good ends would be promoted by our following the example, the course of Nature cannot be a proper model for us to imitate. Either it is right that we should kill because nature kills; torture because nature tortures; ruin and devastate because nature does the like; or we ought not to consider at all what nature does, but what it is good to do. (ibid., p. 31)

When reading what Mill writes here, one could object: "You say that the cosmic forces go straight to their end, without regarding what or whom they crush on the road, but what would it mean for them to regard this? You say that killing is something Nature does once to every being that lives, but should one really use intentional terms when speaking about 'Nature' in general? Does nature *do* anything ? Specifically, does it *kill?*" Such an objection underlines my point. It shows that nature cannot be copied, as if it were some kind of moral manual; I face questions "Nature" does not face.

5 See Strandberg, *Escaping My Responsibility*, esp. ch. 3 and 5.
6 Part of the problem is the phrase "struggle for existence". Charles Darwin (*On the Origin of Species by Means of Natural Selection, or, The Preservation of Favoured Races in the Struggle for Life* (London: John Murray, 1860), 62) points out that "I use the term Struggle for Existence in a large and metaphorical sense" and then goes on (ibid., pp. 62–63):

> Two canine animals in a time of dearth, may be truly said to struggle with each other which shall get food and live. But a plant on the edge of a

> desert is said to struggle for life against the drought, though more properly it should be said to be dependent on the moisture. A plant which annually produces a thousand seeds, of which on an average only one comes to maturity, may be more truly said to struggle with the plants of the same and other kinds which already clothe the ground.

This is somewhat misleading, though. The two animals may struggle with each other in the literal sense, but they may not; even if one of them dies and the other one survives, they could be said to struggle in the metaphorical sense. And why the plant "may be more truly said to struggle" I cannot see; this is also a metaphorical use. The important point – however broadly one uses the phrase "struggle for existence" and whatever one's view on metaphor and literality – is simply that one should pay attention to the *differences* between all these cases. Furthermore, cf. David Hume, *Dialogues concerning Natural Religion*, ed. Stanley Tweyman (London: Routledge, 1991), p. 146.

7 Cf. Jacques Ellul, *The Technological Society*, trans. John Wilkinson (New York: Vintage Books, 1964), pp. 3–7, 19–22.

8 Martin Heidegger, *Die Frage nach der Technik*, in *Vorträge und Aufsätze*, 10th ed. (Stuttgart: Klett-Cotta, 2004), pp. 9–40.

9 And in ch. 4.

10 Arne Næss, "The Shallow and the Deep, Long-Range Ecology Movement", *Inquiry* 16 (1973): pp. 95–100.

11 Arne Næss, *Økologi, samfunn og livsstil: Utkast til en økosofi*, 5th ed. (Oslo: Universitetsforlaget, 1976).

12 Arne Næss, *Ecology, Community and Lifestyle: Outline of an Ecosophy*, trans. and ed. David Rothenberg (Cambridge: Cambridge University Press, 1989).

13 Næss, "The Shallow and the Deep, Long-Range Ecology Movement", p. 99.

14 Here one could return to my discussion in ch. 3: Seeing someone as not cut off from that love is internal to holding her responsible. It is not something one infers from her behavior.

15 Næss, *Økologi, samfunn og livsstil*, pp. 274–78. (Corresponds roughly to Næss, *Ecology, Community and Lifestyle*, pp. 171–75.)

16 However, Næss does mention "togetherness" (*Ecology, Community and Lifestyle*, 175), but understands it as synonymous with "identification".

17 A previous version of a part of this chapter has been published as "Det är vilseledande att betona djupekologins djup", *Ikaros* 4, no. 3 (2007).

Chapter 9

1 Richard Swinburne, *Providence and the Problem of Evil* (Oxford: Oxford University Press, 1998), p. 161.

2 See, e.g., J. L. Mackie, "Evil and Omnipotence", *Mind* 64 (1955): pp. 200–12; J. L. Mackie, *The Miracle of Theism: Arguments for and against the Existence of God* (Oxford: Oxford University Press, 1983), p. 150. Notice that it is irrelevant for my subsequent discussion whether these additional premises are true or not, or whether they are at all needed or not; rather, the question is what the "premises" mean.

3 See, e.g., Nelson Pike, "Hume on Evil", *Philosophical Review* 72 (1963): pp. 180–97; Alvin Plantinga, *God, Freedom, and Evil* (Grand Rapids: Eerdmans, 1977).

4 See, e.g., Stephen T. Davis, "Free Will and Evil", in *Encountering Evil: Live Options in Theodicy*, ed. Stephen T. Davis, 2nd ed. (Louisville: Westminster John Know Press, 2001), 74: "(1), (2), and (3) are consistent and can all be rationally believed. ... I think it is largely due to the work of Plantinga that one rarely hears any longer the problem presented as if it were a purely logical problem, as if the theists were contradicting themselves."

5 See, e.g., Michael Martin, "Is Evil Evidence against the Existence of God?" *Mind* 87 (1978): pp. 429–32; William L. Rowe, "The Problem of Evil and Some Varieties of Atheism", *American Philosophical Quarterly* 16 (1979): pp. 335–41.

6 See, e.g., Alvin Plantinga, "The Probabilistic Problem from Evil", *Philosophical Studies* 35 (1979): pp. 1–53.

7 See, e.g., Swinburne, *Providence and the Problem of Evil.*

8 Cora Diamond, *The Realistic Spirit: Wittgenstein, Philosophy and the Mind* (Cambridge: MIT Press, 1991), ch. 3.

9 See, e.g., David R. Cerbone, "How to Do Things with Wood: Wittgenstein, Frege and the Problem of Illogical Thought", in *The New Wittgenstein*, ed. Alice Crary and Rupert Read (London: Routledge, 2000), pp. 293–314; Lars Hertzberg, "The Sense Is Where You Find It", in *Wittgenstein in America*, ed. Timothy McCarthy and Sean Stidd (Oxford: Oxford University Press, 2001), pp. 90–103. (Phillips discusses this in *Religion and Friendly Fire*, pp. 65–67.)

10 See Gottlob Frege, *Die Grundlagen der Arithmetik: Eine logisch mathematische Untersuchung über den Begriff der Zahl* (Breslau: Wilhelm Koebner, 1884), x.

11 Wittgenstein, *Philosophical Investigations*, § 500.

12 Lars Hertzberg, "On Excluding Contradictions from Our Language", in *Wittgenstein and the Method of Philosophy*, ed. Sami Pihlström (Helsinki: Acta Philosophica Fennica, 2006), p. 176. Cf. Ludwig Wittgenstein, *Wittgenstein's Lectures on the Foundations of Mathematics, Cambridge, 1939*, ed. Cora Diamond (Ithaca: Cornell University Press, 1976), p. 176.

13 The following discussion is partly inspired by D. Z. Phillips, *The Problem of Evil and the Problem of God* (London: SCM Press, 2004), ch. 1, but it also parts from his discussion on many points.

14 Cf. how Peter Winch (*Ethics and Action* (London: Routledge and Kegan Paul, 1972), pp. 24–26) discusses what it means to say that Azande contradict themselves, that there is a contradiction in their practice: it is the European, who presses the Zande to go in thought where he does not usually go, who makes a mistake. Cf. also Wittgenstein, *Lectures on the Foundations of Mathematics*, p. 138.

15 Cf. Wittgenstein, *Philosophical Investigations*, § 188.

16 Wittgenstein, *Culture and Value*, p. 29:

> Someone can be told for instance: "Thank God for the good you receive but don't complain about the evil: as you would of course do if a human being were to do you good and evil by turns." Rules of life are dressed up in pictures. And these pictures can only serve to *describe* what we are to do, not *justify* it. Because they could provide a justification only if they held good in other respects as well. I can say: "Thank these bees for their honey

as though they were kind people who have prepared it for you"; that is *intelligible* and describes how I should like you to conduct yourself. But I cannot say: "Thank them because, look, how kind they are!" – since the next moment they may sting you.

Some of what Wittgenstein is saying here is somewhat misleading – "dressed up in pictures", the transition from justification to description, "as though they were kind people" – but the main point is this, I take it: the kind of gratitude Wittgenstein is talking about is not based on a hypothesis, as if there in it were an idea about what will and will not happen.

17 Michael Dummett has said something similar to this. See *The Logical Basis of Metaphysics* (Cambridge: Harvard University Press, 1991), ch. 4.

18 Phillips, *Religion and Friendly Fire*, p. 11. However, Phillips is right if confusion here does not refer to logic, but, for example, to morality. I will return to this. (One example Phillips returns to now and again is Wittgenstein's remarks on the scapegoat ritual (D. Z. Phillips, *Belief, Change and Forms of Life* (Atlantic Highlands: Humanities Press, 1986), pp. 29–32; Phillips, *Religion and Friendly Fire*, pp. 100–02). Phillips points out that the confusion is not merely a logical or linguistic one. But still he does not pay enough attention to the moral side of it. For such a discussion, although not unproblematic, see René Girard, *Things Hidden since the Foundation of the World*, trans. Stephen Bann and Michael Metteer (Stanford: Stanford University Press, 1987), ch. 1, 5; René Girard, *The Scapegoat*, trans. Yvonne Freccero (Baltimore: Johns Hopkins University Press, 1986)).

19 Cf. Winch, *The Idea of a Social Science*, pp. 49–51, 99–100.

20 Cf. ibid., pp. 100–01.

21 Cf. Gottlob Frege, *Grundgesetze der Arithmetik, begriffsschriftlich abgeleitet*, vol. 1 (Jena: Hermann Pohle, 1893), xix; Edmund Husserl, *Logische Untersuchungen*, vol. 1, *Prolegomena zur reinen Logik*, 2nd ed. (Halle an der Saale, 1913), § 21. (Cf. also Ludwig Wittgenstein, *Bemerkungen über die Grundlagen der Mathematik*, ed. G. E. M. Anscombe, Rush Rhees, and G. H. von Wright (Frankfurt am Main: Suhrkamp, 1984), 95.) Moreover, if we try to justify logic by referring to its alleged truth, the question arises in what sense a sentence in logic is true, as its opposite is not false but not even a conceivable candidate for truth. Nor is logic possible to justify by referring to efficiency or some kind of means/end-rationality, since something contradictory may in some situations be as effective as the non-contradictory (cf. Wittgenstein, *Lectures on the Foundations of Mathematics*, 175).

22 Cf. Wittgenstein, *Tractatus*, §§ 5.473, 5.5563–5.557; Wittgenstein, *Lectures on the Foundations of Mathematics*, pp. 231–32.

23 See Wittgenstein, *Tractatus*, § 5.473; Wittgenstein, *Notebooks, 1914–1926*, ed. G. H. von Wright and G. E. M. Anscombe, 2nd ed. (Chicago: University of Chicago Press, 1979), p. 2.

24 See, e.g., Plantinga, *God, Freedom, and Evil*, pp. 28–29, 64; Davis, "Free Will and Evil," pp. 79–88.

25 See, e.g., Marilyn McCord Adams, "Redemptive Suffering: A Christian Solution to the Problem of Evil", in *Rationality, Religious Belief and Moral Commitment: New Essays in the Philosophy of Religion*, ed. Robert Audi and

Williams J. Wainwright (Ithaca: Cornell University Press, 1986), pp. 250–51; Marilyn McCord Adams, "Horrendous Evils and the Goodness of God", *Aristotelian Society Supplementary Volume* 63 (1989): pp. 302–04. (And even in this case, the problem is phrased in a way which intimates that it is understood in terms of logic: the problem is still about what is possible to combine. To be sure, the problem is no longer understood as a question about whether the belief, as a set of propositions, is compatible with the proposition that evil exists, but still the problem is understood as a question about whether my belief is compatible with my experience of evil. A good example of this tendency: William Hasker, "On Regretting the Evils of This World", *Southern Journal of Philosophy* 19 (1981): pp. 425–37.)

26 Cf. Lars Hertzberg, "The Limits of Understanding", *Sats: Nordic Journal of Philosophy* 6 (2005): pp. 5–14.

27 See ch. 3.

28 Irving Greenberg, "Cloud of Smoke, Pillar of Fire", in *Holocaust: Religious and Philosophical Implications*, ed. John K. Roth and Michael Berenbaum (St. Paul: Paragon House, 1989), p. 315. Cf. also Adorno's (much misunderstood) sayings about the possibility of poetry after Auschwitz: *Negative Dialektik*, in vol. 6 of *Gesammelte Schriften*, ed. Rolf Tiedemann, 3rd ed. (Frankfurt am Main: Suhrkamp, 1984), p. 355; *Prismen: Kulturkritik und Gesellschaft*, in vol. 10, bk. 1, of *Gesammelte Schriften*, ed. Rolf Tiedemann (Frankfurt am Main: Suhrkamp, 1977), p. 30; *Ohne Leitbild: Parva Aesthetica*, in vol. 10, bk. 1, of *Gesammelte Schriften*, ed. Rolf Tiedemann (Frankfurt am Main, 1977), pp. 452–53; *Noten zur Literatur IV*, in vol. 11 of *Gesammelte Schriften*, ed. Rolf Tiedemann, 3rd ed. (Frankfurt am Main: Suhrkamp, 1990), p. 603.

29 Cf. Ludwig Wittgenstein, *Lectures and Conversations on Aesthetics, Psychology and Religious Belief*, ed. Cyril Barrett (Oxford: Blackwell, 1966), p. 43.

30 Karl Marx, *Zur Kritik der Hegelschen Rechtsphilosophie: Einleitung*, in vol. 1 of *Marx Engels Werke*, 7th ed. (Berlin: Dietz, 1970), p. 378.

31 Cf. Friedrich Engels, *Der deutsche Bauernkrieg*, in vol. 7 of *Marx Engels Werke*, 3rd ed. (Berlin: Dietz, 1969), pp. 400–02.

32 On the other hand, Marx claims that we do only give ourselves tasks, the solutions to which are within reach (Karl Marx, *Zur Kritik der Politischen Ökonomie*, in vol. 13 of *Marx Engels Werke*, 3rd ed. (Berlin: Dietz, 1969), p. 9). If that is so, the religious understanding of the problem is not a matter of posing a problem it is not (yet) historically possible to solve. In the end, phrases like "historically possible" and "historically impossible" are far more unclear than helpful, I would say: what would it be to show that something is historically (im)possible or not?

33 See Kierkegaard, *Kjerlighedens Gjerninger*, pp. 185–90.

34 Kierkegaard, *Opbyggelige Taler i forskjellig Aand*, pp. 40–45.

35 Of course, here one should notice that stressing the difference, as well as stressing the similarity or the identity, of the experiences, gets its significance in the light of the intended contrast. This means that it is correct, in the light of another question, to stress the similarity and the identity, as I actually did above: "what we are going through is the *same*." As I said in ch. 6, it is important to notice the difference between going through something together and going through something, how ever identical it may seem to be, each one on one's own.

36 Cf. Rowan Williams, "Redeeming Sorrows", in *Religion and Morality*, ed. D. Z. Phillips (Basingstoke: Macmillan, 1996), pp. 133–34; Stanley Cavell, *Must We Mean What We Say?* (Cambridge: Cambridge University Press, 1976), ch. 9.

37 Of course, it is possible – in both of these cases – that I find the reactions exaggerated and false – a *pretended* hopelessness and joy respectively – but it is clear that the reactions do not have to be of that character. What I discuss are those cases where they are not of that character.

38 See Strandberg, *Escaping My Responsibility*, ch. 8.

39 Cf. de Sade's "proof" that virtue does not pay and God does not exist in *Justine; or, Good Conduct Well Chastised* (in *Justine, Philosophy in the Bedroom and Other Writings*, trans. Austryn Wainhouse and Richard Seaver (London: Arrow Books, 1965)). By returning evil for good, the people Justine meets on her way tries to show her the folly of goodness, and when she, being tortured, begins to pray to God, her torturer takes this to show that God, or the God she believes in, does not exist: "[H]e doesn't much aid you, your God, does he? and thus he allows unhappy virtue to suffer, he abandons it to villainy's hands; ah! what a bloody fine God you've got there" (ibid., p. 675). (But it should be pointed out that Justine's virtue has obviously shady aspects. De Sade seems to have been unable to portray real goodness).

40 Weil, *Gravity and Grace*, p. 76.

Chapter 10

1 Ch. 2.

2 Wittgenstein, *Philosophical Investigations*, §§ 240–42.

3 Ibid., §§ 201–02.

4 Winch, *The Idea of a Social Science*, pp. 55–57.

5 Winch has the example from Lewis Carroll, "What the Tortoise Said to Achilles", *Mind* 4 (1895). See also W. V. Quine, *The Ways of Paradox, and Other Essays* (New York: Random House, 1966), pp. 96–99.

6 Winch, *The Idea of a Social Science*, p. 57.

7 Hertzberg, "On Excluding Contradictions from Our Language," p. 176. Cf. Wittgenstein, *Lectures on the Foundations of Mathematics*, p. 176.

8 The latter one is much more complicated that it might look like. The difficulty is not only the apparent contradiction in the saying, but that the person who says this is himself or herself divided. As Ovid says, "[H]e who says o'er much 'I love not' is in love" (*Remedia Amoris; The Remedies for Love*, in *The Art of Love, and Other Poems*, trans. J. H. Mozley, 2nd ed. (London: William Heinemann, 1979), p. 221). I have touched upon this in ch. 5.

9 For a lengthier discussion of these issues, see ch. 9.

10 See, e.g., Bertrand Russell, *Our Knowledge of the External World, as a Field for Scientific Method in Philosophy* (London: George Allen and Unwin, 1914), ch. 4; Rudolf Carnap, *Der logische Aufbau der Welt* (Berlin: Weltkreis-Verlag, 1928), §§ 67–68, 179.

11 Cf. Hegel, *Phänomenologie des Geistes*, pp. 82–107, for the point that there is an insoluble tension in the concept of sense-data: they are supposed to be both conceptual and nonconceptual.

12 The idea that language constructs reality, and that there is some kind of fundamental insecurity and instability to language, entailing that everything said must
be said within quotation marks, is simply the other side to that understanding
of language I criticized above. Both the idea of linguistic transparency and this
idea see the relation between language and reality as an external one; it is only
the point from which the relation is seen which is another one. That the relation is not an external one means that it is not language which makes something
clear or unclear, but what I say which is clear or unclear. For that reason, it is
misleading to say that there are no limitations.

13 In other words, conceptual analysis – understood as the laying down of necessary and sufficient condition for the application of some concept – is never as
such the solution to a philosophical problem.

14 The examples are numerous. See, for example, the title and subtitle to this
book: Max Black, *Critical Thinking: An Introduction to Logic and Scientific Method*
(New York: Prentice-Hall, 1946).

15 Cf. Augustine, *On Christian Doctrine*, trans. J. F. Shaw, in vol. 2 of *A Select Library of
the Nicene and Post-Nicene Fathers of the Christian Church*, ed. Philip Schaff (Grand
Rapids: Eerdmans, 1956), p. 551:

> There are also valid processes of reasoning which lead to false conclu-
> sions, by following out to its logical consequences the error of the man
> with whom one is arguing; and these conclusions are sometimes drawn by
> a good and learned man, with the object of making the person from whose
> error these consequences result, feel ashamed.

And cf. Collingwood, *The Principles of Art*, pp. 106–07: "Philosophers, especially
those with an academic position, inherit a long tradition of arguing for the sake
of arguing; even if they despair of reaching the truth, they think it a matter of
pride to make other philosophers look foolish." That "argue" sometimes means
"quarrel" is no coincidence.

16 Rudolf Carnap, "Überwindung der Metaphysik durch logische Analyse der
Sprache", *Erkenntnis* 2 (1931): pp. 229–32.

17 Martin Heidegger, *Was ist Metaphysik?* in *Wegmarken*, Gesamtausgabe 9, 3rd ed.
(Frankfurt am Main: Vittorio Klostermann, 2004), pp. 103–22.

18 Heidegger is explicit about this: ibid., p. 107.

19 According to Heidegger (ibid., pp. 114–15, 120–21), it is anxiety which discloses
being as something whole, it is anxiety which makes us transcend something,
thereby making it into something to investigate.

20 Simone Weil, *The Need for Roots: Prelude to a Declaration of Duties towards Mankind*
(London: Routledge and Kegan Paul, 1952), p. 242.

21 However, it should be noted that a line of thought similar to Weil's for once shines
through in this very text of Heidegger's, when he talks about the joy at the presence of a human being one loves (*Was ist Metaphysik?*, p. 110). And in another
place (*Brief über den "Humanismus"*, p. 316) he seems to be even closer to Weil, even
though it is not that clear how what he there says should be understood. See also
Heidegger, *Einführung in die Metaphysik*, 6th ed. (Tübingen: Max Niemeyer, 1998),
p. 1; Heidegger, *Grundprobleme der Phänomenologie*, Gesamtausgabe 58, 2nd ed.

(Frankfurt am Main: Vittorio Klostermann, 2010), p. 185; Heidegger, *Heraklit: 1. Der Anfang des abendländischen Denkens, 2. Logik: Heraklits Lehre vom Logos*, Gesamtausgabe 55, 3rd ed. (Frankfurt am Main: Vittorio Klostermann, 1994), pp. 212–13.

22 Pl., *Grg.* 469b and passim.

23 Pl., *Grg.* 508e.

24 Pl., *Grg.* 475c–e, 480e.

25 Pl., *Grg.* 482e.

26 See, e.g., Pl., *Grg.* 476d–477a.

27 Pl., *Grg.* 483b–484b.

28 See, e.g., Pl., *Grg.* 488c–489c, 490a, 498b–499b, 512c–513c.

29 This shows that love – a central concept in this book – is not a moral "position" or the like, but that which makes morality possible. Cf. Beehler, *Moral Life*, ch. 1 and 6. I have come back to this now and then, for example, in ch. 5. Furthermore, this shows that it is unclear, to say the least, whether a person who does not care at all for others is really possible; see ch. 3.

30 Cf. Gaita, *Good and Evil*, pp. 310–13.

31 See Anscombe, *Human Life, Action and Ethics*, p. 162.

32 Anscombe stresses this (ibid., p. 163, 167).

33 Cf. ch. 6.

34 Cf. Mao Tse-tung, *On Contradiction*, in vol. 1 of *Selected Works* (Peking: Foreign Languages Press, 1965), pp. 343–475; Mao Tse-tung, *On the Correct Handling of Contradictions among the People*, in vol. 5 of *Selected Works* (Peking: Foreign Languages Press, 1977), pp. 384–96.

35 Friedrich Engels, *Zur Wohnungsfrage*, in vol. 18 of *Marx Engels Werke*, 3rd ed. (Berlin: Dietz, 1969), p. 237 (my translation).

36 See, e.g., Friedrich Engels, *Herrn Eugen Dührings Umwälzung der Wissenschaft (Anti-Dühring)*, in vol. 20 of *Marx Engels Werke*, 2nd ed. (Berlin: Dietz, 1968), pp. 87–88.

37 This is Engels unable to see, however. In the quotation, he seems to be seeing morality as an exclusively argumentative matter, something you can *only* make sermons about. This confusion is a result of some philosophical prejudices he has, about what morality *must* be to be something real. Engels's moral relativism and moral skepticism are based on the fact that morality is not explanatory and predictive (ibid., pp. 87–88, 138–39, 248–49) and on the fact that human beings have, and have had, different opinions in moral matters (ibid., p. 86, 145). But Marxism is not a relativism, generally speaking. Marx and Engels do not satisfy themselves with presenting a theory, as good as any other, but claim that what they say is correct (even though the difficulties of seeing that it is correct, if it is, may be ideologically conditioned). Therefore, his moral relativism must be based on a clear-cut distinction between, on the one hand, history, economics, philosophy, and so forth, and, on the other hand, morality. This distinction – which is not the same as the one between base and superstructure – Engels makes without discussion, however; furthermore, it is confused (see Strandberg, *Escaping My Responsibility*). Nevertheless, it is right that there are no moral movements on a *collective* level – this is what is meant by collectivity – only on a personal one. (Cf. G. W. F. Hegel, *Vorlesungen über die Philosophie der Geschichte*, Werke, ed. Eva Moldenhauer and Karl Markus Michel, vol. 12 (Frankfurt am Main: Suhrkamp, 1986), p. 457 (my translation): "Piety is outside

history and without history.") In that sense, one could say that the historical/ societal side to the struggle – if this side is understood as the collective side – is about economics, even though the forms in which a group becomes conscious of the conflicts and fights them out are different (cf. Marx, *Zur Kritik der Politischen Ökonomie*, p. 9).

Another way of approaching this confusion of Engels's is by noticing the difference between what I said in sec. III and a vulgar form of Marxist materialism, made explicit when Engels *contrasts* thinking and fact (*Ludwig Feuerbach und der Ausgang der klassischen deutschen Philosophie*, in vol. 21 of *Marx Engels Werke*, 2nd ed. (Berlin: Dietz, 1969), p. 306). Another typical example is this quote from V. I. Lenin's *Materialism and Empirio-Criticism: Critical Comments on a Reactionary Philosophy* (New York: International Publishers, 1927), p. 106 (but the whole book could be an example): "[T]hings exist outside us. Our perceptions and ideas are their images." And another quote from Engels ("Einleitung zur englischen Ausgabe (1892) der *Entwicklung des Sozialismus von der Utopie zur Wissenschaft*," in vol. 22 of *Marx Engels Werke*, 2nd ed. (Berlin: Dietz, 1970), p. 297 (my translation)):

> Not in one single case, as far as till now is known, we have been forced to the conclusion that our scientifically controlled sense-perceptions induce representations of the outer world in our brain that, with respect to their nature, differ from reality, or that there is an inherent incompatibility between the outer world and our sense-perceptions of it.

Both Lenin and Engels share with those they criticize the scheme of thought of "the inner / the outer"; thus they are as philosophically confused as them. Marx, however, is, as far as I can see, aiming at something else than such a vulgar materialism. In the theses on Feuerbach, especially theses 1 and 3, it is not a matter of knowledge as representation/image, not of passive observation or letting oneself be causally affected, but of action (Marx, *Thesen über Feuerbach*, in vol. 3 of *Marx Engels Werke*, 4th ed. (Berlin: Dietz, 1969), pp. 5–6, 533–34). (In that respect, Lenin's materialism is not a *dialectical* materialism; the one he primarily refers to is Feuerbach, not Marx.)

On the other hand, Engels definitely expresses himself, with regard to questions in the theory of science, in a nonempiricist way on other occasions (see, e.g., "Vorwort zum zweiten Buch des *Kapital*," in vol. 24 of *Marx Engels Werke*, 3rd ed. (Berlin: Dietz, 1970), pp. 21–25). Furthermore – if we leave dialectical for historical materialism – he stresses that the laws of history are few in number and have primarily merely retrospective and specific validity (Engels, *Anti-Dühring*, pp. 82–83, 136–37; cf. Marx, *Zur Kritik der Politischen Ökonomie*, p. 8; Marx, *Das Kapital*, vol. 1, in vol. 23 of *Marx Engels Werke*, 5th ed. (Berlin: Dietz, 1970), pp. 26–27), which means that historical materialism should not be understood as a thesis, some kind of general law for human history, but as a description of one kind of investigation the result of which must be judged from case to case. To be sure, Engels says things which point in another direction too, but him being vague when he is pressed about what historical materialism is – his infamous saying, "das *in letzter Instanz* bestimmende Moment" ("Brief an Joseph Bloch," in vol. 37 of *Marx Engels Werke* (Berlin: Dietz, 1967), p. 463) – is an expression of his unclarity as to these kinds of questions. For Engels, the emphasis on what is material is, in the end, simply a matter of how one should *explain* the success, or failure, of some historical political struggle (*Anti-Dühring*, p. 146). But since it is in the form of a moral question we become conscious of the antagonism and this consciousness does not arise until a successful struggle is possible (ibid., pp. 138–39, 248–49; cf. Marx, *Zur Kritik der Politischen Ökonomie*, p. 9), that means that one could say that the political struggle *for those who struggle* is *essentially* a moral one.

However, that the struggle could be said to be a moral one should not be understood in a too simple way. Economics is not something purely external, but is, in different ways, an expression of how we, on a collective level, *understand* some of our interactions. To that extent, it is not possible to distinguish sharply between an oppressive economic condition and an oppressive understanding of human interaction, and it is not possible to change one's understanding of human interaction in isolation from a change of this very condition. But these are not causal relations, but relations of meaning.

38　Mao Tse-tung, *Problems of War and Strategy*, in vol. 2 of *Selected Works* (Peking: Foreign Languages Press, 1965), p. 224.

Bibliography

Adams, Marilyn McCord. "Horrendous Evils and the Goodness of God." *Aristotelian Society Supplementary Volume* 63 (1989): pp. 297–310.

———. "Redemptive Suffering: A Christian Solution to the Problem of Evil." In *Rationality, Religious Belief and Moral Commitment: New Essays in the Philosophy of Religion*, eds Robert Audi and Williams J. Wainwright, pp. 248–67. Ithaca: Cornell University Press, 1986.

Adorno, Theodor W. *Ästhetische Theorie.* Eds Gretel Adorno and Rolf Tiedemann. Frankfurt am Main: Suhrkamp, 1970.

———. *Negative Dialektik.* In vol. 6 of *Gesammelte Schriften*, ed. Rolf Tiedemann, 3rd ed., pp. 7–412. Frankfurt am Main: Suhrkamp, 1984.

———. *Noten zur Literatur IV.* In vol. 11 of *Gesammelte Schriften*, ed. Rolf Tiedemann, 3rd ed., pp. 493–606. Frankfurt am Main: Suhrkamp, 1990.

———. *Ohne Leitbild: Parva Aesthetica.* In vol. 10, bk. 1, of *Gesammelte Schriften*, ed. Rolf Tiedemann, pp. 289–453. Frankfurt am Main: Suhrkamp, 1977.

———. *Prismen: Kulturkritik und Gesellschaft.* In vol. 10, bk. 1, of *Gesammelte Schriften*, ed. Rolf Tiedemann, pp. 9–287. Frankfurt am Main: Suhrkamp, 1977.

———. *Stichworte: Kritische Modelle 2.* In vol. 10, bk. 2, of *Gesammelte Schriften*, ed. Rolf Tiedemann, pp. 595–782. Frankfurt am Main: Suhrkamp, 1977.

Anscombe, G. E. M. *Faith in a Hard Ground: Essays on Religion, Philosophy and Ethics.* Eds Mary Geach and Luke Gormally. Exeter: Imprint Academic, 2008.

———. *Human Life, Action and Ethics.* Eds Mary Geach and Luke Gormally. Exeter: Imprint Academic, 2005.

Arendt, Hannah. *The Human Condition.* 2nd ed. Chicago: University of Chicago Press, 1998.

Aristotle. *Physics.* Translated by Robin Waterfield. Oxford: Oxford University Press, 1996.

Augustine. *On Christian Doctrine.* Translated by J. F. Shaw. In vol. 2 of *A Select Library of the Nicene and Post-Nicene Fathers of the Christian Church*, ed. Philip Schaff, pp. 513–97. Grand Rapids: Eerdmans, 1956.

Beehler, Rodger. *Moral Life.* Oxford: Basil Blackwell, 1978.

Benjamin, Walter. *Über den Begriff der Geschichte.* In vol. 1, bk. 2, of *Gesammelte Schriften*, eds Rolf Tiedemann and Hermann Schweppenhäuser, pp. 691–704. Frankfurt am Main: Suhrkamp, 1974.

———. *Zur Kritik der Gewalt.* In vol 2, bk. 1, of *Gesammelte Schriften*, eds Rolf Tiedemann and Hermann Schweppenhäuser, pp. 179–203. Frankfurt am Main: Suhrkamp, 1977.

Bergson, Henri. *Les deux sources de la morale et de la religion.* Paris: Librairie Félix Alcan, 1932.

Black, Max. *Critical Thinking: An Introduction to Logic and Scientific Method.* New York: Prentice-Hall, 1946.

Buber, Martin. *I and Thou.* Translated by. R. G. Smith. Edinburgh: T&T Clark, 1957.

Cameron, Euan. *The European Reformation.* Oxford: Oxford University Press, 1991.

Caputo, John D. *On Religion.* London: Routledge, 2001.

Carnap, Rudolf. *Der logische Aufbau der Welt.* Berlin: Weltkreis-Verlag, 1928.

————. "Überwindung der Metaphysik durch logische Analyse der Sprache." *Erkenntnis* 2 (1931): pp. 219–41.

Carroll, Lewis. "What the Tortoise Said to Achilles." *Mind* 4 (1895): pp. 278–80.

Cavell, Stanley. *Must We Mean What We Say?* Cambridge: Cambridge University Press, 1976.

Cerbone, David R. "How to Do Things with Wood: Wittgenstein, Frege and the Problem of Illogical Thought." In *The New Wittgenstein*, eds Alice Crary and Rupert Read, pp. 293–314. London: Routledge, 2000.

Chrétien, Jean-Louis. "The Wounded Word: The Phenomenology of Prayer." Translated by Jeffrey L. Kosky. In *Phenomenology and the "Theological Turn": The French Debate*, pp. 147–75. New York: Fordham University Press, 2000.

Collingwood, R. G. *An Essay on Metaphysics.* Rev. ed. Oxford: Oxford University Press, 1998.

————. *The Principles of Art.* Oxford: Oxford University Press, 1938.

————. *Religion and Philosophy.* London: Macmillan, 1916.

Darwin, Charles. *On the Origin of Species by Means of Natural Selection; or, The Preservation of Favoured Races in the Struggle for Life.* London: John Murray, 1860.

Davis, Stephen T. "Free Will and Evil." In *Encountering Evil: Live Options in Theodicy*, ed. Stephen T. Davis, 2nd ed., pp. 73–89. Louisville: Westminster John Knox Press, 2001.

Derrida, Jacques. *Margins of Philosophy.* Translated by Alan Bass. Chicago: University of Chicago Press, 1982.

Diamond, Cora. *The Realistic Spirit: Wittgenstein, Philosophy and the Mind.* Cambridge: MIT Press, 1991.

————. "Wittgenstein on Religious Belief: The Gulfs between Us." In *Religion and Wittgenstein's Legacy*, eds D. Z. Phillips and Mario von der Ruhr, pp. 99–137. Aldershot: Ashgate, 2005.

Dilman, İlham. "Psychoanalysis and Ethics: Some Reflections on the Self in Its Relationships to Good and Evil." In *Commonality and Particularity in Ethics*, eds Lilli Alanen, Sara Heinämää, and Thomas Wallgren, pp. 123–52. Basingstoke: Macmillan, 1997.

Dummett, Michael. *The Logical Basis of Metaphysics.* Cambridge: Harvard University Press, 1991.

Durkheim, Emile. *The Elementary Forms of Religious Life.* Translated by Karen E. Fields. New York: Free Press, 1995.

Edelman, John T. *An Audience for Moral Philosophy?* Basingstoke: Macmillan, 1990.

Ellul, Jacques. *The Technological Society.* Translated by John Wilkinson. New York: Vintage Books, 1964.

Engels, Friedrich. "Brief an Joseph Bloch." In vol. 37 of *Marx Engels Werke*, pp. 462–65. Berlin: Dietz, 1967.

————. *Der deutsche Bauernkrieg.* In vol. 7 of *Marx Engels Werke*, 3rd ed., pp. 327–413. Berlin: Dietz, 1969.

————. "Einleitung zur englischen Ausgabe (1892) der *Entwicklung des Sozialismus von der Utopie zur Wissenschaft.*" In vol. 22 of *Marx Engels Werke*, 2nd ed., pp. 287–311. Berlin: Dietz, 1970.

————. *Herrn Eugen Dührings Umwälzung der Wissenschaft (Anti-Dühring).* In vol. 20 of *Marx Engels Werke*, 2nd ed., pp. 1–303. Berlin: Dietz, 1968.

————. *Ludwig Feuerbach und der Ausgang der klassischen deutschen Philosophie.* In vol. 21 of *Marx Engels Werke*, 2nd ed., pp. 259–307. Berlin: Dietz, 1969.

————. "Vorwort zum zweiten Buch des *Kapital.*" In vol. 24 of *Marx Engels Werke*, 3rd ed., pp. 7–26. Berlin: Dietz, 1970.

————. *Zur Wohnungsfrage.* In vol. 18 of *Marx Engels Werke*, 3rd ed., pp. 209–87. Berlin: Dietz, 1969.

Erasmus of Rotterdam. *On the Freedom of the Will: A Diatribe or Discourse.* Translated by E. Gordon Rupp. In *Luther and Erasmus: Free Will and Salvation*, eds E. Gordon Rupp and Philip S. Watson, pp. 33–97. Philadelphia: Westminster Press, 1969.

Feuerbach, Ludwig. *Das Wesen des Christentums.* Stuttgart: Reclam, 1969.

Fichte, Johann Gottlieb. *Die Bestimmung des Menschen.* In vol. 2 of *Fichtes Werke*, ed. Immanuel Hermann Fichte, pp. 165–319. Berlin: Walter de Gruyter, 1971.

————. *Versuch einer Kritik aller Offenbarung.* In vol. 5 of *Fichtes Werke*, ed. Immanuel Hermann Fichte, pp. 9–174. Berlin: Walter de Gruyter, 1971.

Frank, S. L. *The Unknowable: An Ontological Introduction to the Philosophy of Religion.* Translated by Boris Jakim. Athens: Ohio University Press, 1983.

Frege, Gottlob. *Grundgesetze der Arithmetik, begriffsschriftlich abgeleitet.* Vol. 1. Jena: Hermann Pohle, 1893.

————. *Die Grundlagen der Arithmetik: Eine logisch mathematische Untersuchung über den Begriff der Zahl.* Breslau: Wilhelm Koebner, 1884.

Freud, Sigmund. *Massenpsychologie und Ich-Analyse.* 2nd ed. Leipzig: Internationaler psychoanalytischer Verlag, 1923.

————. *Neue Folge der Vorlesungen zur Einführung in die Psychoanalyse.* In *Vorlesungen zur Einführung in die Psychoanalyse, und Neue Folge.* Studienausgabe, eds Alexander Mitscherlich, Angela Richards, and James Strachey, 1:447–608. Frankfurt am Main: S. Fischer, 1969.

————. *Die Zukunft einer Illusion.* Leipzig: Internationaler psychoanalytischer Verlag, 1927.

Gaita, Raimond. *A Common Humanity: Thinking about Love and Truth and Justice.* London: Routledge, 2000.

————. Critical notice of *Interventions in Ethics*, by D. Z. Phillips. *Philosophical Investigations* 17 (1994): pp. 613–28.

————. *Good and Evil: An Absolute Conception.* 2nd ed. London: Routledge, 2004.

Girard, René. *The Scapegoat.* Translated by Yvonne Freccero. Baltimore: Johns Hopkins University Press, 1986.

————. *Things Hidden since the Foundation of the World.* Translated by Stephen Bann and Michael Metteer. Stanford: Stanford University Press, 1987.

Greenberg, Irving. "Cloud of Smoke, Pillar of Fire." In *Holocaust: Religious and Philosophical Implications*, eds John K. Roth and Michael Berenbaum, pp. 305–45. St. Paul: Paragon House, 1989.

Hägerström, Axel. *Religionsfilosofi*. Stockholm: Natur och Kultur, 1949.

Hanson, Norwood Russell. *Patterns of Discovery: An Inquiry into the Conceptual Foundations of Science*. Cambridge: Cambridge University Press, 1965.

Hare, R. M. *Freedom and Reason*. Oxford: Oxford University Press, 1963.

Hasker, William. "On Regretting the Evils of This World." *Southern Journal of Philosophy* 19 (1981): pp. 425–37.

Hegel, G. W. F. *Entwürfe über Religion und Liebe*. In *Frühe Schriften*. Werke, eds Eva Moldenhauer and Karl Markus Michel, 1:239–54. Frankfurt am Main: Suhrkamp, 1986.

———. *Der Geist des Christentums und sein Schicksal*. In *Frühe Schriften*. Werke, eds Eva Moldenhauer and Karl Markus Michel, 1:274–418. Frankfurt am Main: Suhrkamp, 1986.

———. *Grundlinien der Philosophie des Rechts; oder, Naturrecht und Staatswissenschaft im Grundrisse*. Werke, eds Eva Moldenhauer and Karl Markus Michel, vol. 7. Frankfurt am Main: Suhrkamp, 1986.

———. *Phänomenologie des Geistes*. Werke, eds Eva Moldenhauer and Karl Markus Michel, vol. 3. Frankfurt am Main: Suhrkamp, 1986.

———. *System der Sittlichkeit [Critik des Fichteschen Naturrechts]*. Ed. Horst D. Brandt. Hamburg: Felix Meiner, 2002.

———. *Über die wissenschaftlichen Behandlungsarten des Naturrechts, seine Stelle in der praktischen Philosophie und sein Verhältnis zu den positiven Rechtswissenschaften*. In *Jenaer Schriften, 1801–1807*. Werke, eds Eva Moldenhauer and Karl Markus Michel, 2:434–530. Frankfurt am Main: Suhrkamp, 1986.

———. *Vorlesungen über die Philosophie der Geschichte*. Werke, eds Eva Moldenhauer and Karl Markus Michel, vol. 12. Frankfurt am Main: Suhrkamp, 1986.

———. *Vorlesungen über die Philosophie der Religion I*. Werke, eds Eva Moldenhauer and Karl Markus Michel, vol. 16. Frankfurt am Main: Suhrkamp, 1986.

———. *Vorlesungen über die Philosophie der Religion II*. Werke, eds Eva Moldenhauer and Karl Markus Michel, vol. 17. Frankfurt am Main: Suhrkamp, 1986.

Heidegger, Martin. *Brief über den "Humanismus"*. In *Wegmarken*. Gesamtausgabe 9, 3rd ed., pp. 313–64. Frankfurt am Main: Vittorio Klostermann, 2004.

———. *Einführung in die Metaphysik*. 6th ed. Tübingen: Max Niemeyer, 1998.

———. *Die Frage nach der Technik*. In *Vorträge und Aufsätze*, 10th ed., pp. 9–40. Stuttgart: Klett-Cotta, 2004.

———. *Grundprobleme der Phänomenologie*. Gesamtausgabe 58, 2nd ed. Frankfurt am Main: Vittorio Klostermann, 2010.

———. *Heraklit: 1. Der Anfang des abendländischen Denkens, 2. Logik: Heraklits Lehre vom Logos*. Gesamtausgabe 55, 3rd ed. Frankfurt am Main: Vittorio Klostermann, 1994.

———. *Sein und Zeit*. 18th ed. Tübingen: Max Niemeyer, 2001.

———. *Der Ursprung des Kunstwerkes*. In *Holzwege*, 8th ed., pp. 1–74. Frankfurt am Main: Vittorio Klostermann, 2003.

———. *Was heißt Denken?* 5th ed. Tübingen: Max Niemeyer, 1997.

———. *Was ist Metaphysik?* In *Wegmarken*. Gesamtausgabe 9, 3rd ed., pp. 103–22. Frankfurt am Main: Vittorio Klostermann, 2004.

Henry, Michel. *I Am the Truth: Toward a Philosophy of Christianity*. Translated by Susan Emanuel. Stanford: Stanford University Press, 2003.

Hertzberg, Lars. "The Limits of Understanding." *Sats: Nordic Journal of Philosophy* 6 (2005): pp. 5–14.

———. "On Excluding Contradictions from Our Language." In *Wittgenstein and the Method of Philosophy*, ed. Sami Pihlström, pp. 169–83. Helsinki: Acta Philosophica Fennica, 2006.

———. "The Sense Is Where You Find It." In *Wittgenstein in America*, eds Timothy McCarthy and Sean Stidd, pp. 90–103. Oxford: Oxford University Press, 2001.

Hobbes, Thomas. *Leviathan*. Ed. C. B. Macpherson. London: Penguin Books, 1968.

Horkheimer, Max. *Eclipse of Reason*. New York: Oxford University Press, 1947.

Horkheimer, Max, and Theodor W. Adorno. *Dialektik der Aufklärung: Philosophische Fragmente*. 2nd ed. Frankfurt am Main: Suhrkamp, 1984.

Hume, David. *Dialogues concerning Natural Religion*. Ed. Stanley Tweyman. London: Routledge, 1991.

———. *An Enquiry concerning Human Understanding*. Ed. Tom L. Beauchamp. Oxford: Oxford University Press, 1999.

Husserl, Edmund. *Ideen zu einer reinen Phänomenologie und phänomenologischen Philosophie*. Bk. 1, *Allgemeine Einführung in die reine Phänomenologie*. Ed. Walter Biemel. Husserliana 3. Haag: Martinus Nijhoff, 1950.

———. *Logische Untersuchungen*. Vol. 1, *Prolegomena zur reinen Logik*. 2nd ed. Halle an der Saale: Max Niemeyer, 1913.

———. *Logische Untersuchungen*. Vol. 2, *Untersuchungen zur Phänomenologie und Theorie der Erkenntnis*. Pt. 1. 2nd ed. Halle an der Saale: Max Niemeyer, 1913.

Hutcheson, Francis. *An Inquiry into the Original of Our Ideas of Beauty and Virtue*. 2nd ed. London, 1726.

James, William. *Pragmatism, a New Name for Some Old Ways of Thinking: Popular Lectures of Philosophy*. New York: Longmans, Green and Co., 1907.

———. *The Will to Believe, and Other Essays in Popular Philosophy*. New York: Longmans, Green and Co., 1903.

Jantzen, Grace M. *Becoming Divine: Towards a Feminist Philosophy of Religion*. Bloomington: Indiana University Press, 1999.

Jünger, Ernst. *Annäherungen: Drogen und Rausch*. Stuttgart: Ernst Klett Verlag, 1970.

Kant, Immanuel. *Anthropologie in pragmatischer Hinsicht*. In *Schriften zur Anthropologie, Geschichtsphilosophie, Politik und Pädagogik*. Werkausgabe, ed. Wilhelm Weischedel, 11-12:399-690. Frankfurt am Main: Suhrkamp, 1968.

———. *Grundlegung zur Metaphysik der Sitten*. In *Schriften zur Ethik und Religionsphilosophie*. Werkausgabe, ed. Wilhelm Weischedel, 7–8:11–102. Frankfurt am Main: Suhrkamp, 1968.

———. *Kritik der praktischen Vernunft*. In *Schriften zur Ethik und Religionsphilosophie*. Werkausgabe, ed. Wilhelm Weischedel, 7–8:107–302. Frankfurt am Main: Suhrkamp, 1968.

———. *Kritik der reinen Vernunft*. Werkausgabe, Ed. Wilhelm Weischedel, vol. 3–4. Frankfurt am Main: Suhrkamp, 1968.

———. *Kritik der Urteilskraft*. Werkausgabe, Ed. Wilhelm Weischedel, vol. 10. Frankfurt am Main: Suhrkamp, 1974.

———. *Die Metaphysik der Sitten*. In *Schriften zur Ethik und Religionsphilosophie*. Werkausgabe, ed. Wilhelm Weischedel, 7–8:303–634. Frankfurt am Main: Suhrkamp, 1968.

———. *Practical Philosophy*. Translated and ed. Mary J. Gregor. Cambridge: Cambridge University Press, 1996.

———. *Die Religion innerhalb der Grenzen der bloßen Vernunft*. In *Schriften zur Ethik und Religionsphilosophie*. Werkausgabe, ed. Wilhelm Weischedel, 7–8:645–879. Frankfurt am Main: Suhrkamp, 1968.

Kierkegaard, Søren. *Afsluttende uvidenskabelig Efterskrift*. 2 vols. Samlede Værker 9–10. Copenhagen: Gyldendal, 1963.

———. *Dømmer selv!* In *En opbyggelig Tale; To Taler ved Altergangen om Fredagen; Til Selvprøvelse, Samtiden anbefalet; Dømmer selv!* Samlede Værker 17:125–230. Copenhagen: Gyldendal, 1964.

———. *Indøvelse i Christendom*. Samlede Værker 16. Copenhagen: Gyldendal, 1963.

———. *Kjerlighedens Gjerninger*. Samlede Værker 12. Copenhagen: Gyldendal, 1963.

———. *Opbyggelige Taler i forskjellig Aand*. Samlede Værker 11. Copenhagen: Gyldendal, 1963.

———. *Philosophiske Smuler; eller, En Smule Philosophi*. In *Philosophiske Smuler; Begrebet Angest; Tre Taler ved tænkte Leiligheder*. Samlede Værker 6:7–99. Copenhagen: Gyldendal, 1963.

———. *Purity of Heart, Is to Will One Thing: Spiritual Preparation for the Office of Confession*. Translated by Douglas Steere. New York: Harper and Brothers, 1948.

———. *Works of Love: Some Christian Reflections in the Form of Discourses*. Translated by. Howard Hong and Edna Hong. New York: Harper and Row, 1962.

Kojève, Alexandre. *Introduction to the Reading of Hegel*. Ed. Allan Bloom. Translated by James H. Nichols. Ithaca: Cornell University Press, 1980.

Lenin, V. I. *Materialism and Empirio-Criticism: Critical Comments on a Reactionary Philosophy*. New York: International Publishers, 1927.

Lessing, Gotthold Ephraim. *Die Erziehung des Menschengeschlechts*. In *Die Erziehung des Menschengeschlechts, und andere Schriften*, pp. 7–31. Stuttgart: Reclam, 1965.

———. *Über den Beweis des Geistes und der Kraft*. In *Die Erziehung des Menschengeschlechts, und andere Schriften*, pp. 31–38. Stuttgart: Reclam, 1965.

Levinas, Emmanuel. "The Ego and the Totality." In *Collected Philosophical Papers*, translated by Alphonso Lingis, pp. 25–45. Pittsburgh: Duquesne University Press, 1998.

———. *God, Death, and Time*. Translated by Bettina Bergo. Stanford: Stanford University Press, 2000.

———. *Otherwise Than Being; or, Beyond Essence*. Translated by Alphonso Lingis. Pittsburgh: Duquesne University Press, 1998.

Luther, Martin. *On the Bondage of the Will*. Translated by Philip S. Watson. In *Luther and Erasmus: Free Will and Salvation*, ed. E. Gordon Rupp and Philip S. Watson, pp. 99–334. Philadelphia: Westminster Press, 1969.

Lyotard, Jean-François. *The Postmodern Condition: A Report on Knowledge*. Translated by Geoff Bennington and Brian Massumi. Minneapolis: University of Minnesota Press, 1984.

Mackie, J. L. *Ethics: Inventing Right and Wrong*. Harmondsworth: Penguin Books, 1977.

———. "Evil and Omnipotence." *Mind* 64 (1955): pp. 200–212.

———. *The Miracle of Theism: Arguments for and against the Existence of God*. Oxford: Oxford University Press, 1983.

Macquarrie, John. *Principles of Christian Theology*. 2nd ed. New York: Charles Scribner's Sons, 1977.

Mao Tse-tung. *On Contradiction*. In vol. 1 of *Selected Works*, pp. 311–47. Peking: Foreign Languages Press, 1965.

———. *On the Correct Handling of Contradictions among the People*. In vol. 5 of *Selected Works*, pp. 384–421. Peking: Foreign Languages Press, 1977.

———. *Problems of War and Strategy*. In vol. 2 of *Selected Works*, pp. 219–35. Peking: Foreign Languages Press, 1965.

Marion, Jean-Luc. *God without Being: Hors-Texte*. Translated by Thomas A. Carlson. Chicago: University of Chicago Press, 1991.

Martin, Michael. "Is Evil Evidence against the Existence of God?" *Mind* 87 (1978): pp. 429–32.

Marx, Karl. *Das Kapital*. Vol. 1. In vol. 23 of *Marx Engels Werke*, 5th ed., pp. 3–802. Berlin: Dietz, 1970.

———. *Thesen über Feuerbach*. In vol. 3 of *Marx Engels Werke*, 4th ed., pp. 5–7, pp. 533–35. Berlin: Dietz, 1969.

———. *Zur Kritik der Hegelschen Rechtsphilosophie: Einleitung*. In vol. 1 of *Marx Engels Werke*, 7th ed., pp. 378–91. Berlin: Dietz, 1970.

———. *Zur Kritik der Politischen Ökonomie*. In vol. 13 of *Marx Engels Werke*. 3rd ed., pp. 3–160. Berlin: Dietz, 1969.

Mill, John Stuart. *Three Essays on Religion*. London: Longmans, Green, Reader, and Dyer, 1874.

Moore, Gareth. *Believing in God: A Philosophical Essay*. Edinburgh: T&T Clark, 1988.

Murdoch, Iris. *Existentialists and Mystics: Writings on Philosophy and Literature*. Ed. Peter Conradi. Harmondsworth: Penguin Books, 1997.

Novalis. *Blütenstaub*. In *Gesammelte Werke*, ed. Hans Jürgen Balmes, pp. 390–416. Frankfurt am Main: Fischer, 2008.

Nygren, Anders. *Den kristna kärlekstanken genom tiderna: Eros och agape*. Vol. 1. 2nd ed. Stockholm: Svenska kyrkans diakonistyrelses bokförlag, 1938.

Næss, Arne. *Ecology, Community and Lifestyle: Outline of an Ecosophy*. Translated and ed. David Rothenberg. Cambridge: Cambridge University Press, 1989.

———. *Økologi, samfunn og livsstil: Utkast til en økosofi*. 5th ed. Oslo: Universitetsforlaget, 1976.

———. "The Shallow and the Deep, Long-Range Ecology Movement." *Inquiry* 16 (1973): pp. 95–100.

Ovid. *Remedia Amoris; The Remedies for Love*. In *The Art of Love, and Other Poems*, translated by J. H. Mozley, 2nd ed., pp. 178–233. London: William Heinemann, 1979.

Pascal, Blaise. *Great Shorter Works*. Translated by Emile Cailliet and John C. Blankenagel. Westport: Greenwood Press, 1974.

———. *Pensées*. Translated by A. J. Krailsheimer. Rev. ed. London: Penguin Books, 1995.

Peterson, Michael, William Hasker, Bruce Reichenbach, and David Basinger, eds. *Philosophy of Religion: Selected Readings*. 2nd ed. Oxford: Oxford University Press, 2001.

Phillips, D. Z. *Belief, Change and Forms of Life*. Atlantic Highlands: Humanities Press, 1986.

————. "Ethics and Humanistic Ethics: A Reply to Dilman." In *Commonality and Particularity in Ethics*, eds Lilli Alanen, Sara Heinämää, and Thomas Wallgren, pp. 153–76. Basingstoke: Macmillan, 1997.

————. *Interventions in Ethics*. Albany: State University of New York Press, 1992.

————. *Philosophy's Cool Place*. Ithaca: Cornell University Press, 1999.

————. *The Problem of Evil and the Problem of God*. London: SCM Press, 2004.

————. *Recovering Religious Concepts: Closing Epistemic Divides*. Basingstoke: Macmillan, 2000.

————. *Religion and Friendly Fire: Examining Assumptions in Contemporary Philosophy of Religion*. Aldershot: Ashgate, 2004.

————. *Religion and the Hermeneutics of Contemplation*. Cambridge: Cambridge University Press, 2001.

Pike, Nelson. "Hume on Evil." *Philosophical Review* 72 (1963): pp. 180–97.

Plantinga, Alvin. *God, Freedom, and Evil*. Grand Rapids: Eerdmans, 1977.

————. "The Probabilistic Problem from Evil." *Philosophical Studies* 35 (1979): pp. 1–53.

Plato. *Complete Works*. Ed. John M. Cooper. Indianapolis: Hackett, 1997.

Quine, W. V. *The Ways of Paradox, and Other Essays*. New York: Random House, 1966.

Rawls, John. *A Theory of Justice*. Oxford: Oxford University Press, 1972.

Rorty, Richard. *Objectivity, Relativism, and Truth: Philosophical Papers, Volume 1*. Cambridge: Cambridge University Press, 1991.

————. *Philosophy as Cultural Politics: Philosophical Papers, Volume 4*. Cambridge: Cambridge University Press, 2007.

Roth, John K. "Critique of David Ray Griffin." In *Encountering Evil: Live Options in Theodicy*, ed. Stephen T. Davis, 2nd ed., pp. 125–28. Louisville: Westminster John Knox Press, 2001.

————. "A Theodicy of Protest." In *Encountering Evil: Live Options in Theodicy*, ed. Stephen T. Davis, 2nd ed., pp. 1–20. Louisville: Westminster John Knox Press, 2001.

Rowe, William L. "The Problem of Evil and Some Varieties of Atheism." *American Philosophical Quarterly* 16 (1979): pp. 335–41.

Russell, Bertrand. *Our Knowledge of the External World, as a Field for Scientific Method in Philosophy*. London: George Allen and Unwin, 1914.

Sade, Marquis de. *Justine; or, Good Conduct Well Chastised*. In *Justine, Philosophy in the Bedroom, and Other Writings*, translated by Austryn Wainhouse and Richard Seaver, pp. 447–743. London: Arrow Books, 1965.

Sartre, Jean-Paul. *Being and Nothingness: An Essay on Phenomenological Ontology*. Translated by Hazel E. Barnes. New York: Philosophical Library, 1956.

————. *Critique of Dialectical Reason: Volume One, Theory of Practical Ensembles*. Ed. Jonathan Rée. Translated by Alan Sheridan-Smith. London: Verso, 2004.

Schelling, F. W. J. *Über das Wesen der menschlichen Freiheit, und die damit zusammenhängenden Gegenstände*. Ed. Thomas Buchheim. Hamburg: Felix Meiner, 1997.

Schleiermacher, Friedrich. *Über die Religion: Reden an die Gebildeten unter ihren Verächtern*. Ed. Günter Meckenstock. Berlin: Walter de Gruyter, 2001.

Shestov, Lev. *Kierkegaard and the Existential Philosophy*. Translated by Elinor Hewitt. Athens: Ohio University Press, 1969.

Stjernfelt, Frederik. "Overskridelsens vulgærmetafysik: Den negative æstetiks erstatningskriterier." In *Kritik af den negative opbyggelighed: 7 essays af Frederik Stjernfelt og Søren Ulrik Thomsen*, 2nd ed., pp. 9–31. Copenhagen: Vindrose, 2008.

Strandberg, Hugo. "Det är vilseledande att betona djupekologins djup." *Ikaros* 4, no. 3 (2007).

———. *Escaping My Responsibility: Investigations into the Nature of Morality*. Frankfurt am Main: Peter Lang, 2009.

———. "Från död till liv: Om religionsfilosofins natur." *Svensk teologisk kvartalskrift* 83 (2007): pp. 32–40.

Swinburne, Richard. *Providence and the Problem of Evil*. Oxford: Oxford University Press, 1998.

Vattimo, Gianni. *Belief*. Translated by Luca D'Isanto and David Webb. Cambridge: Polity Press, 1999.

———. *Beyond Interpretation: The Meaning of Hermeneutics for Philosophy*. Translated by David Webb. Stanford: Stanford University Press, 1997.

Weber, Max. *Wissenschaft als Beruf*. In *Gesammelte Aufsätze zur Wissenschaftslehre*, 7th ed., ed. Johannes Winckelmann, pp. 582–613. Tübingen: J. C. B. Mohr (Paul Siebeck), 1988.

Weil, Simone. *Attente de Dieu*. Paris: La Colombe, 1950.

———. *Gravity and Grace*. Translated by Emma Craufurd. London: ARK Paperbacks, 1987.

———. *Lettre à un religieux*. Paris: Gallimard, 1951.

———. *The Need for Roots: Prelude to a Declaration of Duties towards Mankind*. London: Routledge and Kegan Paul, 1952.

Williams, Rowan. "Redeeming Sorrows." In *Religion and Morality*, ed. D. Z. Phillips, pp. 132–48. London: Macmillan, 1996.

Winch, Peter. "Asking Too Many Questions." In *Philosophy and the Grammar of Religious Belief*, eds Timothy Tessin and Mario von der Ruhr, pp. 200–214. New York: St. Martin's Press, 1995.

———. *Ethics and Action*. London: Routledge and Kegan Paul, 1972.

———. *The Idea of a Social Science, and Its Relation to Philosophy*. 2nd ed. London: Routledge, 1990.

Wittgenstein, Ludwig. *Bemerkungen über die Grundlagen der Mathematik*. Eds G. E. M. Anscombe, Rush Rhees, and G. H. von Wright. Frankfurt am Main: Suhrkamp, 1984.

———. *Culture and Value*. Ed. G. H. von Wright. Translated by Peter Winch. Chicago: University of Chicago Press, 1980.

———. "A Lecture on Ethics." In *Philosophical Occasions, 1912–1951*, eds James Klagge and Alfred Nordmann, pp. 37–44. Indianapolis: Hackett, 1993.

———. *Lectures and Conversations on Aesthetics, Psychology and Religious Belief*. Ed. Cyril Barrett. Oxford: Blackwell, 1966.

———. *Logisch-philosophische Abhandlung; Tractatus Logico-Philosophicus*. Translated by D. F. Pears and B. F. McGuinness. London: Routledge and Kegan Paul, 1961.

———. *Notebooks, 1914–1926*. Eds G. H. von Wright and G. E. M. Anscombe. 2nd ed. Chicago: University of Chicago Press, 1979.

————. *Philosophie; Philosophy.* Translated by C. G. Luckhardt and M. A. E. Aue. In *Philosophical Occasions, 1912–1951*, eds James Klagge and Alfred Nordmann, pp. 160–99. Indianapolis: Hackett, 1993.

————. *Philosophische Untersuchungen; Philosophical Investigations.* 4th ed. Translated by G. E. M. Anscombe, P. M. S. Hacker, and Joachim Schulte. Chichester: Wiley-Blackwell, 2009.

————. *Wittgenstein's Lectures on the Foundations of Mathematics, Cambridge, 1939.* Ed. Cora Diamond. Ithaca: Cornell University Press, 1976.

Žižek, Slavoj. *The Fragile Absolute; or, Why Is the Christian Legacy Worth Fighting For?* London: Verso, 2000.

Index

                    Index

CPSIA information can be obtained at www.ICGtesting.com
Printed in the USA
LVOW10s1824111213

364879LV00005B/146/P